SPEED READING
THAT YOU CAN DO YOURSELF

You may know people who are able to read a newspaper in a few minutes, flip through yot thoroughly absorb a book in an hour, or effortlessly finish skimming a report before you even suspected they were done. Quite possibly you have thought that these people were born with a natural talent for speed reading that you do not possess.

Nothing could be further from the truth.

Speed reading actually consists of a series of simple skills that can be mastered and applied by anyone willing to take the short time and minimal effort needed to master these so-called "secrets" and "tricks." Now they are no longer either secret or tricky—but completely comprehensible and available in the finest speed reading guide on the market today—

SPEED READING MADE EASY

CRITICAL ACCLAIM

"Readable and persuasive."
> —*Cleveland Plain Dealer*

"An excellent, self-improvement manual . . . by a specialist."
> —*Los Angeles Times*

"Examples and self-applicable tests are provided every step of the way . . . Even the reader who thinks his speed and grasp adequate will benefit."
> —*Saturday Review Syndicate*

"It is possible for anybody to read faster with increased pleasure and profit."
> —*San Francisco Call-Bulletin*

SPEED READING MADE EASY

by Nila Banton Smith, Ph.D.

WARNER BOOKS

A Time Warner Company

WARNER BOOKS EDITION

Copyright © 1957, 1958, 1963 by Prentice-Hall, Inc.
All rights reserved.

Published by CBS Inc. by arrangement with
Prentice-Hall, Inc., Englewood Cliffs, New Jersey 07632

Warner Books, Inc.
1271 Avenue of the Americas
New York, N.Y. 10020

A Time Warner Company

Printed in the United States of America

First Warner Books Printing: July, 1983

Reissued: August, 1987

20 19 18 17 16

CONTENTS

Acknowledgment

Grateful acknowledgment is made to the following able instructors at The Reading Institute of New York University, who tested and successfully used the procedures described in this book in teaching adults to read better:

Harry L. Donahoe, Justin H. Miller, Harold H. Ferster, Donald S. Leeds, Irwin L. Joffe, Robert Chamberlain, Edward T. Clark, and James Devine.

Special acknowledgment is given to Justin H. Miller and James Devine for valuable assistance in helping to prepare testing questions which accompany several of the practice selections in the book.

This book has one basic purpose—to help you read as well as you want to read. Regardless of your age or occupation or the kind of reading that you have to do, you *can* learn to read more rapidly and with better understanding.

But how?

There *is* a new art of reading. This new art has arisen in response to a deeply-felt need of people everywhere to read faster and better. In this book you will find explanations of the basic techniques in this new art of rapid, effective reading, together with selections to which you may apply these new techniques for practice. *If you follow the instructions faithfully and practice their application conscientiously, you can achieve whatever goals in reading efficiency you may desire.*

First Step in Reading Improvement

First, take an inventory of your present skills in reading.

When you begin any self-improvement course you should know where you are at the start and the progress you make as you go along. If you take a weight-reducing course, you weigh and measure at the beginning and at frequent intervals thereafter to find how much you are losing in pounds and girth. In a reading course you should measure frequently to find how much you are gaining in speed and comprehension.

Chapter 1 contains the *instructions and materials you need to find out where you stand in regard to these reading skills at the beginning of your work in this book.*

"Discovery"—What Is It?

The discovery discussed in Chapter 2 is that good readers read for ideas and take in several words at each glance, while poor readers read in short units, taking in only one, two, or three words at each pause of the eyes. So long as a person reads in this latter manner, he cannot pick up much speed. The larger thoughts are cut up into so many small units that it is hard to get the full meaning of a passage.

All of this is explained to you in Chapter 2, where you are given practice in stretching your own reading units. This chapter equips you with the *foundation for all the speed work* in the remainder of the book.

Do You Long to Read More Rapidly?

If speed is your chief objective you'll get a lot of satisfaction in working with Chapter 3. It is in this chapter that you really take off!

The title of the chapter is "Faster! Faster!" This title tells you straight from the shoulder that you should abandon your present rate of reading and take on a new tempo.

But you aren't simply given this instruction. You're told how to put yourself in the right physical setting for fast reading, how to set up a purpose for faster reading, what to do mentally in starting your speed reading program.

Then you are given an opportunity to apply these instructions in the selections provided for rapid reading practice.

A special feature which appears for the first time in this chapter is "Vocabulary Development." Increasing your vocabulary contributes to your speed and comprehension. So you will find *vocabulary helps* in this chapter, and in all the following chapters except the last two.

What Are Signposts in Reading?

There are words that tell you to keep on going straight ahead in your reading—that there will be more of the same thing. There are other words that warn you of a change in thought, that tell you to slow down, there's a sharp turn ahead. It's important for you to know *how to use these word signals.*

In Chapter 4 you will find out what these signposts are, and how to make the most of them in your reading.

What Is Meant by "Shopping Before You Read"?

You shop before you buy clothes, food, or a house. In other words, you *take a preview*. This same general technique applies to an article or book before you buy it, meaning "before you read it."

In Chapter 5 you will learn how to "Shop Before You Read." This is one of the most useful reading procedures you can acquire.

Sight-Seeing!

Everyone loves to sight-see. This is the basic reason why millions of dollars are spent every year in traveling.

Think of the last trip *you* took. What sights do you recall? No doubt a few outstanding ones. The lesser ones have faded.

In the chapter on "Sight-Seeing As You Read" you will learn how to find the outstanding thoughts quickly in printed material. You will learn *how to "spot" the main idea in paragraphs.*

When you have acquired this skill, you will be well on the road to becoming an expert reader.

Do You Grasp Details Readily?

Some of us have no trouble reading easy narrative material. Nowadays, however, most of us have to do much informative reading which is packed with numerous details. These can be confusing. We can't give equal attention to all of them, and often we end up not grasping any of them. Do you have this experience when reading detailed factual or technical material?

There are special techniques for *grasping details readily and reading difficult factual material faster* than you have been accustomed to do. You will learn how to "Mine for Details" in Chapter 7.

Patterns of Writing

There are patterns in tool-making, patterns in dress-making, and patterns in writing.

Every author has some purpose in mind when he starts to write. Different purposes require different patterns of writing. Certain techniques are helpful in reading certain patterns. If you learn how to recognize the most common of these different patterns, and how to deal with each pattern, you will increase your reading competency.

You will learn *the most common patterns of writing, and how to read them,* under the chapter title "Riding Along with the Author."

What About Skimming?

Most people skim in a hit-or-miss fashion. This skill, however, has a potential for tremendous development. It is an art in itself and can be perfected to a high degree.

Skimming is based upon and makes use of all the other skills; consequently, it is the most complex of all. You'll be ready, though, to rise to *new horizons in your skimming techniques* when you reach Chapter 9.

The Author's Wish For You

You have had a glimpse of what this book holds for you. Now let me speed you on your reading way with good wishes. I trust that you may achieve whatever goals you have set for yourself in becoming an expert reader.

Happy journey in reading improvement!

NILA BANTON SMITH

Chapter 1

Taking Inventory

How Do You Rate Yourself?

What do you have to start with? That's the first thing to find out. You've been adding to or, more likely, depleting your stock of reading skills for the past one, two, three, or more decades. Without specific checking you probably have a general idea that you're a good reader, an average reader, or a poor reader.

Mr. H., a famous newspaper columnist, said to me when he came in: "I think I am a very good reader. I've never had any trouble at all in reading. But if I could learn to cover double the amount of material in the time at my disposal, this would just be a matter of plain efficiency. Mind you, though, this isn't because I'm a poor reader to start with. I'm an excellent reader already."

Miss G., a story reader at a moving-picture studio, said: "I read about fifty pages an hour. Isn't that pretty good?"

John M., a high school student, reasoned this way: "I understand that most colleges nowadays give a reading test as a part of their entrance exams. I'll never pass that test unless I do something about my reading right now. I'm a miserable reader."

Sarah M., a college student, declared, "I'm a grind. I have to study hours while others are having a good time. I'm a terribly slow reader."

Mr. M., a businessman, said, "I never can wade through all the white stuff on my desk. I'm a fair reader but the amount of reading that I have to do overpowers me."

Professor R., a college teacher of English, told me with pride: "I can read a novel in one sitting. That's really pretty fast reading, isn't it?"

"I never finish a novel," complained Mrs. B. "I read too slowly to cover books, so I've given them up entirely. About all I can do is to follow the headlines in a newspaper. I must be the world's worst reader."

And so it is that we "grade" ourselves. These impressions, however, are too general to be a basis for making any precise judgment in regard to reading competency. Maybe you, like the columnist, have "never had any trouble in reading." Does that mean that you are an excellent reader as compared with highly-skilled adult readers who have learned the modern techniques of reading?

Even if you do read fifty pages an hour, how well do you get the thought out of what you read? As for the professor, was the book a thin volume with small pages printed in large type like Steinbeck's *Sweet Thursday?* Or was it a huge, compact volume printed in relatively small type such as *Not as a Stranger?* And how long was the "sitting"? Two hours? Six hours? Twelve hours?

Obviously there are many fallacies in attempting to grade oneself in reading. If you wish to find out exactly how well you read and how much improvement you achieve as you go along, then you must make more careful measurements than general impressions.

Measuring Your Reading Growth

Measuring your own growth in reading is comparable to measuring your child's physical growth. If you want to know how fast your child is growing, you periodically weigh him and measure his height. Then you make your comparisons in terms of exact units—pounds and inches. You must do the same sort of thing in evaluating your growth in reading.

Reading is not a "lump sum," as so many people seem to think. It is a very complex mental process involving many different skills. A horse uses one set of muscles when pulling a heavy load uphill and an entirely different set when trying to hold back that load on his way downhill. So it is with reading. We use different sets of skills when we read different kinds of material for different purposes. You will have opportunities to practice several of these different sets of skills as you work through this book.

Regardless of how varied the skills may be, there are always two fundamental skills which are in operation. Growth in reading is judged in terms of progress in these two basic skills as commonly as physical growth is judged in terms of height and weight. And like height and weight these two skills should grow together simultaneously and in relation to each other.

One of these basic skills is *speed*. It is the rate with which you can cover printed material through reading. The basic unit used in measuring speed is the number of words per minute. The abbreviation W.P.M. is written after the number indicating a score, as 275 W.P.M. The other basic skill which easily lends itself to measurement is understanding of what is read. This is *comprehension*. The terms *speed* and *comprehension* have special meanings in a reading-instruction vocabulary. You may as well right now become accustomed to these terms as used in this book.

The writer was one day amused when a gentleman came in with this complaint: "I want to talk with you about my wife. I'm very much worried. She's having a dreadful time with her apprehension."

He might have been told not to seek improvement of his wife's "apprehension" lest he have occasion to worry still more. But instead he was told to bring her in for a check-up of her speed and *comprehension*.

The average reader covers about 250 words per minute. Very good readers read 500 or 600 words per minute. Occasionally there is a person who reads at the phenomenal rate of 1,000 words per minute, or in rare instances even faster. However, ability to cover printed words rapidly is quite valueless unless the reader gathers meaning as his eyes travel over the lines of print.

Fortunately, these two basic skills, speed and comprehension, can be developed with guidance and practice. But they must increase together. Like height and weight in the growing child, comprehension must keep pace with speed in the reading growth of an adult. If you should increase your speed to 600 words per minute and drop your comprehension from 80 to 40 per cent, your speed would do you more harm than good. Therefore, in all the chapters in this book you will be asked to work on *both* speed and comprehension.

First you need to find out what your normal rate of speed is and also get some idea of how well you are comprehending. You can then use these first scores as a basis for comparison to see later on how much you have improved.

For checking purposes you are asked to read two selections. One is very easy, and you will read it simply for entertainment. The other is more difficult, and you will read it for the information it contains.

You'll have to time yourself in taking both of these tests, so get out a watch with a second hand. Note the hour and the minute that you begin to read each of the selections and jot this data down in the space provided. This test is given to check your present speed and comprehension in reading easy, narrative material.

Reading for Entertainment

Don't try to read fast for test purposes. Just read at your comfortable normal rate and for the purpose of enjoying the story.

Ready! Start!

Selection 1

BEGINNING TIME:——————
HR.—————— MIN.——————

THE GREAT MOLASSES FLOOD[1]

From early Colonial days on, ships loaded with wooden hogsheads of thick, dark molasses came regu-

[1] Ralph Frye, "The Great Molasses Flood," *Reader's Digest*, August 1955, pp. 63-67.

larly from the West Indies to unload at Boston's wharves. Molasses took the place of sugar, which few colonists could afford, and it made Yankee rum. It was a keystone of Boston's prosperity and trade for almost three centuries—until January 15, 1919.

I was a reporter on the *Boston American* on that fateful day. The stories coming in over the wire were predicting, rightly, that on the morrow Nebraska would become the 36th state to vote dry, thus bringing nationwide Prohibition upon this country (and rendering great quantities of molasses virtually useless). But even before the news could be printed, the biggest molasses storage tank in all Boston burst and sent an angry deluge of the stuff rampaging through the old North End, tearing down the elevated railway, demolishing buildings, drowning and crushing 21 persons and dozens of horses, wreaking property damage of more than a million dollars.

For years the tank, a bulging giant 50 feet tall and 282 feet in girth, had loomed above the freight-loading depots, stables, and firehouse on Commercial Street, near Boston's inner harbor. Three days before, the pumps of tankers from Puerto Rico had filled it right up to the brim with 2,320,000 gallons—14,000 tons—of molasses.

At five minutes to noon on that mild winter morning, a telephone rang in the molasses plant's office in the shadow of the tank. Superintendent William White picked up the receiver and heard his wife insist he join her uptown for lunch. White took a cursory look at the frowning tank, ignored the molasses sweating ominously through the riveted seams, and left—thus undoubtedly saving his life. But the busy market district was thronged with people destined to be less fortunate.

Along Commercial Street, new-fangled motor trucks and horse-team drays clattered on the cobblestones beneath the elevated railway. In the doorways of shops and brick dwellings across the street from the tank, residents were taking advantage of the warm weather to sun themselves. In stables of nearby draying companies, dozens of workhorses were placidly munching hay. Teamsters chatted over their lunch boxes on the freight-loading platforms. Mrs. Bridget Clougherty, 68, stood watching them from the doorway of her frame house at the corner of Copp's Hill and Commercial. Her big son Martin, a well-known boxer and referee, lay in his third-floor bedroom, sleeping soundly. The time was 12:41.

At this moment Patrolman Frank McManus was making a routine duty call at a police-signal box down the street. Suddenly he heard a "grinding, rumbling" noise. Looking up, he saw a dark sea of liquid gush from the bottom of the tank. He saw the big tank open out and fall apart, and a towering wall of molasses roll over the ground with a seething, hissing sound. Going 35 miles an hour with a push of 25 tons, it enveloped the fire station; then buildings began to collapse. McManus yelled for all the ambulances and policemen available.

At the same moment, the brakeman of a northbound train coming around the curve on the elevated yanked his emergency cord. "All I could see was molasses rushing toward me," the brakeman later said. The train stopped just as the elevated structure ahead sagged into the raging molasses below; the forward wheel trucks of the first car were lifted off the rails.

Mrs. Mary Musco, watching from the window of her house when the "explosion" came, saw the three-story Clougherty house rise from its foundations and "fly into the air," then disappear beneath the El in a caldron of floundering horses, people, jagged timbers, splintered wagons, huge crates of goods and—molasses. "I ran for help," Mrs. Musco said. "It was awful. People were running every which way all covered with molasses."

To many people the breaking of the tank came with a tearing sound, like the ripping of a huge sheet of paper. To a Navy gunner on a ship in the harbor it was like a succession of reports from an impossibly-enormous machine gun. The tearing sound was caused by the initial giving-away of the tank at its base; the machine-gun reports were rivets bursting upward from the bottom, like buttons popping off a vest.

Then the very steel of the plates themselves sundered and burst outward. One 400-square-foot section of steel weighing two and one half tons was catapulted 182 feet into North End Park. Another murderous ribbon of half-inch steel plate swept across Commercial Street, sheared through a tree-trunk-size steel El column like a knife through butter. A few hours later, boxer Martin Clougherty, bandaged like a mummy, was able to tell reporters: "I was asleep on the third floor, and I awoke in several feet of molasses. A little way from me I saw my sister. I struggled out from under the wreckage and pulled my sister onto a board. Then I began to look for my mother." But the roof had fallen on Mrs. Clougherty and crushed her.

Russel McLean, a commuter from Waverly, Mass., was on his way to North Station when the tank burst. The next thing he remembered he was lying in a doorway across the street with a young woman unconscious in his lap. "All around me horses and men were struggling in the thick molasses." One man, running from the on-rushing molasses when it overtook him, landed sitting and was swept right out into the harbor. Crewmen of the Naval tug *U.S.S. Pawnee* picked him out of the water sticky and frightened, but unharmed.

We at the *Boston American* knew nothing of any of this at the time. I was on my way to lunch when a single alarm came in. Henry Daily, assistant city editor, called to me: "Ralph, take a look at this fire. Probably nothing to it, but there are a lot of old firetraps down there."

I cut north to Commercial Street. At first there was no sign of trouble until, away up past Constitution Wharf, I saw it. What looked like a moving wall of volcanic lava filled the street and was moving relentlessly toward me. Everything it overtook—horses, automobiles, people—disappeared. I telephoned Henry. "Where's the fire?" he said.

"Wait!" I yelled. "This is no fire. I don't know what it is. Shoot some cameramen and legmen down here fast. Listen—there seems to be an awful stink of molasses around here. Maybe molasses has something to do with it."

"Molasses?" Henry was outraged. When I got nearer I realized that this was the story of all stories. . . . Sailors, firemen, and policemen, wallowing thigh-deep in the wreckage, were coated from head to foot with molasses; it gave them a weird copper color.

The big old firehouse had been shoved off its foundation and stood with its tower canted at a crazy angle. Inside several firemen were still trapped. It took nearly four hours before their comrades freed the last of them —and discovered George Layhe dead at the foot of the sliding pole, with the firehouse piano and pool table piled on top of him.

Even in the shallow places the molasses was dangerous. It was worse than quicksand. It held your feet.
Well-meaning bystanders waded in to help floundering
victims and couldn't get out. Scores of persons trapped
in the upper floors of buildings kept up a plea to be
rescued. Fire lines were strung around the area, but the
crowd pressed so hard against the ropes that some persons slipped into the goo. Ambulances manned by molas-
ses-stained interns were continually carrying away victims.

One ambulance outfit of Red Cross girls arrived in
Oxford-gray uniforms with shiny black puttees and
pretty white shirtwaists. They were very beautiful and
very earnest, and they plunged into the flood. When firemen dragged them out, swollen and tottering with the
weight of molasses, they looked like loathsome creatures
of the primordial slime.

By midafternoon the flood had settled. Hundreds of
residents and curious spectators went slipping and slop-
ping through the mess and tracked it all over the metro-
politan district. The next day if you sat down in any
public place or conveyance in the city of Boston, you
stuck to the seat. Riders in streetcars and buses in
Worcester, 44 miles away, found them smeared. There
wasn't a telephone booth in Boston where the instrument didn't stick to your fingers.

Streams of water were played on the molasses to wash
it into the sewers and the harbor. But ordinary fire hoses
proved useless to dissolve the muck. Firemen discovered
that salt water managed somehow to "cut" the molasses.
Fireboats and pumping equipment were called into play.
Police used huge hydraulic siphons to pump molasses
out of flooded cellars. It was nearly a week before all of
the bodies were recovered, and months before signs of the
disaster disappeared.

The distillery owners tried to wash their hands of responsibility for the disaster, only to find this as sticky a
task as the molasses itself. Accident-insurance underwriters, too, tried not to get stuck. "They do not believe," reported the *Boston Globe*, calmly, "that the aggregate claims will be very great, as the persons affected
were for the most part of the wage-earning class."

The courts of Massachusetts took a different view.
One hundred and nineteen separate damage suits were

filed. Hearings, continued as late as 10 p.m. to give work-men a chance to be heard, consumed 309 days. Three thousand witnesses spoke more than six million words of testimony, filling 40,000 pages of court record.

The defendant distillers spent more than $50,000 on expert witnesses, built three tanks and blew them up in an effort to show the disaster had been caused by an "anarchist bomb." But when it was shown that the molasses tank had been built of thinner plates than were specified in the plans filed with the Boston Building Commission, the defense collapsed. In 1925 the company settled the suits out of court, for a total of more than one million dollars.

Cleaning up the mess took longer than the litigation. Men scraped and scrubbed and painted, but the taint of molasses persisted. It is said that even now, on humid days, a sickly sweetish aroma surrounds some of the older buildings of Boston's North End.

Began   Finished No. words: 1500

$$\frac{\qquad}{\qquad} \times 60 = \underline{\qquad} \text{W.P.M.}$$

No. seconds:

Write your finishing time in the appropriate space in the form above. If you finished at 34 minutes and 10 seconds after 9, write 9:34:10 under *Finished*. Next, turn back to find your beginning time which you recorded when you started to read the article. Let us suppose that this was 28 minutes after 9. Then write 9:28 under *Began*. Subtracting the beginning time from the finishing time you have 6 minutes and 10 seconds.

Now use the formula given above in computing your reading rate. Divide 1500, the number of words in the selection, by the number of seconds that it took you to read the article. Multiply the answer by 60 to convert to minutes, and the answer will give you the number of words per minute that you read.

Following through with the example above: suppose it took you 6 minutes and 10 seconds to read the article. This would amount to 370 seconds. Dividing 1500 by 370 would give you 4.05. You would then multiply 4.05 by 60 and get 243. This would be the number of words per minute which you read and should be written in the space preceding W.P.M.

Compute your rate according to this procedure and record it in the appropriate space.

Checking Comprehension

Read each of the exercises below. Choose the answer which you think is correct. Write the corresponding letter in the appropriate answer space at the end of the exercises.

1. The article says that one of the uses to which the Colonists put molasses was (a) to pour it on their pancakes, (b) to make candy, (c) to mix with cattle feed, (d) to make Yankee rum.

2. The first person to call ambulances and policemen was (a) Mrs. Bridget Clougherty, (b) Superintendent White, (c) Patrolman Frank McManus, (d) Mrs. Mary Musco.

3. The tank contained about (a) 5,000,000 gallons, (b) 25,000 gallons, (c) 2,300,000 gallons.

4. The writer approached the scene of the disaster (a) because of his own curiosity, (b) because one of the editors of the *Boston American* asked him to do so, (c) hoping to offer some aid, (d) wanting to take pictures.

5. It can be correctly inferred that the time of day when the disaster occurred was (a) early morning, (b) midafternoon, (c) about noon, (d) late evening.

6. As far as clean-up work is concerned the statement least true is (a) the Fire Department helped greatly in the clean-up work, (b) the Police Department directed the activities, (c) the Red Cross was on hand, (d) the Navy helped.

7. The *Boston Globe* (a) declared that the fault lay with the distillers, (b) quoted the underwriters in their underestimation of contingent claims, (c) believed that the underwriters had overestimated the probable claims, (d) made no comments about this matter.

8. The cause of the disaster was traced to (a) the failure of the builders to adhere to specifications, (b) the

Building Commission's standards, (c) an anarchist's bomb, (d) none of these.

9. The company finally settled the suits (a) with the state, (b) with the city of Boston, (c) in the Supreme Court, (d) out of court.

10. The cleaning up (a) lasted until after everyone immediately concerned with the flood was dead, (b) was a quick job, (c) lasted longer than the litigation, (d) is not yet completed.

Answers: 1)——, 2)——, 3)——, 4)——, 5)——, 6)——, 7)——, 8)——, 9)——, 10)——.

Check your answers with the Answer Key on page 276. Multiply the number of correct answers by 10. Record your score.

Rate: W.P.M. ——— Comprehension Score: ———

Reading for Information

The following test is provided for the purpose of checking your speed and comprehension in reading more difficult material. Read the article in your normal manner for obtaining its information.

Selection 2

BEGINNING TIME:————
HR.———— MIN.————

LIFE ON OTHER PLANETS[2]

Although climate is chiefly a matter of winds, ocean currents, sunshine, rains, and snow, it involves also the responses of plants and animals to these physical factors. Plants grow on the mountainsides and control the evaporation and contribute to the cloudiness. One industrious animal affects the weather by diverting the water courses, thereby producing lush vegetation in arid regions. Clearly life and climate interact on each other. If life had never appeared on the earth's surface, the local climates would have been different from those which have

[2] Harlow Shapley, "Life on Other Planets," *The Atlantic Monthly*, November 1953, pp. 29-32.

prevailed. And if the climate had everywhere been unchanging throughout geologic time, the variety of life we know—the millions of species—might not have come about; possibly the organisms would never have got their start in the dim Pre-Cambrian ooze. . . .

Let us consider the solar system and its climatic problems. The existence of life on Mars is still an open question although astronomers have for years rather uncritically assumed that the seasonal color changes on the surface must mean that life is present. An observer looking at the planet Earth from a moderate distance, say a scientist on the Moon, would also see our winters come and go. He should be able to locate the positions of the poles of the earth by watching the alternating color changes due to winter snowfall and summer melting in our northern and southern hemispheres. He would note that we have much water on the surface, in strong contrast to the small amount on Mars, where it is weakly recorded by the skin of hoarfrost in the polar caps. The color changes on the surface of the earth, visible to the observer on the Moon, could be quite independent of vegetable or other forms of life. Even in the absence of snow, the moisture on desert lowlands should produce color that would fade out with the drying up in the annual rainless season. Fog on a lifeless desert could produce a widespread color change. In other words, variations in the color of Mars do not necessarily mean that vegetation is present. The Martian problem is still open.

II

Some of the climatic changes on Mars can be readily deduced. The surface is relatively free of high elevations and certainly free of large bodies of water. Air and water currents must be relatively uncomplicated. The mass is low, and the air is rare even at the Martian surface. The inclination of the equator to the plane of the orbit is like that of the earth and consequently the seasonal phenomena are similar. The rotation of the planet is a little more than 24 terrestrial hours; the year is 1.9 terrestrial years, and the months may be ignored because the two little moons are ineffective, both tidally and photometrically. We can predict the daily and annual meteorological changes from our own experience after making allowance for the low temperatures and the weak effects of air currents on the lowland elevations. The orbit of Mars has an eccentricity of 0.093, compared with 0.017 for the earth; and therefore the Martian temperature (and climate) will be somewhat affected by the fact that Mars is 26 million miles nearer the sun at perihelion than at aphelion—a change of 18 per cent in the distance. The perihelion effect on the earth's temperature and climate is relatively small, in comparison with the many other contributing factors to terrestrial climatic change, for the perihelion to aphelion difference in distance is only 3.4 per cent.

If we knew how life got started on our own planet, we could better guess whether the Martian conditions have been hostile or friendly to the origin of organisms. Certainly the mean temperature is painfully low, the atmosphere at the surface is rarer than on our highest mountaintops, and both oxygen and water vapor are scarce. Carbon dioxide has been detected and we all agree that argon, produced by the radioactivity of one of the isotopes of potassium, is almost certainly a constituent of the thin Martian atmosphere. The dominant gas presumably is nitrogen, which has not yet been recorded. Could it be detected without going to the planet? Dr. Rupert Wildt of Yale suggests that Martian aurorae may at some time be observed, and, if so, they would probably indicate the presence of a deep but low-density atmosphere composed mostly of nitrogen surrounding the dry, cool planet.

The Moon, of course, is lifeless, waterless, and essentially airless. Hydrogen, helium, nitrogen, and oxygen gases would all leak away from the surface of this small-mass satellite. The Moon might not permanently retain by gravitation even the inert argon, produced radioactively from Potassium 40. Very little of it could get to the surface in the absence of water erosion and volcanic action. The writer interpolates the suggestion, however, that the ever-impinging meteors, with their consequent explosions, would produce, throughout the three or more thousand million years that the Moon has been under meteoric bombardment, various gasses, including some that are relatively so heavy that they would not easily escape from the surface. The meteoric impacts would also release from the surface some of the entrapped argon. The Moon must therefore have an atmosphere, but in quantity perhaps not many lungfuls and in character not very salubrious.

The cloud-shrouded surface of the planet Venus remains as yet something of a mystery. In general, the students of planetary atmospheres find little likelihood of life of the terrestrial sort on that planet, notwithstanding its earthlike mass and its fairly suitable location with respect to the sun. Is it covered with oceans of water? Does the rotation period permit an equable night and day alteration? Is the oxygen situation suitable for air-breathers? Some of the astrochemists have rather positive answers to some of the questions of this sort, but doubts still prevail and we must await improved technologies before we penetrate the shroud and agree on the living conditions on the planet Venus.

The other planets of the solar system are too hot or too cold, and they have other limitations. For example, Mercury is too hot on the sun side, too cold in the endless night of the hemisphere that is never exposed to the sun; and life of our sort would be impossible in Mercury's twilight zones because of the lack of atmosphere and water. Jupiter, Saturn, and the other distant planets, out in the icy cold that is inevitable so far from the sun, have poisonous atmospheres, heavy with methane and ammonia; and they have other hostile characteristics.

III

Climate is not the only important factor that determines the possibility of life on a planetary surface. The following are necessary for the origin and continuance of life:

1. Water, the practical solvent for living processes, must be available in liquid form.

2. The planet must have a suitable rotation period so that the nights do not overcool nor the days overheat.

3. The orbital eccentricity must be low to avoid excessive differences in the isolation as the planet moves from perihelion out to aphelion and back. Most cometary orbits would be lethal for organisms.

4. The chemical content of air, ocean, and land surface must be propitious, not perilously polluted with substances inimical to biological operations.

5. The controlling star must not be variable by more

than 4 or 5 per cent; it must not be a double star, and of course must not be subject to catastrophic explosions like those of the novae.

6. Finally, life must get started, and it must establish a tenacious hold on the seas, shores, or inland.

Certainly many adjustments could be made by organisms on a planetary surface to physical conditions unlike those we experience, but the major requirements still stand. The most important requirement is, of course, that life must in some way get started.

Began *Finished* No. words: 1300

$$\frac{}{} \times 60 = \underline{} \text{ W.P.M.}$$

_____ _____ No. seconds:

Compute your rate in the same way as described above, and record the number of words per minute in the appropriate space.

Checking Comprehension

Mark the letter of each correct answer in the appropriate answer space below the statements.

1. Climate (a) exists quite independent of plants, (b) exists quite independent of animals, (c) has no effect on life, (d) interacts with life.

2. Astronomers have assumed that there is life on Mars because (a) it has canals which they think men have excavated, (b) because Mars has a climate much like our own, (c) because of the color changes on Mars, (d) because Mars apparently has seasons.

3. The length of the Martian year is: (a) about half of our year, (b) about one and three fourths as long as our year, (c) about twice our year, (d) about three times our year.

4. Mars is 26 million miles nearer the sun (a) at aphelion, (b) at perihelion, (c) in the middle of a Martian year, (d) at the end of each axial revolution.

5. The dominant gas on Mars is probably (a) oxygen, (b) carbon dioxide, (c) argon, (d) nitrogen.

6. The moon has (a) a damp atmosphere, (b) no atmosphere, (c) an atmosphere highly limited in quantity, (d) an atmosphere heavily saturated with oxygen.

7. A planet which has a poisonous atmosphere is (a) Venus, (b) Mercury, (c) Jupiter, (d) Mars.

8. One of the conditions for life on a planet is that (a) the planet must revolve around its orbit every 12 months, (b) it must have seasons, (c) it must have a suitable rotation period to prevent extremes of heat and cold, (d) it must have high orbital eccentricity.

9. Another condition necessary for life on a planet is that (a) it must have a chemical content inimical to biological operations, (b) it must be lethal for organisms, (c) its chemical content must be propitious to life, (d) it must have catastrophic explosions.

10. The most important requirement for life is (a) that it be able to adjust to physical conditions different from ours, (b) that it be intelligent enough to survive, (c) it be strong enough physically to survive, (d) that it get started.

Answers: 1)——, 2)——, 3)——, 4)——, 5)——, 6)——, 7)——, 8)——, 9)——, 10)——.

See Answer Key on page 276. Allow 10 for each correct answer.

Rate: W.P.M. ——— Comprehension Score: ———

Using Your Test Scores

Now you have at least some idea of your speed and comprehension in reading easy narrative material and also in reading difficult material. These are your basic beginning scores. You will wish to refer to them frequently in making comparisons with successive scores that you achieve as you proceed through the book.

You may have found that your rates of reading easy material and of reading difficult material are about equal at this time, but they shouldn't be. As you work through this book you will be taught to "shift your gears" when you read different types of materials for different purposes. You will, however, need always to go back to these two sets of beginning scores to ascertain your gains.

Checking Your Physical Habits

Now you should do some informal checking of physical habits which may interfere with attempts to increase speed.

As you continue to read on this page, notice whether or not you point to words or follow the lines of print along with your fingers as you read. If so, break yourself of this habit. One way to do this is to hold the book or magazine with both hands, one on each side of the open pages. Your fingers, then, will not be free to point.

Note whether you move your head from side to side as you read. If so, nest your chin in one hand and hold it firmly. This will prevent your head from moving.

Watch yourself to see if you vocalize the words while reading silently. If your lips move as you read each word, then you are a vocalizer, and this will interfere seriously with your speed. Perhaps you do not actually say the words with your lips, but you may still vocalize to the extent that a slight movement of the muscles in the throat can be detected. If you find yourself vocalizing in either of these ways, place your fingers on your lips or the part of the throat which is moving. Whenever you feel the movement starting, stop it! You can break yourself of this habit by conscious and persistent attention.

Analyze your reading habits to see if you reread a great deal. Note how many times you go back to read a word, phrase, or sentence a second time. If you do not reread at all in pursuing nontechnical material, such as you find on this page, then all is well and good. If you frequently reread, then this is another habit which you must dispense with. When you feel the urge to reread, just proceed straight ahead. You'll probably be surprised to find that you didn't miss anything after all, and in the meantime you will have saved yourself a lot of time.

Perhaps you found that you do not have any of these habits to begin with. If you are free of them, so much the better. If you found that you do have some of them, then consciously break yourself of these practices. With undesirable physical habits cleared away, there is nothing to prevent you from increasing your reading speeds to any goals that you may set for yourself.

Chapter 2
Discovery

A Stick and a Drumhead

Back in 1879 there was a Frenchman by the name of Javal who became interested in investigating eye movements. He thought that, if he could ascertain exactly how the eye behaves when a person is reading, this would afford some insight into the mental activities that go on as reading takes place.

First he tried observing the eyes of people who were

reading just by looking at them with his own naked eyes. But the eyes of the readers moved so fleetingly that Javal couldn't tell just what did take place. He then tried placing a mirror in front of the reader, watching the reader's eyes in the mirror. But this didn't work either. Finally Javal concluded that the movements of the eyes could not be detected accurately by another pair of naked eyes.

He continued to work on the problem for some time. His thought was that it might be possible to rig up some sort of contrivance which could be used in obtaining really objective evidence in regard to movements of the eyes. He consulted his friends, asking them to help him invent some way of checking the eye movements of a person reading. "Nonsense," said they. "Why bother about something that everybody already knows? The eyes have to look at each letter in every word as they move across a line of print. Otherwise, how could the reader tell one word from another?"

This theory had been accepted as a fact throughout the centuries. The whole methodology of teaching reading was based for many years on the assumption that a person looks at each separate letter as he reads. Hence children were always taught their ABC's as a first step in learning to read.

Javal, however, doubted that a person recognized printed sentences letter by letter, so he persisted in trying to figure out some method by which he could detect and record the movements of the eyes under reading conditions. At last he hit upon it—a stick and a drumhead!

In developing his experimental equipment, Javal first fashioned a cup of plaster of Paris which was to fit over the eyeball of the person reading. He made an aperture in the middle of the cup through which the page could be seen.

While the plaster of Paris was still damp and pliable, Javal inserted one end of a long, slender stick into the outer side of the cup. When the cup dried, of course the stick was securely rooted in the plaster of Paris.

Next, Javal smoked a drumhead as people sometimes prepare a piece of glass for use in looking at an eclipse of the sun. The smoke left a heavy black coating on the drumhead.

When this equipment was ready, Javal asked a man to sit close to the drumhead and read. The plaster of Paris cup was placed over one eye of the subject, and as he read the stick traced a design in the smoke on the drumhead.

What did this design reveal? That the eyes did not look at one letter at a time or even at one word at a time. Rather, they proceeded in a series of pauses and jerks, stopping only three or four times in covering an entire line. Thus it was that a startling discovery about reading was made, one that is the very foundation of modern speed reading—namely, that the good reader quickly moves his eyes along over the lines of print, grasping whole meaningful units at each glance, rather than stopping to scrutinize each letter or even each word.

Other investigators, stimulated by Javal's experiment, began to make studies of their own. Huey improved upon Javal's equipment by using an ivory cup on the eye. The ivory cup was lighter and more comfortable than the plaster of Paris cup. Others used still different kinds of experimental equipment. Finally a huge camera was devised which would actually take photographs of the eye movements. This camera was designed by a professor who devoted full time for a year to its perfection, and it cost $6,000.

When using this camera, a bead of mercury was placed on the eyelid of the reader. If you have ever dropped a thermometer and broken its glass you have seen that little beads of mercury, almost as light as air and as round as balls, rolled about here and there in response to the slightest movement. Because of these properties, mercury was a highly satisfactory medium for this experimental work with eye movements. Furthermore, rays of light were reflected from these bright mercury beads. These rays were photographed as they were reflected on the lines of print while the reader was in the act of reading.

Once this thoroughly scientific procedure for detecting and recording eye movements had been developed, hundreds of studies were made with all kinds of readers at various age levels. Voluminous evidence piled up, showing beyond the shadow of a doubt that there were decided differences between the way poor readers read and the way excellent readers pursue the printed page. These studies revealed that the poor reader perceives just one word or perhaps a part of a word at a time, while the excellent reader takes in an entire group of words at a glance.

The plate[1] on page 34 is a composite photographic reproduction of the eye movements of eight different adults as each one read the same line of print.

The vertical lines represent the points at which the eyes rested as they moved across the line. These are called *fixation pauses*. It is during these fixation pauses that the eyes "pick up" the content. We do not "read" while the eyes are moving from one fixation point to another. The movements are just waste motion in so far as actual reading is concerned, but they are necessary in conveying the vision to another point on the line where the eyes again pause "to do some reading." During the fixation pauses the eyes of the good reader perceive two or three words on both sides of the pause; that is, the pause is in the middle of the cluster of symbols which the reader perceives. The width of this portion of a sentence which the eyes perceive at one glance is called the *span of recognition*.

The number at the top of each vertical line represents the order in which the fixations took place. For example, the numbers 1, 2, 3 above the vertical marks in the first line indicate that the reader paused three times in reading this line and that the pauses occurred in the numerical order. The figure under each vertical line represents the length of time the fixation endured in sixteenths of a second. For example, the reader's first fixation in the first line of the diagram lasted $9/16$ of a second.

Now that the symbols in the diagram have been ex-

[1] Guy Thomas Buswell, *How Adults Read*. Supp. Educ. Monograph, Univ. of Chicago, 1937.

Subject

655 After the war he gave the Negro a little house on

582 After the war he gave the Negro a little house on

790 After the war he gave the Negro a little house on

455 After the war he gave the Negro a little house on

491 After the war he gave the Negro a little house on

427 After the war he gave the Negro a little house on

747 After the war he gave the Negro a little house on

846 After the war he gave the Negro a little house on

plained, we should consider the larger implications of this photographic reproduction.

Subject 655 was the most skillful of the readers whose eye movements were photographed. This adult made only three fixations in covering the line. These were in exact order straight across the line and were of about the same duration. The first fixation lasted $9/16$ of a second; the second $7/16$ of a second; and the third $5/16$ of a second. The pauses became somewhat shorter as he got under way with his reading. His total reading time for the line was only $21/16$ or $1-5/16$ of a second.

Subject 582 was also a very good reader. His eyes paused only four times in passing across the line, in the right order. He was not able, however, to take in quite so much at one glance as Subject 655, and therefore he required more time to read the line. His first pause endured for $16/16$ or 1 full second; his second pause for $12/16$ of a second. His total reading time amounted to $42/16$ or $2-10/16$ of a second as compared to $1-5/16$ of a second for Subject 655.

In the photographic representation of the other subjects on the page, each succeeding diagram represents a less competent reader.

The eye movements of the poorest reader, Subject 846, are represented in the diagram at the bottom of the page. This reader made 20 fixations while reading the line, as compared with 3 fixations made by Subject 655. His total reading time for the line was $163/16$, or $10-3/16$ seconds as compared with $1-5/16$ of a second for the first reader.

Furthermore, this Subject 846 did not proceed regularly across the page as did Subject 655. He made his first fixation on the g in *gave;* then he swept his eyes backward and made his second fixation on the r in *after.* Then he proceeded ahead with his third fixation which centered between the t and h in *the.* His next eye movement was a regressive one, and his third pause took hold at the point of t in *after.*

In similarly studying his other fixations you will note about 7 times as many fixations as those of Subject 655. Besides, he took about ten times as much time to read the line as did Subject 655, and he made several backward or regressive movements instead of proceeding straight ahead.

The fundamental difference between the good and poor readers whose eye movements are shown in these photographic representations is that the good readers grasped a large, meaningful unit of thought at each fixation; whereas the poor readers fixated each time upon a single letter or a small group of letters which had little or no meaning in itself. These latter subjects were frequently forced to go back over the line to figure out what the text was saying.

The Fallacy of Treating Symptoms

Following these scientific studies of eye movements, instructors in some quarters began striving to train people to change their eye movements. For a time, this was considered the chief panacea for slow reading.

The writer recalls watching Dr. R., a psychiatrist, while under instruction designed to increase his reading speed. Since Dr. R.'s professional field was developing so rapidly that it was impossible for him to do all the necessary reading and also take care of his patients, he had applied at a reading laboratory. He was told over and over again that he "must widen his eye span" and was put through the routine of exercises designed to "increase his span." He sat in a tense position, clutching a book and straining every effort to widen his eye span. His eyelids were opened wide, and his eyes were fairly bulging out of their sockets. He soon became fatigued and remarked, "Well, I think I forced a pretty good span. The only trouble is, I was concentrating so hard on making my eyes work right that I don't know what I was reading about."

There you have in a nutshell the fallacy of striving to change the physical movement of the eyes only. When a patient is ill, the doctor takes his temperature and his pulse. If the temperature is high and the pulse rapid, he sees these as symptoms of the degree of illness. However, he looks for the cause of the illness and treats that rather than the symptoms.

So with reading. The eye movements are simply symptoms of the mental processes which a person uses while reading. The eyes are the servants of the mind and do its bidding in reading, just as the hands do the bidding of the mind when you tell them to "shell those peas rapidly and get it over with."

So don't make the mistake of concentrating on the mechanics of changing your eye span to accomplish faster and better reading. In other words, don't try to treat the symptom; work on the fundamental mental process itself.

Read for Ideas

The great value of investigations in eye movements is the picture they furnish of the different ways the mind works in perceiving reading symbols. They tell us that the mind of the poor reader loafs along, picking up very small units at a time, while the eyes of the excellent reader race over the lines, gathering an entire meaningful idea at each glance.

Cultivating the habit of reading for ideas not only increases speed, but it also increases understanding. A person who reads one word at a time thinks in terms of the meanings of these separate words and thus he "can't see the woods for the trees." The synthesis of important meanings is lost in any meticulous perception of the meanings of separate words or small units.

The first and most important instruction is *Read for ideas!* If you can cultivate the habit of rapidly picking up one complete thought unit after another, the eye movements will take care of themselves.

Try yourself out. Read each of the sentences below. As you go along determine which pattern you are using. Have your mind bid your eyes to pause at each slanting line and "take in" the meaning in so far as you can see on each side of the line. The pattern which you feel most comfortable in using is no doubt the one which best represents your own habits.

Poor

Many/adults/are/now/suffering/from/habits/which/ became/fixed/during/the/early/stages/in/which/they/ were/learning/to/read.

Average

Many/adults are/now suffering/from habits/which became/fixed during/the early stages/in which/they were/ learning/to read.

Good

Many adults/are now suffering from habits/which became fixed during the early stages/in which they were/ learning to read.

Even though you find you are reading according to the third pattern, there is still room for improvement. Everyone can with practice learn to pick up longer thought units.

Several short selections are provided on the following pages for your use in learning to read in increasingly longer units of meaning. You are not asked to time yourself in doing these exercises. The first step in your reading improvement program is to get yourself into the habit of taking in large groups of words at a glance. Therefore, in these exercises concentrate on just one thing—your intake of increasingly longer units of meanings.

To ascertain whether you are getting the meaning as you lengthen the span of words that you perceive at a glance, checks of comprehension are provided. These checks are based largely on your ability to grasp meanings in increasingly longer word groups.

Selection 1

Move your eyes down from top to bottom as you read

these columns. Follow the vertical line straight down without moving your eyes either to the right or left. Try to grasp the full meaning of each group of words as you impel your eyes down through the center of each list of phrases.[2]

Here is	This profit	Our best	If any
an idea	is entirely	knowledge	young man
for every	aside from	is that which	will get
young man	the money	we absorb	this thought
who works	that changes	as a result	well rooted
for a living.	hands	of work.	in his mind
The worker	in the	It is	he will
gets the	transaction.	part of us.	increase
biggest profit	It is	We do not	his chances
out of	the profit	forget it.	for recognition
any job	of increased	It is ours	and promotion
that is	ability.	to command.	100 per cent.
well done.			

Checking Comprehension

Write the letter which appears before the correct answer in the blank spaces below. Follow this same procedure in taking all the other comprehension tests throughout this book.

1. This article is directed primarily to (a) old men, (b) middle-aged men, (c) young men, (d) all men.

2. The worker gets the greatest profit out of (a) increases in salary, (b) promotions, (c) investments in the company, (d) any job well done.

3. The profit of increased ability (a) includes money that changes hands in the transaction, (b) includes money earned by promotions, (c) is entirely aside from the money that changes hands in the transaction, (4) is concerned only with the money that changes hands in the transaction.

4. Our best knowledge is that which (a) we get in college courses, (b) absorb as a result of work, (c) learn

[2] *Reader's Digest*, August 1955, p. 133, quoted from *The William Feather Magazine*. (Rearranged.)

through self-study, (d) pick up from others who possess the "know-how."

5. Chances for recognition and promotion can be increased 100 per cent by (a) cultivating someone who will give you a "pull," (b) asking for a raise, (c) doing something spectacular, (d) realizing that increased ability resulting from the job is one's most important asset.

Answers: 1)——, 2)——, 3)——, 4)——, 5)——.

Check your answers with the Answer Key, page 276. Allow yourself a score of 20 for each correct answer.

Comprehension Score:————

Selection 2

These thought units are longer than those in the preceding exercise. Use the same technique in reading these units as suggested for Selection 1.

PUSHBUTTON RAIN[3]

For many years drought-stricken farmers have sought relief by praying for rain. Now they are beginning to answer their own prayers. With aluminum pipe the average farmer can have rain if and when he wants it.

Of course, it will be much easier for some farmers than for others. The important thing is to have an accommodating creek, river, strong well, or some other convenient source from which water can be obtained.

The farmer will hook up a pump with a long pipe and put that water where it will do the most good. He will no longer have to look toward the clouds and wistfully hope for the heavens to spill out their moisture.

Checking Comprehension (*Selection 2, above*)

1. This article concerns the farmer's problem of obtaining (a) seed, (b) better fertilizer, (c) top-grade soil, (d) water.

2. The method with which a farmer may now obtain water when he wants it is by (a) running it to his fields with a pipe, (b) "seeding" clouds to make rain, (c) praying for rain, (d) using water from large dams built by the government.

³ Ross L. Holman, "Pushbutton Rain," *Science Digest*, August 1955, p. 61. (Rearranged and adapted.)

3. The factor that will largely determine each farmer's ease or difficulty in obtaining water will be (a) the shape of his fields, (b) the altitude of his fields, (c) the availability of a source of water, (d) the ease or difficulty of digging drainage ditches.

4. Water will be made to flow through the pipes by means of (a) gravity, (b) a pump, (c) siphons, (d) the force of the water flowing downhill.

5. From now on, farmers will no longer have to worry about (a) poor crops, (b) low prices, (c) drought, (d) insects.

Answers: 1)——, 2)——, 3)——, 4)——, 5)——.

Check your answers with the Answer Key, page 276. Allow yourself a score of 20 for each correct answer.

Comprehension Score:———

Checking Comprehension (Selection 3, page 42)

1. The custom of shaking hands is (a) purely American (b) practiced in most parts of the world, (c) a New-World custom, (d) mainly a custom of English-speaking countries.

2. In England and Holland shaking hands is (a) considered an affront, (b) done daily with each employee, (c) reserved for introductions, (d) done on every conceivable occasion.

3. In Italy, Turkey, and Greece (a) everyone shakes hands everywhere, (b) people never shake hands, (c) a firm grip is the custom, (d) people shake hands only at introductions.

4. In many countries, an American who normally uses a firm grip may find it wise to (a) refrain from handshaking, (b) not change his habit at all, (c) wait until the other party offers to shake hands, (d) ease off his grip.

5. In the Orient, shaking hands is (a) done in imitation of American ways, (b) more widespread than in the United States, (c) reserved for special occasions, (d) something to beware of.

Answers: 1)——, 2)——, 3)——, 4)——, 5)——.

Selection 3

On Shaking Hands[4]

Shaking hands
is an old custom
in almost every part
of the world.
In feudal times
it was the symbol
of homage and fealty.
Today the glad hand
is an exchange
between equals,
but there are shades
of variation in its use.
In Holland and England
the handshake
is reserved for introductions.

In France and Portugal
employers shake hands daily
with each employee.
In Italy, Turkey, and Greece,
everyone shakes hands everywhere
—in street, cafe, office, home—
on meeting and leaving
his friends.
The American who is
proud of his firm grip,
and normally uses
an energetic one,
may find it wise
to ease off
in many countries.

In the Middle East,
for example,
the proper handshake
is just a gentle pressure.
And in the Orient, beware of
personal contact,
including shaking hands.
Holding the arm
or tapping the shoulder
is an affront.
Instead, practice a bow
and you'll have
as firm a grip
on the situation
as is required.

[4] "On Shaking Hands," *Holiday*, September 1955, p. 93.

Selection 4

DON'T GET SEASICK[5]

A century ago
Sir Henry Bessemer
built an English Channel steamer
in which the cabins
were hung on brackets.
Through a mechanism
which was manipulated
by a crew member
when the water was rough,
the cabins would swing
so as to offset
the uncomfortable roll
of the little vessel.

Since then, engineers
have tried out scores
of ingenious arrangements
intended to free travelers
aboard sea-going vessels
and other conveyances
from the usual hazard
of motion sickness.
They have eliminated
numerous jolts and twists
but not motion sickness.
Fortunately, engineers are not
the only ones concerned
with this problem.

The traveler of today
has no occasion
to fear motion illness,
for in recent years
active chemical investigators
have found useful drugs
that make the passenger
immune to the unpleasantness
which he otherwise
would feel in his stomach.
Outstanding among these drugs
is one called Bonamine,
a unique, long-acting
anti-motion sickness compound.

[5] Milton Liebman, *Mechanics Illustrated*, April 1954, p. 76.

Check your answer with the Answer Key on page 276. Allow yourself a score of 20 for each correct answer.

Comprehension Score:———

Checking Comprehension (*Selection 4, page 43*)

1. Sir Henry Bessemer tried to eliminate seasickness by (a) preventing ships from rolling, (b) using drugs, (c) allowing the cabins to swing, (d) increasing the speed of the ship.

2. Since Bessemer's time, engineers have (a) given up the attempts to prevent motion sickness, (b) continued to work out ingenious arrangements, (c) succeeded in their attempts to prevent passengers from getting motion sickness, (d) not given any more thought to the problem.

3. Through the years, attempts to keep parts of ships from moving have resulted in (a) the elimination of numerous jolts and twists, but not motion sickness, (b) the elimination of motion sickness, (c) no improvement because of theoretical impossibility of cutting down motion in a moving conveyance, (d) failure because of the expense involved.

4. People who travel today (a) face the same hazards of motion sickness as travelers faced years ago, (b) are better off only because they grow used to motion, (c) are more subject to motion sickness than people were years ago, (d) have no occasion to fear motion sickness.

5. Today's improved protection against motion sickness is largely the result of (a) the success of engineers in reducing motion, (b) the development of antimotion drugs, (c) the greater size and speed of modern ships and planes, (d) the fact that modern diet has made us more resistant to motion sickness.

Answers: 1)——, 2)——, 3)——, 4)——, 5)——.

Check your answers with the Answer Key on page 276. Allow yourself a score of 20 for each correct answer.

Comprehension Score:———

Selection 5
Mark this selection into phrases yourself. Divide the

sentences so that, as often as possible, each meaningful unit is four or five words long. Then read the selection, trying to grasp each one of these long, meaningful phrases at a glance.

VANISHING AMERICAN SOUNDS[6]

The other afternoon when the house was temporarily quiet, I found myself remembering the sounds of my childhood.

Missing now is the sound of carpet-sweeper and broom, of eggs being beaten with a fork in a platter, of suds being squeezed through wet cloth, with an occasional rib-rub on the scrub board, the slow tick-tock of the grandfather's clock at the foot of the stairs.

In summer, the lop-lop-lop of the ceiling fan, the gentle creak of the porch swing. Or the sound of ice being shaved in the kitchen. From the street came the clip-clop of the vegetable man's horse, the ding-dong of his bell, the wonderful high call of the strawberry man walking along the sidewalk.

Rhythmic sounds, comforting sounds—a relaxing fabric of sound for a child to read against or dream against.

Today's children are under constant bombardment of noises. Clocks don't tick-tock any more; they hum endlessly. Instead of the broom there is the whine of the vacuum cleaner. Instead of the fork against the egg platter, there is the higher whine of the mixer. Instead of the gentle creak of the porch swing, the roar of the power lawn mower. Instead of the rocking chair and soft talk, the blare of television or radio on full blast. Outside, in the place of the clip-clop or the strawberry call, we have the jet plane, the squeal and roar of a teenager's car.

No, houses don't sound the same as they used to.

No comprehension check is given for this exercise. Since you were asked to mark the selection into meaningful units before you read it, you are no doubt so familiar with the meaning that a check of comprehension would be valueless.

[6] Marguerite Johnston, *Reader's Digest*, August 1955, p. 85. (Quoted from the *Houston Post*.)

Selection 6

Read this entire selection without marking it into meaningful word groups. Try to grasp a sizable unit of meaning with each glance as you read across the lines of print. Force yourself to take in as large an "eyeful" of meaning as possible at each fixation pause. You will be given a comprehension check at the end of the selection.

NEBRASKA'S FABULOUS FISHWORM FARMER[7]

Meet Pete Scheidt, of McCook, Nebraska, the one farmer in America today without a gripe, subsidy, or worry to his name, with one exception. "Doggone it!" Pete grumbles every day of his life. "I ain't had time to go fishin' only once in two years."

Pete didn't really intend to get into the big farming business. It just caught up with him in an accidental sort of way. All Pete asked of life was just something to tinker around with after he'd retired from the railroad in 1951. "If you would live longer and happier, get a hobby," he'd read over and over again in a hobby magazine, and so Pete was in quest of his fountain of youth and happiness with a hobby—when it happened.

One Spring morning a little red wriggler stuck his head out of the soft warm earth in Pete's back yard and smiled at Pete. Pete smiled back, and then it struck him like a bolt from the blue!

That very morning Pete started digging pits, then digging worms to fill them. He calculated he had close to 20,000 big red wrigglers to start with. A female worm lays 100 to 120 eggs a year, and each egg, which looks like a small brown seed, hatches five little wrigglers—so that's exactly how big business caught up with Pete.

The first year he sold more than 140,000 worms wholesale at $4.20 per box of 12-pint cartons. Each pint contained 60 to 70 worms. And he retailed thousands of worms at 60 cents a pint, or approximately one cent per worm.

To get all the eggs possible, Pete keeps 150,000 breeder worms in boxes in his hatchery. Every six weeks they are transferred to new boxes, and the eggs are deposited in hatchery boxes made especially for that purpose. Pete's

[7] Pearl P. Puckett, *The American Mercury*, June 1954, pp. 23-24.

hatchery is a frame building on the rear of his lot, with hundreds of clean sunny south windows across the entire front of the structure. The hatchery is immaculate, and a heater is kept burning night and day at the right temperature to raise worms. Each box is watered with care and regularity. Under normal conditions maintained in the hatchery, Pete has a box of eggs hatching every 30 days, and in this way he is able to select one-year-old worms for his breeding stock.

Pete has had to hire a lot of help, too, because his worm pits are a little out of the ordinary. Each pit is lined with a soft mulch of leaves, barnyard fertilizer, and then alfalfa "leavings."

Last spring he started something new. He bought fifty old white-enamel washing-machine tubs, something that a dealer had had to take in on trade and intended to junk. Each tub was placed in a pit, and grape vines were planted around each pit to run arbors over the tubs. This will, as Pete says, "kill two birds with one stone": keep his worms from cooking in summer heat and produce the finest grapes known. The soil is extremely rich, and the worms act more or less as cultivators in keeping it stirred up deep down in the pits.

Not long ago a young chemical engineer from Sun Valley saw Pete's sign along Highway 6 and stopped in to find out about fishworm farming. Before he left, he bought 100,000 worms.

Pete ships worms all over America today, and he just can't keep up with the demand. In fact, it requires more than one man to count and box them for shipment. The worms are sent parcel post. He lines waxed-paper pint cartons with peat moss, puts in his worms and adds just enough water; then punches holes in the lid so that the worms can breathe.

Counting worms for his shipments is the hardest part of the business, because it is necessary to dig your hands down into the warm mulch, and the worms move very fast. Let a little light in, and they swarm over to the dark side of the box quick and slippery.

"Takes me exactly 13 days to count out 96 boxes," Pete says. "So I bring my radio out here to make the job more pleasant."

Pete is possibly the largest fishworm farmer in the world today, as orders pour in from the 48 states and

Canada. He has pits all over his yard with more than 100,000 worms per pit. Pete believes that the reason there aren't more fishworm farmers in America today is because it's a squeamish business and time consuming; then, too, the big resorts and fellows who love to fish would rather pay one cent a piece for their worms than stop and dig them.

Pete doesn't have to worry about subsidies, overproduction, or embargoes. He quotes his own prices, and so far there hasn't been any ceiling placed on worms or worm eggs. Fishworm farming is pretty big business. It can be handled on a small acreage, and a million worms a year at approximately one cent each adds up to a five-figure income.

Checking Comprehension

Write the letter which appears before the correct answer in the appropriate answer space following each statement.

1. Peter Scheidt got into the business of raising worms through his search for (a) a hobby, (b) a means of obtaining a modest living without too much work, (c) a means of making a lot of money quickly, (d) a means of getting rid of some worms which had been tearing up his land.

2. Pete raises his worms in (a) the soft, warm soil in his barnyard, (b) in one of his fields, (c) in pits lined with special materials, (d) in black soil in his garden.

3. Pete obtains most of his worms by (a) searching for them, (b) paying boys to find them for him, (c) getting them from people who want to get rid of them, (d) breeding them himself.

4. Pete's idea of "killing two birds with one stone" involves (a) getting rid of worms on the neighbors' land when he sells them, (b) raising grapes near the breeding soil, (c) fertilizing neighbors' gardens with worms he is raising, (d) raising vegetables in the breeding soil.

5. The young chemical engineer who visited Pete Scheidt (a) bought a lot of worms, (b) wrote a paper on worm breeding, (c) gave Pete valuable advice on

the chemistry of soils, (d) set up another farm next to Pete's.

6. The market for Pete's worms (a) extends all over the United States and Canada, (b) is local, (c) has to be kept to a small area because worms would die if shipped a long distance, (d) is kept in the United States by laws which prohibit shipment of worms over national borders.

7. Pete has found that the demand for his worms (a) has fallen off lately, (b) was not good when he began his business but has improved, (c) is so great he can't keep up with it, (d) would be better if he did not have so much competition.

8. The most difficult job that Pete Scheidt faces in his work is (a) breeding the worms, (b) counting them for shipment, (c) hiring help, (d) finding customers.

9. Pete gives some reasons for the fact that there are not more fishworm farmers in America. One of these reasons is that (a) it is a squeamish business, (b) it is difficult to raise worms efficiently, (c) the market is not large enough for additional producers, (d) raising worms requires too much hired help.

10. One of the many advantages that Pete Scheidt's farm has over more conventional farms is that (a) his machinery lasts longer, (b) he can do all the work himself, (c) he does not need to water his crop, (d) he is free of governmental regulation.

Answers: 1)——, 2)——, 3)——, 4)——, 5)——, 6)——, 7)——, 8)——, 9)——, 10)——.

See Answer Key, page 276. Allow yourself a score of 10 for each correct answer.

Comprehension Score:————

Follow-Up Suggestions

You have now learned one of the basic secrets of rapid, meaningful reading—that of grasping large thought units at each glance. If you wish to read fast you must gulp—not nibble!

There are three avenues open to you for further development of your ability to grasp sizable meaningful units at each momentary pause of your eyes.

1. You are given opportunity to practice this technique throughout the remainder of this book. Many other skills will be developed, but each new skill will be added to this basic skill, and each one will be founded upon the assumption that you are continually striving to improve your ability to grasp larger thought units at each glance.

2. You should try to apply this technique in all your outside reading, as well as while working with this book. Whenever you have to read something in connection with your work, consciously look for wide groups of words, each of which expresses a significant idea. Do the same thing when you read casually from a newspaper, magazine, or novel. In other words, apply the technique continuously in *all* the reading you do.

3. In addition to the two suggestions above, set aside a definite time for practice each evening. Devote from fifteen to thirty minutes regularly to practice reading in increasingly larger thought units. You may use any material you have at hand. It is advisable, however, to begin practicing with easy material such as that used in this chapter, then gradually to work with more difficult material.

Chapter 3

Faster! Faster!

An amusing story is told about Puccini, the great Italian composer. One day he dashed out of his flat in Milan, fifteen minutes late for an appointment. As he rushed up the street he encountered an organ-grinder who was drowsily turning the crank of his organ under the spell of the warm Italian sunshine. The disturbing thing to Puccini was that the aria which the grinder was so indolently reproducing was one from his own *Madame Butterfly*.

Puccini, deeply irritated by the agonizingly slow movement of his masterpiece, cried out impatiently, "Heavens, man, faster, faster!" without slackening his pace. As he ran, however, he momentarily attempted to set a tempo by waving his right hand rapidly back and forth in true maestro fashion.

The next week Puccini again met this same organ-grinder. This time he was grinding out *Madame Butterfly* in the rapid, sprightly tempo which Puccini's hand had indicated. Even more surprising, however, was the sign suspended from the grinder's neck: "Pupil of Puccini."

For you who would speed your reading, this story holds more than passing amusement at the organ-grinder's capitalizing on his brief contact with the great master. Maybe you, too, have fallen into the habit of "grinding out the tune" in a slow tempo when you read. Perhaps you need to be startled out of your lethargy by having someone shout at you, "Heavens, man, faster, faster!"

Working for Speed

You have learned in the preceding chapter that the rapid reader's eyes move fleetingly across the lines, pausing briefly two or three times on each line and picking up an "eyeful" of words at each pause. Speed is achieved by increasing the rapidity of the eye movements, decreasing the length of the pause, and taking in a large number of words during each pause.

While these are the mechanics of eye movements, you have been warned that it is the mind which controls the reading process, and better eye movements are but a reflection of increased mental tempo in absorbing the meaning from printed symbols. So, first of all, set your mind to take in long, meaningful units, with fleeting eye pauses that gather in everything within the range of vision. Don't point, don't say the words with your lips, and don't move your head. Free your mind from all bodily accompaniments. Let it race ahead unimpeded.

Now that you know what to do, make up your mind that you must practice. A person learns to type rapidly and accurately by practicing; he learns to play the piano excellently by practicing; he learns to skate skillfully by practicing. So it is with reading. As a busy man or woman you must definitely resolve to tackle your reading improvement in the same way that you would tackle skill improvement in any other area. Desire, determination, practice—these are the basic ingredients in your recipe for reading improvement. Once you've put yourself in the frame of mind to work, you've made a good start.

Choose the right physical setting for this practice. Don't start your improvement program in the midst of a busy office where phones are ringing, employees are asking questions, and people are coming and going. And don't start it in the living room at home where television is shouting out attention-arresting phrases and the children are playing cops and robbers. You probably can withstand such distractions when you become a highly proficient reader. But to start with, go into a room by yourself—and close the door! Shut out the distractions.

Once you are in a room free from distractions, look for a chair which isn't too comfortable. Your period of reading practice is no time to loll on a chaise lounge or to recline on soft pillows in a bed. You have a job to do. You are about to sharpen one of your most important tools. With the importance of your new job in mind, find a straight-backed chair. Seat yourself so that you know you have a spine, square your shoulders, and go to work.

At this stage in your program, you should practice on easy material. Practice with difficult material will come later on. Easy material will serve you best while you are breaking the old tempo and establishing new habits. Consequently, each of the selections which follow in this chapter will be very easy—so easy that you'll dare to "let go" and sweep your eyes across the lines with a speed you've never tried before. As you are about to begin each of the selections, set your own purpose for reading it. A strong purpose helps to pull your eyes rapidly along over the lines, and it gives you something to tie to in gathering meanings as you go along.

So when you are ready to read, make up your mind just why you want to read that particular selection. Just to follow the plot of the narrative? To get some ideas that might be useful to you? To find out what happened in a current event? Whatever the reason, phrase it concisely and keep it uppermost in your mind throughout the reading of the selection. Your purpose is the pilot light which guides you over the sea of print with a well-filled dragnet of ideas at the end of the journey. It is a magnet which attracts useful information to satisfy your business and pleasure needs.

Above all, force your speed! Consciously push your eyes across the line as fast as you can make them go and still know what you are reading about. Across, back, across, back, across, back, in rapid, rhythmic sweeps! Make those eyes leap over each line. They are your servants. You can control them. Don't let them loaf along in the old lazy way.

Practicing and Checking

Now see if you can apply all the things you've learned while reading the next selection. It is about banks, a topic in which all people are interested.

After seating yourself in the right physical setting, look at the title. What specific information do you think will be presented in regard to banks? For what purpose would you like to read this article? To obtain general information about the differences between the banks of "Yesterday" and "Now"? To find out if differences between old and new banking procedures have parallels in your own business? To get additional insights into changes in banking procedures which might be beneficial to you in making greater use of the bank in furthering your own business interests? Or what?

Whatever your purpose, phrase it concisely and keep it uppermost in your mind throughout the reading of the article.

Resolutely determine to read *fast, faster than you've ever read before.*

Jot down the beginning time on an even minute. Ready! Go!

Selection 1

BEGINNING TIME:————
HR.———— MIN.————

BANKS—YESTERDAY AND NOW[1]

Time was—and not so many years ago, either—when the average citizen took a pretty dim view of banks and banking. That this was so, it should be said, was to no small extent the fault of banks and bankers themselves. Banks used to be—and a few still are—grim and forbidding structures, where business was conducted in a sort of genteel gloom, atmospherically and personally. Be-

[1] *New York Times,* February 17, 1954, p. 30.

hind the little barred windows were, more often than not, elderly gentlemen whose cordiality—and that may be an over-generous word to apply—reflected the size of the customer's account, and nothing less than a few hundred thousand on deposit could have inspired the suggestion of a smile. As for the officers and junior members of the firm—well, the man on the street rarely saw them and perhaps even more rarely thought seriously of speaking to them in a business way.

Now, that appraisal may be a bit too harsh. And yet the average bank for many years was, to the average citizen, an awesome if necessary instrument for the transacting of business—usually big business. But somewhere in the past quarter century—perhaps in the wake of the depression—banks began to grow human, even pleasant, and started to woo the little man, the man who had been in awe of banks and bankers. It is possible that this movement began in medium-sized towns, or in small towns where people know each other by their first names, and spread to big towns. At any rate, the results have been spectacular.

The movement to "humanize" banks, of course, received a big push during the war, when more and more women were employed to do work previously performed by men. Also more and more "little people" found themselves in need of personal loans, as taxes became heavier and as the institution of installment buying broke down the previously long-held concept that there was something almost morally wrong about being in debt. All sorts of people began to discover that the intelligent use of credit could be extremely helpful—and this idea was encouraged to grow by forward-looking banks that saw a great future in aiding large numbers of small depositors and borrowers to meet their financial problems.

Today's banks present a picture startlingly different from that offered by the banks of yesterday. For the most part their officers are accessible and are known to a surprisingly large number of small depositors whom even vice-presidents can call by their first names. Some banks even have women—not unattractive, either—as personal loan interviewers. And, of course, at many cashier's windows—most of which are now bar-less—pretty young women greet the customer with a smile regardless of the size of his account. Banks today make personal loans that few, if any, banks perhaps a quarter of a century ago would have considered. For example, not long ago a young man moved to a large city to embark on a new job and appealed to a bank for help in obtaining funds sufficient to move his family to the new location, some distance from his former home. He had no collateral—only a bright future and a creditable past. One bank did turn down his petition—in a friendly way—but another studied his problem and decided to invest in his future. He got the loan. In a not-too-distant past he'd have been regarded as a poor risk by any bank.

In view of the public's increasing acceptance of banks and bankers as friendly counselors, it is indeed surprising to discover that banks feel it necessary to embark on an elaborate public relations program to make people more conscious of their place in the community and the national scene. It may well be that the role of banks in keeping the nation's financial arteries functioning properly is not as well understood by the public as it might be. But in most communities today's banks and bankers have "sold" themselves and their services at the local level. It may be that the local banker has not yet established himself as firmly as a source of help and counsel as has the family doctor, and it may be also that by the nature of his services he never will, but he is making rapid strides in that direction.

Began Finished No. words: 735

$$\frac{\rule{2cm}{0.4pt}}{\rule{2cm}{0.4pt}} \times 60 = \rule{1cm}{0.4pt} \text{ W.P.M.}$$

_____ _____ No. seconds:

Checking Comprehension

1. The author believes that the unfriendly atmosphere in banks of many years ago was due to (a) economic pressures of the times, (b) hostility of customers toward banks, (c) the attitudes of bankers and people who worked in the banks, (d) the physical structure of bank buildings.

2. The bank of many years ago paid the bulk of its attention to (a) businessmen, (b) large depositors, (c) small depositors, (d) none of the above.

3. Which of the following was not stated as a cause of the bank's more "human" policies of recent years:

(a) business growth, (b) increased installment buying, (c) employment of women in banks, (d) increased needs of "little people."

4. The author believes that the movement to "humanize" banks may have begun in (a) large cities, where more banks are located, (b) all over the country, (c) small and medium-sized towns, (d) Federal Reserve banks.

5. During the war, banks saw new possibilities in (a) accounts of war industries, (b) only large accounts, (c) manufacturers' accounts, (d) large numbers of small depositors and borrowers.

6. One common example of banks' friendlier attitude is (a) smaller-sized banks, (b) more-expensive decorations, (c) better-dressed employees, (d) greater accessibility to officers.

7. The example of the young man's loan was intended to show that (a) banks must be careful when making loans, (b) banks will now make loans that they would not have made years ago, (c) there is no set policy on loans, (d) people now need more money than they did in times past.

8. The author feels that bankers are approaching the role of (a) businessmen, (b) lawyers, (c) brokers, (d) doctors.

9. Perhaps the present public-relations program of banks is necessary because (a) banks want to drain off surplus earnings, (b) they want to complete a planned program, (c) they are sorry for poor people, (d) people do not understand the role of the banks in keeping the nation's financial arteries functioning properly.

10. It is probable that today's banks have sold themselves at local levels (a) to big business, (b) in most communities, (c) in a few towns, (d) in a few large cities.

Answers: 1)——, 2)——, 3)——, 4)——, 5)——, 6)——, 7)——, 8)——, 9)——, 10)——.

Check your answer with the Answer Key on page 277. Multiply the total correct items by 10.

Rate: W.P.M. ——— Comprehension Score: ———

Selection 2

Set yourself a purpose for reading this article, and try to read it even faster than you read the first one.

BEGINNING TIME:———————
HR.——————— MIN.———————

WHY DO THEY MOVE? [2]

The Population Reference Bureau says that about 3 per cent of the nation's population move from one state to another each year. Many more persons undoubtedly move intrastate; the Institute of Life Insurance estimates that this year 31,000,000 people will pull up stakes and move to other homes. It is difficult to see why this is so. If moving one's household from one home to another in the same city, or from one city to another, were as simple as changing a pair of shoes, those figures pertaining to Americans on the move would not be surprising. But moving, and especially long-distance moving, is an incredibly complex, uncomfortable, unsettling, wearisome, expensive and distasteful operation.

Here in City A, for example, are old friends and neighbors, old haunts—familiar faces, familiar schools, familiar church, comfortable if not plush house—and firmly fixed habits. There in City B, are neighbors of as yet undetermined humours, new surroundings and perhaps customs; strange schools and—at first glance—gimlet-eyed teachers, a church with perhaps different hymnbooks (very unsettling) to say nothing of a wholly strange order of worship. And high on the list of painful adjustments is the necessity of forming new habits, of finding new restaurants, perhaps changing one's mode of transportation. And then there is the little matter of the new house.

The matter of the new house appears on the agenda early in any moving operation. The lady of the (old) house says that the new house must be larger, nearer to stores, nearer to schools, with a large yard, with fireplaces, a sunny kitchen, etc., etc. And the head of the (old) house finds himself saddled not only with the

——————
[2] *New York Times*, March 15, 1954, p. 24.

task of adjusting himself to new associates in what may be a totally strange place but also with the responsibility of finding a new house answering the foregoing description. If he is wise, the head of the (old) house will somehow turn the important (and time-consuming) business of discovering a new house to the distaff side so that in the event matters turn out poorly he, and not she, can say, "Well, I didn't think much of the house in the first place, but I didn't like to say so."

But no matter what, the new house will be a problem. Even the most careful inspection of a house does not prepare one fully for living in it. Inspection before moving in does not prepare one for the discovery that the movers with their van load of furniture—and what looks more worn and frazzled than worn furniture being carted across a pavement, from truck to house, in the cold light of day?—and a small army of painters have arrived at the new house at the same time. Inspection before moving does not prepare one for the discovery that the previous occupants have decamped with all but three window shades, leaving the new residents and all their dusty furniture and their undisguised misery fully exposed to curious eyes.

Inspection does not disclose that, although one may come from a place where trash, ashes, and garbage were picked up twice a week, here at the new house trash is picked up once every two weeks on one day, ashes on another day, and garbage on still another. Or that the paper boy's aim at the new house is worse than a certain lad's aim at the old. Or that the new house's windows rattle alarmingly even in a light breeze. Or that there are fewer shelves in the kitchen than one had supposed. Or that one of the garage doors—a heavy, heavy door—is about to fall off.

But there is the new house—and its larger yard, just as the lady of the (old) house wanted it. With more grass to cut. A nice, big hedge to trim. Lots of trees to shed their leaves in season. And a lot of neighbors, who, as yet, do not appear to be the type eager to share any of their belongings with newcomers who have no shades on their windows and appear to be, for all the world, a bunch of gypsies with a heap of broken-down or at least badly-bent furniture. The new house will be all right some day, but when the movers have gone and the door is closed (stickily), the old house looks pretty good, wherever it was.

Began Finished No. words: 680

——— ——— No. seconds: —— × 60 = —— W.P.M.

Checking Comprehension

1. The author seems to believe that moving is an operation (a) as simple as changing shoes, (b) much easier than it used to be, (c) not at all expensive nowadays, (d) complex and distasteful.

2. According to the Population Reference Bureau, the percentage of people that move from one state to another each year is (a) one per cent, (b) three per cent, (c) five per cent, (d) seven per cent.

3. *Not* mentioned as one of the adjustments which must be made in a new neighborhood is. (a) finding new restaurants, (b) forming new habits, (c) attending another church, (d) finding suitable stores.

4. It is suggested that the head of the (old) house (a) find a new house himself, (b) leave the choice to his wife, (c) have the family do it together, (d) depend upon a real estate agent.

5. It is likely that the lady of the house will want a new house that is (a) larger and more conveniently located than the old one, (b) a duplicate of the old one, (c) more conveniently located but smaller in order to require less work, (d) one having one floor only so that she won't have to climb stairs.

6. The author seems to believe that the difficulties of getting settled in a new home (a) can be practically eliminated by careful planning, (b) will take care of themselves, (c) are so numerous that it is no use trying to cope with them, (d) will arise no matter what.

7. Furniture being moved from a truck to a house looks (a) good to the neighbors, (b) the way it looked in the old house, (c) worn and frazzled, (d) suitable for the old home but not for the new one.

8. The previous occupants of the new house were said

to have taken (a) the lawnmower, (b) all Venetian blinds, (c) all but three window shades, (d) a screen-door.

9. At the new house, pick-up service of trash, ashes, and garbage may be (a) more frequent than at the old, (b) less frequent than at the old, (c) same as at the old, (d) nonexistent.

10. The new neighbors seem to be (a) very friendly, (b) destructive, (c) helpful, (d) not eager to share their belongings.

Answers: 1)——, 2)——, 3)——, 4)——, 5)——, 6)——, 7)——, 8)——, 9)——, 10)——.

See Answer Key, page 277. Allow 10 for each correct answer.

Rate: W.P.M. ——— Comprehension Score: ———

Selection 3

See if you can beat all your records so far in covering this with high speed and increased comprehension.

BEGINNING TIME:————
HR.———— MIN.————

WIZARD OF THE VEGETABLE PATCH[3]

It all started with "the carrot job." The Campbell Soup Company wanted a drastically remodeled carrot, one with no yellow in its core, and uniform in size and shape. The company found that pale-yellow cubes among deep-orange cubes in vegetable soup cut down eye appeal and that odd-shaped carrots left too much waste when they went through the dicing machines. They asked the C. C. Morse Seed Company what could be done about it.

For centuries carrots had matured with yellow cores and in assorted shapes. Changing their growing habits called for horticultural magic. So Lester Morse, head of the firm, sent for a ruddy-cheeked young Scot, Frank G. Cuthbertson, who had bred flowers but had never tried to restyle a vegetable to order.

[3] Frank J. Taylor, *Reader's Digest*, July 1954. (Reprinted from *Town Journal*, July 1954.)

He tackled the job, and over the years his efforts have burgeoned into a widespread vegetable-remodeling drive. In three decades Cuthbertson and his team of hybridizers have redone so many truck crops that it is almost impossible to sit down to dinner without enjoying at least one of his restyled vegetables. Last year the American Seed Trade Association honored him with a medallion for "outstanding contributions to horticulture."

The carrot job back in the '20's confronted Cuthbertson and his colleague, Walter Nixon, with unique obstacles. To breed a strain with orange cores, they first had to find one carrot with orange "blood," the seedman's term for a trait. To find that one carrot they grew thousands.

To get a peek at the cores without checking the carrots' further growth they plugged each root with a small glass tube. Whenever the plug revealed a darker-than-usual core they replanted the carrot, put a marker beside it and waited patiently until the plant bore seed. Then they planted again, repeating the tedious hunt for a darker-cored carrot.

Eight years and thousands of carrots later Cuthbertson had ten carrots with no trace of yellow in their cores. Furthermore, their size was just what the soup makers wanted. Today progeny from those ten carrots produce enough seed annually to plant 100,000 acres.

Home gardeners, canners, and produce merchants wanted a beet that was red all the way through and would resist mildew. So Cuthbertson and Nixon induced beets to give up the characteristic pink rings in their flesh, then grew a generation in fields of mildewed beets. The plants that defied mildew became the parent stock for a mildew-resistant strain known as Morse's Detroit Dark Red. This year U. S. seed growers will produce 300,000 pounds of seed of this made-to-order beet.

But gardeners who grow beets for the greens as well as for the roots were still unsatisfied. So the Morse team built a red-fleshed beet with many tender leaves, called Green-Top Bunching. Now everybody in the beet patch is happy.

Ironically, after the seed of a restyled vegetable is introduced to growers and gardeners, any competitor can grow seed. Most of them do, sometimes giving the variety another name. The vegetable designer takes his reward in prestige among seedsmen and commercial growers.

Born in Scotland, Frank Cuthbertson came to San Francisco in 1911 with 20 borrowed dollars in his pocket. His first job, at $2.50 a day, was "roguing"—pulling out the off-foliage plants on the Morse farm.

With the eye of a perfectionist, the young Scot rogued so mercilessly that he made a shambles of the company's sweet-pea fields. His ruthlessness paid off. Before long the seed of Morse sweet peas was selling for four times the previous price. (The Cuthbertson sweet pea is now famous.) Impressed, Morse offered Cuthbertson an interest in the firm, merged in 1930 with the Ferry Seed Company. Today Cuthbertson is executive vice-president of Ferry-Morse and boss of all the concern's seed-growing farms.

Sometimes a Cuthbertson made-to-order vegetable launches an entirely new appetite. In the 1920's, when a team started to work on broccoli, it was called "sprouting calabrese" and eaten mainly in Italian homes. Instead of its present-day large head it produced small buds which sprouted on many stems along the stalks; they were tasty but very difficult to pick. Frozen-food processors wanted a variety that bore the buds in clusters, like those of cauliflower—a vegetable easy to harvest and pack.

Cuthbertson planted broccoli by the acre. His fieldmen went down the rows, whacking out all plants except the few that showed a tendency to develop "umbrella heads." Repeating this season after season, nine years later they had narrowed their selections down to a new-style broccoli that delighted growers and packers. Pickers could harvest the umbrella heads with one sweep of a knife; at the processing tables cutters easily sliced off the stem, broke up the head and left the clusters of buds ready for packing. In the rapidly developing frozen-food trade the new broccoli grew from nothing in 1939 to 89 million pounds last year. Broccoli now ranks among the frozen-vegetable Big Four, along with peas, limas and snap beans.

"We made broccoli an American vegetable that has

almost pushed spinach off the frozen-food table," says Cuthbertson, his eyes sparkling. "Now I guess we'll have to do something about spinach."

Correcting a vegetable's bad habits sometimes takes ten or more plant generations. Canners, for instance, wanted the curve bred out of stringless snap beans. Straight beans would go through their cutting machines 25 per cent faster than the naturally curved bean. The Cuthbertson team launched their bean-straightening project in 1941; 12 years later they delivered Blue Lake FM-1, a bean without a curve; it met canners' specifications exactly.

As the frozen-food business boomed, lima beans became a problem vegetable. About one per cent of the beans had thick skins, through which the flesh showed in a bluish color. These are known as "blue beans" or "oyster beans." They are just as edible as other limas, but the processors reported, "Frozen foods sell on appearance, and if the housewife sees one blue bean in the pot she is unhappy."

Getting rid of that one blue bean is about the most exasperating project that Cuthbertson and his team have tackled. They started by planting the seeds from a single vine free of blue beans. The offspring of this plant were carefully scrutinized by fieldmen who, on hands and knees, opened pods on every vine. If a single bean looked blue the plant was yanked out. Each year of this tedious roguing unearths fewer throwbacks. Shortly Cuthbertson expects to have a strain free of blue beans. It is a worthwhile search; packers freeze and ship 100 million pounds of limas each season.

In this amazing modernization program nearly every vegetable presents a different problem. Growers wanted a corn that would mature in the Pacific Northwest, which isn't corn country because the nights are too cold. By 1950 Johnny McCabe, who is the corn expert on Cuthbertson's team, had a hybrid that could take the cold nights and whose kernels remained sweet and soft even after the stalks dried. That same year John Moran, the tomato man, came up with the heavy-yield deep-red tomato for which canners had been praying.

A partial list of the commercial vegetables restyled under Cuthbertson's direction during the last three decades includes more than 70 varieties of 14 vegetables. Cuthbertson contends that no vegetable is so good that it cannot be made better. "Vegetables are like autos," he says. "They become obsolete—but there is no used-vegetable market."

Began Finished No. words: 1260

—— × 60 = ——W.P.M.

—— —— No. seconds:

Checking Comprehension

Select the correct answer for each statement and write the corresponding letter in the appropriate answer space.

1. Cuthbertson did his "carrot job" because (a) he had a special interest in experimenting with vegetables, (b) Morse Company wanted him to develop a carrot that had a taste flavor which more people would enjoy, (c) Walter Nixon wanted him to develop a carrot that could be raised in poor soil, (d) Campbell Soup Company wanted carrots that had more eye appeal.

2. The process of producing carrots with orange cores involved (a) coloring carrot roots with a dye, then using the seeds from these carrots to produce others, (b) searching the world over for a patch of orange-cored carrots, then producing seeds from these carrots, (c) plugging the roots of carrots until a darker-than-usual one was found, then replanting the seed from such carrots, (d) calling upon home gardeners to search for a carrot with "orange blood," then reproducing it.

3. The problem with the snap bean was that (a) it was too big, (b) it was too small, (c) it was the wrong color, (d) it was curved.

4. A "blue bean" is undesirable because (a) its food value is good, but its taste is bad, (b) its appearance hurts sales, (c) it is unfit for human consumption, (d) it cannot be quick-frozen.

5. A special corn was needed which could take cold nights in (a) the Northwest, (b) the Southwest, (c) the Northeast, (d) the Southeast.

6. Cuthbertson's restyling of one vegetable created a

new appetite in Americans for (a) string beans, (b) beets, (c) spinach, (d) broccoli.

7. When a grower develops a new vegetable he (a) patents it, (b) allows others to produce it on a royalty basis, (c) protects it by a "gentleman's agreement" with other companies, (d) does nothing to prevent competitors from growing the seed.

8. An industry that caused lima beans to become a problem vegetable was (a) canning business, (b) frozen-food business, (c) development of super-markets, (d) advertising.

9. Mr. Cuthbertson rose from the position of "roguing" to that of (a) director of research, (b) president, (c) executive vice-president, (d) salaried employee doing experimental work.

10. Mr. Cuthbertson contends that the need for more improved vegetables will (a) end soon, (b) end when all vegetables are grown to suit packers' specifications, (c) never end, (d) grow less as processing improves.

Answers: 1)——, 2)——, 3)——, 4)——, 5)——, 6)——, 7)——, 8)——, 9)——, 10)——.

See Answer Key, page 277.

Rate: W.P.M. ——— Comprehension Score: ———

Vocabulary Study

A knowledge of word meanings will contribute much to your improvement in reading. If you cannot pronounce an unfamiliar word, or if you do not know the meaning of a word, you are apt to stop and pause over that word, thus interrupting your flow of speed. Your comprehension is hampered also by lack of a specific word meaning. Misunderstanding or ignoring even one word may change the import of a sentence or paragraph or of an entire selection. Since vocabulary is important in reading growth, you are given some practice in vocabulary building in this chapter and in the successive chapters of this book.

The words presented in the vocabulary section of each

chapter will be taken from the given selections. Follow carefully the instructions which accompany each vocabulary section, and check your work with the appropriate Answer Key. If you make mistakes in some of the exercises, study the word list and its definitions again, to see if you can find why you made each mistake.

Here is a list of words taken from the selections which you have just read, with their definitions. Study the words and their definitions. Then read the following sentences, and for each one select from the word list the word which best completes the meaning. Write that word in the blank space. You may have to add *ing* to some of the words.

abrasion	wearing away in shreds
burgeon	to put forth buds, to sprout
decrepit	worn out
agenda	memoranda of things to be done
prestige	power to command admiration
obsolete	gone out of use
horticulture	art of growing fruits, vegetables, etc.
paradox	an idea opposed to common sense
hybrid	offspring of specially-selected species
congeals	changes from a liquid to a solid
derelict	neglectful, not attended to
engrossing	monopolizing all attention
primordial	first in order of time, primitive
progeny	offspring
irony	humor which implies the opposite of what is meant
intrastate	not outside the state
concept	a thought, opinion, or idea
distaff	woman's authority or domain
collateral	something of equal value
disintegrate	to destroy the wholeness of

1. The prestige of the Roman Empire was rapidly _____.

2. With sufficient _____, a large loan may be negotiated.

3. The old gardener still maintains his interest in _____.

4. Quill pens are no longer used. They are _____.

5. A mother skunk and her numerous ——————— ambled serenely from the garden.
6. Asian affairs are scheduled for discussion on this week's ———————.
7. To be ——————— in so important a duty is dangerous to security.
8. Bob and his father were in disagreement with the ——————— side of the family.
9. The house, a ——————— structure, had broken windows, sagging shutters, and missing shingles.
10. The plant wizard becomes very busy when buds ——————— in the springtime.

Check your answers with those given in the Answer Key on page 277. Allow yourself 10 for each correct answer.

Vocabulary Score: ———————

Follow-Up Practice

You have had some experience in trying to increase your speed. You should avail yourself of much more practice, however, than that afforded in the three selections which you have just covered.

Using materials of your own selection. Now begin your speeded reading practice in earnest. This practice should be of two types: (1) general informal practice throughout the day; and (2) specific practice within stated periods of time.

Your general informal practice will consist of forcing yourself to read faster everything that you have to read all day long. Try the same techniques that you used in reading the articles in this chapter on *everything* you read. Regardless of whether you are reading memos or ads that are piled up on your desk, news items, magazine articles, or chapters in books, push your eyes along as fast as you can make them go, and speed up your mental process of absorbing meanings rapidly.

You have to work at this business of increasing speed. Nothing short of continuous and abundant practice will develop the new rapid reading habits which you wish to acquire. So jolt yourself out of the old complacency and force yourself to read faster every time you have or can make an opportunity to read. Take in whole meaningful groups of words at each fleeting glance.

You won't be able to read technical material so rapidly as nontechnical material, so while you are breaking old habits and establishing new ones try to devote the bulk of your reading practice to subjects of general interest and material which is easy. Don't shy away from any technical reading that you have to do, however. If this is a must in your daily program, apply the same speed-reading techniques to this that you do to reading easy material. Try to read even technical material at a higher tempo.

Don't let a low comprehension score slow you down at this stage. Keep right on pushing yourself to a high speed. Let yourself go, whether or not you are getting the meaning of every sentence. The important thing at this time is to accustom yourself to a new tempo.

Of course if you continue to do badly with comprehension after, let us say, ten different sittings of practice, then for a time you should devote more attention to this phase of your improvement. You will be given a great deal of help on comprehension in the remaining chapters of this book. With the aid of the additional techniques suggested, your comprehension should keep pace with your speed improvement, once your new speed habits become established.

If during your speed practice you meet a word which you cannot pronounce or for which you do not know the meaning, skip over it for the time being. After you have finished your speed reading, go back over the selection, pick out any such words, and look them up in the dictionary. There is no surer way of building your reading vocabulary.

Chapter 4

Heeding the Signposts

A story is told of Rollo, the illiterate mountain boy who received a letter one day and asked the postman to read it to him. "Can't you read the writing?" asked the postman. "No," replied Rollo. "I have trouble with words. I can get along a lot better with numbers. When I see the signposts I can tell how fur to but not whur to." Surely signposts were not of much use to Rollo. And signposts aren't of much use to any of us, even though we can read the "whur to" words, unless we watch for them and make use of them.

Ordinarily when you are driving in unfamiliar territory, you keep yourself on the alert for road signs. You have a definite destination, and you are acutely aware of the fact that the quickest and surest way to reach this destination is to heed the signs which tell you when to turn left, when to turn right, and when to go straight ahead. If you become preoccupied with other thoughts and fail to note the signposts as you roll complacently along, you will later on find that you are on the wrong road. Then time and gasoline and driving energy are all wasted as you retrace the route to the very important sign which you should have observed in the first place.

Printways are similar to trailways in that they, too, are posted with signs which aid the reader in finding his way quickly and surely to his reading destination. If the reader ignores these signs, he, like the motorist, is apt to find it necessary to retrace his steps.

The signposts in reading warn you when to go straight

ahead, and when to make a sharp turn. If you pay attention to these signposts, you can read much more intelligently and much more rapidly. They warn you what to expect, and thus you are prepared to anticipate the meaning and to adjust quickly to change in the printed stream of thought.

What are these signposts? Usually they are words; occasionally they are phrases. There are two distinct groups.

Go-Ahead Signals

One group of direction words tells you to go ahead with speed. These words assure you that there will be no turns, or bends, or obstacles in your printed pathway. They indicate that there will be more and more ideas added which carry forward the same course of thought.

Some of the most commonly used sign words in this group are *and, more, moreover, more than that, furthermore, also, likewise.*

And is the most common of all of the go-ahead words. It connects ideas of equal importance, or ideas which occur in a certain order. Notice how *and* signals you to go ahead in the sentence below—to read more and more equivalent ideas.

Mr. Jennings was angry and guilty and apologetic and harassed all at the same time.

The three *ands* in this sentence tell you to race right along, that you will find more and similar ideas about Mr. Jennings.

More, moreover, more than that, furthermore, indicate that there is something to be added on the same subject and that the thought will be carried forward in the same direction.

Also literally signifies "all in the same manner." *Likewise* means "in like manner." Both of these words are used to join ideas which have a sameness in the whole, and therefore they tell you that there will be a continuance in the same thought direction.

Underline the direction words or phrases in the paragraphs below, which signal you to go straight ahead. At each one, stop and think about its function in the sentence. Ask yourself, "Does this word *really* warn me that the discussion is going to run along in the same tenor—that there will be no change in the course of thought?"

They reported the usual number of hunting accidents this year. They also reported that mistaking men for game came third in all causes of wounds. More than that, they painted a picture of the type of man who usually commits this most inexcusable of hunting accidents. Furthermore, they stated flatly that this type of person ought to stay out of the woods and view television for his recreational diversion.

Hugh Watson, operator of a substation of the City Power and Light Company, was closing the windows against a sudden gust of rain and wind. Suddenly his lights flickered and went out. The next thing he knew his entire station was dead. Likewise the radio. Likewise the telephone.

Did you note that *furthermore* and *likewise* in the paragraphs above told you to continue right on, that there would be more of the same thing?

There are go-ahead words which belong in a slightly different classification from the ones discussed above, because they have a more specific function to perform. These are words such as *thus, so, and so, therefore, consequently*, and *accordingly*. These words give you a go-ahead signal in so far as the stream of thought is concerned, but they mark the beginning of a more weighty idea—an idea which may be a summary or a consequence of ideas previously presented. While these words signal you to continue without change in thought, they also tell you that something is coming which is of significance—which, indeed, may be the "heart" of the paragraph. Therefore, when you see such words, you think, "I must pay special attention to this sentence. It may summarize the whole paragraph for me."

Note the specific function of these more commanding go-ahead words in the paragraphs below.

One phase of sociology deals with social amelioration. If we know the influences which made any human condition what we find it to be, we can, with scientific precision, point out the influences that must be brought to bear upon that condition to improve it. Thus we have the science called practical or applied sociology.

The world is now reduced to a state of little better than moral anarchy. Consequently, nothing but renewed ideals and good government can bring the people back to the use of their sober senses.

Another group of go-ahead words is even more decisive. They signal you to continue, but they tell you also that you are about to come to a stopping place. They announce that the author has developed all the ideas he intends to use in the discussion and is about to sum up the entire set of ideas, or draw the conclusion. Some of the words and phrases which give you these warnings are *as a result, finally, concluding,* and *in conclusion.*

When you encounter one of these words or phrases, alert yourself for a sudden termination of the flow of thought. You are about to reach the end.

Read the examples below. Note the direction words that warn you of a stopping place and heed these words!

A college girl reports that she has a fear of eyes. She admits that this is unreasonable, yet she cannot look anyone directly in the eyes without experiencing panic. The phrase "fear looking out of her eyes" runs through her thoughts constantly. As a result of this condition, her social relationships and academic achievements are approaching ruin.

The monthly figures are based on a combination of techniques. In some cases, samples are used; sample data are received from banks and from retail outlets, for example. In other areas, where little current information is available, straight-line extension of past trends is used. Finally, estimates are made, based solely on trends in somewhat related credit series.

The double-wedding-ring ceremony, although an old one, continues to be very popular. Jewelers state, however, that it is the rule rather than the exception that the groom discards his ring after a few years. Women wear theirs as long as they live. One firm states that less than one per cent of wedding rings sold to bridegrooms have been made to wear. Conclusion: women are much more sentimental about wedding rings than men.

Turn back to the beginning of this chapter. Underline all the go-ahead words which you can find in the discussions from the beginning of the chapter up to this point. You will of course omit the examples in which you have already underlined the go-ahead words.

Turn-About Signals

The words we have discussed so far are the leading-on words which warn that the stream of thought is flowing straight ahead. In opposition to these go-ahead words another group serves to turn the thought sharply in a different direction.

The most common of these adversative words is *but*. Literature is filled with laments of writers concerning the effect of this word *but*. As an example, here is a quotation from Samuel Daniel, the English poet:

Oh, now comes that bitter word—*but*, which makes all nothing that was said before, that smooths and wounds, that strikes and dashes more than flat denial, or a plain disgrace.

If all readers would heed every warning which this little word *but* signals to them, they would read with much greater ease and more decisive understanding.

Read the quotation below. Keep yourself alert for the word *but*. Note how this one word is the harbinger of a complete change in thought.

Life is like a beautiful and winding lane, on either side bright flowers, beautiful butterflies, and tempting fruits, which we scarcely pause to admire or taste, so eager are we to hasten to an opening which we imagine will be more beautiful still. But by degrees, as we advance, the trees grow bleak, the flowers and butterflies fail, the fruits disappear, and we find we have arrived— to read a desert waste.—*G. A. Sala*

There are other words and phrases which also negate preceding statements with equal effectiveness. Some of these words are *yet, nevertheless, otherwise, although, despite, in spite of, not, on the contrary, however, notwithstanding, rather* and sometimes *still*. When used to divert the current of thought, these words usually occur either at the beginning of a new sentence or in the middle of a two-clause sentence.

When you come upon such words, prepare yourself for an abrupt change. These deflectors tell you to stop going ahead and to change your course to the opposite direction, since the author is about to usher in an idea adverse to those that you have been reading. Don't go jogging along past these signposts on a straight-ahead road. When a signpost says "Sharp Turn," adjust to the change of course which the author is about to take. Travel with the author, and you'll reach your destination more quickly and more accurately.

Read the sentences and paragraphs below. Underline the deflecting words and phrases. Note the effect which these words have on the direction in which the thought is flowing.

Addison was not a good speaker, yet he was an admirable writer.

He has acted an unworthy part; nevertheless, I will be a friend to him as far as I can.

She was glad in a way; still, she felt unhappy.

Treat kindly every miserable truth that knocks at your door. Otherwise you will some day fail to recognize

Truth Himself when He comes in rags.—*Austin O'Halley*

Because of the variability in dyes from color to color, the ratings can give only an indication of the likelihood of getting desired results under a particular set of circumstances. For example, it is probable that if you select a brand which was rated as good for wool, and if you follow the correct procedures, you'll get good results. However, since an overall rating of "good" represents a composite of individual color ratings, there is always a possibility that your selection of color may be one of the less satisfactory shades of a generally good brand.[1]

You decide to reduce. And so you set your jaw as you hurry off to the grocery to lay in a supply of lettuce, asparagus, lamb chops and tomato juice. But even as you vow *this* time you are going to stick with it until you get down to the desired weight, you hear your subconscious whispering to you, "You won't do it. You know you won't. You've tried it before and you never stayed with it."

He who says much says but little in proportion to his thoughts. He selects that language which conveys his ideas in the most explicit and direct manner. He tries to compress as much thought as possible in a few words. On the contrary, the man who talks everlastingly and promiscuously, who seems to have an exhaustless magazine of sound, crowds so many words into his thoughts that he always obscures and very frequently conceals them.—*Washington Irving*

Now turn back to the beginning of the chapter and underline all turn-about words that you can find in the discussion, studying the effect which each such word has on the flow of thought.

Checking Your Awareness of Direction Words

Read the following selection. Underline all the direction words which you think influence the flow of thought one way or the other.

[1] "Household Dyes," *Consumer Reports*, August 1951, p. 359.

Selection 1

Traveling in Summer[2]

It isn't the mere joy of speeding "on spinning rubber shoes" along the broad highways, nor the fellowship of the road, that completes the satisfaction of eating up the landscape in the good old summer days.

Rather is it the glorious sense of freedom, and the peace and quiet, and the invigorating tonic of good fresh air in the great outdoors.

Not on the dusty highroad but in the shaded by-lanes and in the cool woods where we lunch or set our camp—that's where we find our Eden.

Sailing has its thrills, tramping and fishing their own enticements, and golf links have a lure that few can resist.

But when, after a long day's run, we have turned our car into a bosky dell, and settled ourselves down for our own camp meal and bed under the whispering pines by the side of a mountain stream, we are a-tingle and full-tuned to a sense of joy in living that our golfer friend seldom finds, even though he reaches the nineteenth hole. Not that I discount his enjoyment of this sport. There is a world of satisfaction in playing a round in par. On the other hand, the honorable and ancient games may yield only sorrow and vexation of spirit. Therefore golf is not all pleasure.

But here in the enfolding shadows of night, as the sparks fly upward from our own campfire, there is no trouble. We shuffled off the coil of trouble when we left the noisy streets of town. Moreover, here there are no flashing, blinding lights, no crashing trolley cars, no nerve-wracking sounds of any kind. Consequently we have peace and rest, and a few hours of quiet communing with the real, simple things in the midst of which we humans used to live—long, long ago.

And so it's nice to get back there. There we find the oldest fellowship of life, the fellowship that Thoreau, John Burroughs, Muri, Jefferies, Hudson and other sons of nature found—the finest and most enduring fellowship on earth.

[2] W. D. Moffat, "The Open Letter," *The Mentor*, August 1926, p. 68.

And it is all within easy reach today. Our car, "be it ever so humble," will get us there and back. Could the fabled magic carpet of Arabian tales afford us greater pleasure than a trip in the country with our jalopy?

Now that you have underlined the direction words in the selection above, write these two headings on a piece of paper:

Go-Ahead Words   Turn-About Words

Copy each of the words you underlined under the appropriate heading.

Then turn to the Answer Key on page 277 and check your work. This will give you an indication as to whether or not you are fully aware of direction words and their function in reading.

Heeding Signals in Timed Selections

As a result of the study and practice which you have had thus far, you should be ready to heed signals as one means of increasing both your speed and comprehension.

Two selections are provided for your use in timed practice. Read them as rapidly as you can. Jot down your beginning and ending times in the appropriate blank spaces. Speed forward without restraint as long as the go-ahead signals flash out their message to you, *but* take heed when you see a turn-about word and adjust quickly to anticipate a change.

Selection 2

BEGINNING TIME:———————
HR.——————— MIN.———

THE SPIRIT OF PAPER MAKING[8]

For 1,800 years my spirit has gone from land to land, from continent to continent, from China to Turkestan

[8] Royal S. Kellog, "Paper Making, From Papyrus to the Printed Page," *The Mentor*, September 1925, pp. 21-26.

and to Arabia, thence to Spain, Italy, and France; thereafter to Germany, England, and Sweden—and finally to the great new country on the western side of the Atlantic.

And I have everywhere worked with the substances men were familiar with and the tools they knew how to handle. So it was that a hundred years after I made paper from the mulberry tree I taught my own people of the Flowery Kingdom how to make even a stronger and better paper from rags of cotton and flax, and also a cheap paper from the straw of the rice plant.

And it was from rags that the craftsmen of Arabia and of Europe and of America learned to make paper, and for 1,700 years but little paper was made of aught else— and no better paper has ever been made than was made in those days.

Yet a man with much labor and sweat could make only a little pile of sheets a day.

Learning was carried throughout every land, but books were dear and hard to get, and mostly kept in the temples by the priests who wrote the words therein by hand or mayhap printed a page at a time from shapes cut into a block of wood.

A better way must be had if there were to be more books, so one day when I found a man in Germany named Gutenberg, who had more sense than most, I told him that many centuries before, in faraway China, printing had been done with single types each representing a character so that, by making many of these types, they could be put together quickly in the form of words for the page of a book and then set again for another page. This man had much skill with his hands as well as with his head. He printed a sacred book and thereafter there was so much printing that more paper must be had.

Next I caused a Dutchman to make a great vat in which was a heavy wheel with sharp edges, turned by water power so that fibers could be beaten up quickly and more men kept busy with the frames and screens.

Then did I cause a Frenchman, Robert by name, to make a great wire screen moving over pulleys so that the water would fall through the screen and leave the fibers on it, after which the wet sheet was run over hot iron cylinders and dried quickly.

This was the beginning of paper making as people know it today and was during the period of my twenty-second rejuvenation.

And men made new machines for the types so that there was much printing of books and the things called "newspapers," unknown to my people.

But not for long was there enough paper even when it was made by machines, because there could not be found enough rags of cotton and linen. So men did try many strange substances—even grass and leaves and straw and seaweed and stalks of many plants—but with little success for most.

And when I was unable to solve the problem did the spirit of the great Confucius come to me once more during the Moon of the Harvest and say: "Ts'ai Lun, as thou first went to the tree, go thou again, but this time take not the bark, for it is not enough. Take thou the solid wood itself. Hold blocks of it firmly against a turning stone with water thereon so that it is ground finely and yet most of the fibers left unbroken.

"This when washed and screened as thou knowest how to do will give thee much paper-making material—not so good as rags, but cheap and plentiful so that men may have newspapers and papers of divers other kinds."

Thus again spoke the great Confucius. And it was even so. There arose paper mills in the forests and along the streams where there was much falling water to turn the stones, and ten men were making paper where there was one before. Great rolls of paper came from them ready for the other machines that held the little types.

And then men put the forms of the types on great cylinders and turned them even faster so that thousands of books and newspapers were printed where there was one before.

And there were schools; and all the children learned to read and write.

And then other men made a wondrous machine that set more of the little types than seven could do, so that there were more books and newspapers and magazines than ever before; and more paper was used in other ways, so there was not enough paper until more mills with bigger machines were built.

And merchants took much space in the newspapers

and magazines to tell of their wares, and trade was greatly increased thereby.

And all manner of business was done by means of papers, and paper was used in the place of other substances for many purposes.

And then the printing machines were made bigger and swifter, so that twoscore thousand newspapers might be printed in an hour; and the paper machines were made still bigger and swifter, so that one machine might make enough paper in a day to cover four hundred acres of land.

And people began to say again that there was not enough wood to make paper and something else must be found or there would be no more paper.

And then the foresters arose and said that there might be wood enough if men were to grow more trees, so that there would always be plenty of paper.

All-wise Ho-Ti spoke truly when he said that a kingdom of knowledge is greater than a kingdom of arms.

And I shall carry out his charge as long as the world endures, for I am the Spirit of Paper Making.

Began Finished No. words: 1130

$$\frac{\quad}{\quad} \times 60 = \underline{\quad\quad} \text{W.P.M.}$$

_____ _____ No. seconds:

Checking Comprehension

Read each of the paragraphs below. Choose the answer which you think is correct. Write the corresponding letter in the appropriate answer space at the end of the exercise.

1. The spirit of paper-making has traversed the earth for a period of (a) 1000 years, (b) 2300 years, (c) 1800 years, (d) 400 years.

2. The earliest paper makers in the "Flowering Kingdom" made paper from the mulberry tree, from cotton and flax, and a cheap paper from (a) hide of animals, (b) plastics, (c) poppy leaves, (d) straw of the rice plant.

3. The chief ingredient used in paper-making for 1700

years was: (a) wood, (b) rags, (c) straw, (d) a combination of wood and straw.

4. Paper mills arose in forests when it was discovered that good paper could be made of (a) solid wood, (b) bark, (c) leaves, (d) roots.

5. An invention which brought about a great demand for more paper was (a) a machine for running off newspapers quickly, (b) steam engines which made it possible to transport wood pulp great distances, (c) typesetting by Gutenberg, (d) a glue which would hold rag fibers together.

6. A Dutchman's contribution to the manufacture of paper was (a) a newsprint machine which would turn off large sheets of newspapers, (b) a large water-power wheel with sharp edges which would beat the fibers up quickly, (c) a pulp digester which would cook the fibers, (d) a machine for sizing paper.

7. A Frenchman by the name of Robert invented (a) a method of making pulp, (b) straps to guide the pulp as it rolls over cylinders, (c) a reel for winding paper as it comes from the cylinders, (d) a wire screen moving over the pulleys so that water would fall through the screen and leave the fibers on it.

8. An advance in typesetting which gave an impetus to the production of more printed material was (a) making better type, (b) putting forms of types on cylinders that turn rapidly, (c) training compositors to work more rapidly, (d) a machine which increased the production of the type itself.

9. As bigger and better machines were made for typesetting and for manufacture of paper, there was not enough wood to supply the demand, so it was suggested (a) that some way be found to manufacture synthetic wood, (b) that certain chemicals be combined with straw to make paper, (c) that more trees be grown specifically for paper-making, (d) that a search be made for some entirely new paper-making substance.

10. The statement that most closely sums up the gist of this selection is (a) There is an increasing need for paper, (b) Paper-making is an ancient art, (c) There

has been a strong relationship between invention and paper-making, (d) The spirit of paper-making always has been and always will be an inspiration and stimulation to many, (e) The fact that paper today has reached its peak in both production and quality in response to man's resourcefulness in meeting the demands that civilization has placed upon him is not to be interpreted to mean that the spirit of paper-making will not continue to guide man to further achievements, (f) The spirit of paper-making has had far-reaching influences in civilization, noticeably in the realms of education and business, chiefly because it has been the outstanding means of distributing knowledge throughout the world.

Answers: 1)——, 2)——, 3)——, 4)——, 5)——, 6)——, 7)——, 8)——, 9)——, 10)——.

Check your answers with the Answer Key on page 277. Multiply the number of correct answers by 10.

Rate: W.P.M. ——— Comprehension Score: ———

Selection 3

BEGINNING TIME:———
HR.——————— MIN.———————

How to Negotiate for a House[4]

A great many houses are not advertised by the owners, but are listed with brokers (realtors, agents). The broker's commission is usually 5% of the sale price; consequently, elimination of this fee by giving priority inspection to owner-advertised houses may be a justified first step.

But don't ignore broker-advertised houses. If the broker is a man of intelligence, tact, and integrity he can be well worth his fee. The problem is to find a good one. The chances are best with brokers whose advertising copy is matter-of-fact and moderate in tone. If the agent turns out to be unpleasant, take a quick look at a couple of his listings and pass on.

While you are sorting out the brokers you will be seeing houses and getting a preliminary idea of values. Also,

[4] *Consumer Reports,* October 1952, pp. 468-471.

in active neighborhoods, you are likely to meet a number of brokers who are at least not impossible. Moreover, you may be fortunate enough to find one who is both frank and expert in his judgment of houses—but it does not follow that he will be the one through whom you finally buy, for chance plays as great a part in realty transactions as merit and good intentions.

If you have seen a property through a broker or by direct contact with the owner and you are later inadvertently taken to it by another broker, you should immediately so state, and not enter the house with the second broker. Otherwise, if you should later buy the house, you may find yourself involved in a lawsuit.

Factors which sometimes play a part in bidding include the length of time the property has been on the market, and when the present owner acquired it. If he bought it and made improvements in the Thirties or early Forties he can sell relatively cheap and still make a whopping profit. On the contrary, the recent buyer, builder, or improver, having paid top prices, must get a top price in turn if he is not to lose. A property which lingers on the market may sometimes be acquired advantageously by a buyer who comes along just when the owner decides he can't get his price and decides to come down to a more reasonable level. It is advisable, nevertheless, to let the property rest a while longer and investigate to check whether price was the only reason for its failure to move.

In deciding how much you can afford to pay, one rule of thumb is that the total price should not exceed double your annual income. If followed rigorously in the present market, this simply means that few low-income families can own their homes. It is true enough, however, that you should be especially cautious in buying if your income is under say $5,000 a year, or if it is precarious for any reason. And if you have lived in apartments all your life, don't be taken in by the monthly charges quoted in the developers' ads as "covering everything, just like rent." Although these charges do cover interest and amortization or mortgage, real estate taxes, and insurance, there are also heat, electricity, maintenance and repairs, water taxes, special assessments, and other costs, which may come to another 40% and likewise must be paid for—just like rent. Furthermore, if your move is from the city to suburbs, there is the not-inconsiderable cost of commutation and the possibility that you will need another car.

When you find a house in which you are really interested, an offhand estimate of market value is not good enough. You should appraise it yourself, if you feel competent to do so, or get it appraised.

You can get a direct appraisal of the property's value by hiring a professional appraiser but, unless he is both competent and disinterested, his findings may not be very helpful. Be especially careful in a small town, where bank officials and directors, realtors, assessors, and tax collectors, the probate judge, and realty-minded lawyers are all likely to be good friends. You go to the bank for an appraisal and the bank sends out or recommends a man. Neither the bank nor the appraiser will deliberately set out to rob you, of course, but the bank may prefer to see you buy the house for one of a number of reasons—the broker or the owner may be a friend or a director, the bank may want to make a loan, it may favor an active market on general principles, or it may have any of a dozen equally cogent reasons. Appraisal being an art, not a science, there is a normal latitude of perhaps plus or minus 5%. Therefore, if the appraiser is acting in the interest of the bank, the 5% is apt to be minus; if he has reasons for wanting the house sold, it may chance to be plus. The difference—say $2,000 on a $20,000 property—is no slight one.

When a property needs repairs or remodeling, some brokers transform themselves into architects or builders and glibly quote the cost of heating plants, plumbing, masonry, and "streamlined" kitchens. Such estimates are usually a fraction of actual cost. Not many brokers will tell you anything worth listening to about building costs, or any other technical matter. If you are seriously interested in a house that needs extensive remodeling or repair work before it comes up to your standards, call in a builder or contractor and get a firm bid on the cost of the job. Do this before you make any bid, otherwise you may be unpleasantly shocked at how much more the house costs than the amount you thought you were paying for it.

When the difference between bid and asked prices is small but both parties stand firm, the broker can sometimes save the deal by reducing his commission. Before resorting to this final and painful expedient he may enlarge on the possible consequences to him: loss of license, expulsion from his trade association, ostracism, etc. Despite his story these penalties are almost always imaginary; the broker's colleagues will do the same thing when they have to.

Began Finished No. words: 1260

$$\frac{\qquad}{\qquad} \times 60 = \underline{\qquad} \text{W.P.M.}$$

_____ _____ No. seconds:

Checking Comprehension

Select the correct answers and write the appropriate letters in the answer space below.

1. The broker's fee is justified because (a) of his knowledge of houses and property, (b) of his ability to secure houses more cheaply, (c) many houses are for sale which are not advertised, (d) the legal aspect of the situation requires a broker.

2. In regard to broker advertisements, you are advised to accept (a) nothing of what is claimed, (b) everything except that which pertains to future improvements, (c) that which is moderate and matter-of-fact, (d) only that which you would like to believe.

3. In negotiating for a house, you are advised (a) not to consult more than one broker in regard to houses, (b) to sort out your brokers as they show you houses, (c) to consult two reliable brokers as a general rule, (d) to make a visit to the house you may want to buy before consulting any broker at all.

4. Not mentioned in the article as significant in the bidding is (a) the length of time the house has been on the market, (b) when the improvements were made, (c) the financial status of the seller, (d) when the house was purchased by the present owner.

5. The total price in regard to the buyer's income should (a) be less than double his annual income, (b) not exceed double his annual income, (c) be approximately three times his annual income, (d) not necessarily be a major consideration.

6. If the owner of a property which has been lingering on the market comes down to a lower price you are advised (a) to buy it at once before he changes his mind, (b) ask him to sell at a still lower price, (c) disregard the deal entirely, (d) let the matter rest while you investigate to find out if the price was the only reason why the property hadn't been sold previously.

7. Appraisals should be made by (a) yourself, if you feel competent, (b) an appraiser, not necessarily professional, who is connected with the bank but who doesn't know the broker, (c) professional appraisers recommended by both the broker and the bank, (d) a friend who has bought a house.

8. The writer claims that appraising is (a) a science, (b) an art, (c) an inexact science, (d) a combination of art and science.

9. If repairs and remodeling are to be made, the best course to pursue is to (a) consult the owners about the cost, (b) have the real estate man give you an estimate, (c) figure out yourself about how much it would cost, (d) call in a contractor to give a bid.

10. The consequences which the broker tells you may befall him when he offers to reduce his commission in order to make a sale should cause you (a) not to accept his reduction, (b) to worry over the consequences to the broker, (c) to take his story of penalties lightly because they are almost always imaginary, (d) to give him a substantial tip.

Answers: 1)——, 2)——, 3)——, 4)——, 5)——, 6)——, 7)——, 8)——, 9)——, 10)——.

See Answer Key, page 277.

Rate: W.P.M.———— Comprehension Score:————

Vocabulary Study

The following sentences were taken from the selections you just read. Below each sentence you will find three words within parentheses. Underline one of these three words which the author might have used in place of the italicized word in the sentence. Refer to a dictionary if necessary.

1. Paper-making underwent a *rejuvenation* after the invention of the printing press.

(regression, retrograde, reinvigoration)

2. *Craftsmen* from Arabia made paper out of rags.

(artists, artisans, laborers)

3. Men use wood for newspapers and papers of *divers* other kinds.

(scattered, diverse, several)

4. If the broker is a man of intelligence, tact, and *integrity* he can be well worth his fee.

(honesty, expediency, ascendancy)

5. Neither the bank nor the appraiser will deliberately set out to rob you, but the bank may prefer to see you buy the house for any of a dozen *cogent* reasons.

(vexing, inadvertent, convincing)

6. When a property needs repairs or remodeling, some brokers transform themselves into architects or builders and *glibly* quote the cost of heating plants, plumbing, masonry, and "streamlined" kitchens.

(flippantly, sarcastically, insidiously)

7. Before resorting to a final and painful *expedient* the broker may enlarge on the possible consequences to himself.

(appraisal, resource, privilege)

8. The broker may say that he faces expulsion from his trade association, *ostracism*, and financial ruin.

(rejuvenation, exclusion, conversion)

9. Your broker will tell you he is subject to penalties, but his *colleagues* will under pressure do the same thing.

(competitors, associates, probationers)

10. It is true enough that you should be especially cautious in buying if your income is under, say, $5,000 a year, or if it is *precarious* for any reason.

(inconsiderable, insecure, irreparable)

Check your answers with those given in the Answer Key on page 278. Allow yourself 10 for each correct answer.

Vocabulary Score: —————

Follow-Up Practice

Continue forcing your speed in all the reading you do, both in connection with your daily activities and during your specific practice periods. In all this reading, be sure to note the signposts. Now that you are sensitive to the signpost words, let them mean something to you. When you encounter a go-ahead sign, be assured that the course of thought will proceed in the same manner, that more will be said in the same tenor, and that you may continue full speed ahead with no change in thought. On the other hand, when a turn-about word or phrase pops up, be prepared to change your course of thinking, but continue your speed without loss in comprehension.

Chapter 5

Shop Before You Read

Why Shop Before You Read?

Before you buy a car you shop. You look over the various makes and "size up" their appearances, special features, colors, promise of performance, price, etc. Similarly, you should shop before you select an article to read; that is, take a preview. A book, chapter, or article has certain prominent characteristics, just as a car or a suit has outstanding features. If you briefly study these characteristics before you read, your survey may be as valuable to you as your general "sizing up" of a car or suit before you buy it.

In some cases the preview will provide you with all the information you desire, and you won't find it necessary to read the selection at all. In other cases the preview will "whet your appetite," increase your interest, and strengthen your motive for reading. In these latter cases, when you actually do begin to read you will find that your prereading insight has paved the way for speedier and more comprehensive coverage of the printed page.

How to Shop

The first step in making a preview is to study the title. The title holds a world of information, for it gives you a quick cue as to what the topic of discussion is. It may be a deciding factor in determining whether or not you want to read the selection. If you decide that you do want to read it, then you have advance information and can read in terms of the promise that the title holds out to you.

Next, glance through the material to see if subheadings are used. If so, a quick survey of them will be valuable to you. You should consider each one for the information it gives or implies. These subheadings reveal to you the trend of discourse in the article as a whole. There will be occasions in which a preview of these subtitles will tell you all you want to know. At other times they will serve as interest leads to reading the difficult sections and as door-openers to better understanding of the text.

If any visual aids are furnished, study them for their significance. Look at illustrations carefully. They will aid your comprehension by giving you a vivid mental picture of the people, things, and locale dealt with. If maps are provided, study them. Your reading will be more meaningful if you have precise geographical locations in mind. If graphs and charts are provided, study these before you read the article. They will give you a quick grasp of relationships and proportions among data discussed in the text.

Next examine the length of the paragraphs. Turn the pages quickly and find out if most of the paragraphs are short, medium, or long. Remember, each paragraph is a thought unit, and a single idea is developed in each. If there are many short paragraphs, this is a fairly reliable indication that the article will include many ideas but will not be heavy with details. On the other hand, if the paragraphs are long, there will be fewer ideas, but each main idea will be expanded by numerous details. On the whole, this material will be more difficult to read.

Finally, make an estimate of how long it will take you to read the article. Count the words in several lines to ascertain the average number of words per line. Then multiply this number by the number of lines in the article. Once you have estimated the total number of words, decide how long it ought to take you to read it.

Don't be easy with yourself. Set as short a time limit as you think you can possibly meet. Then live up to it!

Applying Preview Techniques to a Selection

After you have previewed the following selection, you will be given a test to enable you to find out how much information you have gleaned as the result of your rapid survey.

Gathering information from title and subheads. Examine the title of the selection that follows on page 93. What does it tell you?

Obviously it tells you that the selection is about an adventure in canoes which took place in Labrador.

Glance at the first subtitle. What additional information does that give you? Since it is "Million-Paddle-Stroke Journey," you now know that the adventurers must have traveled by canoe and that it must have been a long journey.

Skim on to the second subheading: "Rails Soon Will Split Wilderness." You now know that the trip was through a wilderness where there were no railroads as yet.

Glance at the next subheading. From this you gather that the adventurers built fires to warm themselves or to cook, and that at times they had difficulty finding a beach wide enough for a fire to be built.

Now skim on in search of the next subheading. It tells you that the adventurers, accompanied by guides, journeyed to some place so seldom traveled that even the guides were unfamiliar with the route.

Now glance at the subheading "Few Eyes Have Seen Unknown Falls." This gives you the idea that seeing Unknown Falls was something very special—perhaps the goal of the whole adventure.

Move your eyes rapidly on to later subheadings. What do they tell you about the source and kind of food? What was another sight they saw? What did it resemble? What hardship did they encounter? What exciting experience did they have?

Noting lengths of paragraphs. Since the paragraphs are comparatively short, there won't be too much detail; therefore you will be able to move right along in your reading.

Testing yourself. If you should take a test to find out how much you know about this article without having read it, you would probably be surprised to discover the amount of information you have gained simply by making a preview. Turn to page 100 and see how many of the statements you can complete.

Selection 1

BEGINNING TIME:————
HR.———— MIN.————

LABRADOR CANOE ADVENTURE[1]

Two Indians ran dark hands and eyes over our twin aluminum canoes lying outside a warehouse in Burnt Creek, northern Quebec mining camp.

Prospectors, geologists, and drillers strolling by in their iron-reddened clothing expressed doubts about the unfamiliar metal craft. One hairy giant muttered something about "tin-can-oes."

. . . Despite pessimistic comment, we were confident the little canoes could carry us from the Quebec border across hundreds of miles of Labrador wilderness to Atlantic tidewater. It could be disastrous if they let us down! . . .

"Mathieu say the first jagged rock will gash 'em," interpreted John Michelin, one of our trapper guides.

"Well, they weathered a rough test last summer running the Susquehanna River," we pointed out, reassuring ourselves as well as the guides. "We'll go ahead as planned. They'll do better than you think."

By journey's end the 18-foot Gruman aluminum craft were scratched and dented, but watertight and sound. And—final vindication—our guides wanted to buy them.

Million-Paddle-Stroke Journey

In five weeks we paddled 578 miles on waters of Labrador's Hamilton River, trudged 61 miles over portages

[1] Andrew Brown and Ralph Gray, *The National Geographic*, July 1951, pp. 85-99.

and up lookout hills, and navigated 150 fateful yards by raft. From height of land to sea level, each of us dipped a quarter of a million paddle strokes.

We embarked near the heart of the vast peninsula of Labrador-northern Quebec (Ungava). End of our water trail was North West River, trapper's town on Lake Melville, tidal arm of the Atlantic.

A chief objective was North America's next-to-greatest waterfall, the seldom-seen Grand Falls of the Hamilton, a stupendous cataract 245 feet high. Niagara, by its huge volume, alone surpasses it.

We traveled the interior of the land where Europeans probably made their first landfall in the New World. Yet the tides of history have largely swept by this corner of North America. Explorers recoiled from Labrador's barren, arctic coast. The wooded inland, far more pleasing and habitable, still is rarely visited.

In Labrador's wilderness the dense spruce forest marches north, like an immense army, to the edge of subarctic barrens. Myriad lakes break its ranks; also stretches of spongy muskeg and the scars of forest fires. Water laces the country everywhere—twisting rivers, lakes great and small, and grassy marsh.

Moss takes the place of soil. Gray or yellowish caribou moss, really a lichen, covers drier ground with its fluffy mat. Crossing moss-quilted bog and boulder fields, every step is a gamble.

Rails Soon Will Split Wilderness

The Hamilton, Labrador's mightiest river, gathers its flood from this bewildering tangle. Long the domain of snowshoe and canoe, its western sources soon will echo to locomotive whistles and the clatter of cars on rails.

For the upper Hamilton basin encompasses part of a vast, newly-explored iron deposit that straddles the Quebec-Labrador border region. Track-laying has been begun on a 360-mile railroad to carry the ore from semi-barren hills of Labrador and Ungava to the Gulf of St. Lawrence, whence ships will bear it to the market.

It was early summer, 1950, when we set out to see and picture Hamilton River wilds. At Montreal we picked up our trapper guides, John and Leslie Michelin, distant cousins. They had come from North West River, Labrador, by plane. . . .

On a Sunday afternoon we launched our canoes and slipped away into the silent wastes. John Michelin, our head guide, took the helm and Andrew Brown the forward paddle of bright-red *Loon*, Leslie Michelin the stern and Ralph Gray the bow of sky-blue *Trout*. . . .

On Monday, after 25 miles of paddling down Dyke Lake, we clambered up Fault Hill. A mighty sweep of country lay revealed. Long ridges banded the gently rolling land. Lakes filled nearly every depression. Higher hills thrust up bare crowns, overtopping the spruce and fir forest that reached, green and untouched, to the horizon. In silence we gazed out upon the haunting scene.

Beach Barely Wide Enough for a Fire

Skimming down the swift Ashuanipi River next evening, our wool shirts beaded by a steady drizzle, we searched for a campsite.

"We'll try here," John called out at last, indicating a narrow, rocky beach at the foot of a 40-foot sandy bluff.

Our paddles swung the canoes in toward shore. Ralph and Andy jumped out and tied the craft to boulders.

"We'll pitch the tent on top of the bank, I 'low," said Leslie. "It's a good job we've got this beach to unload on, and for our fire."

It took fancy stepping to move around, after the fire was blazing and all the supper things were strewn along that skimpy shore. To pass the fire we had to climb the bank or wade the brimming river. . . .

Long after the sky was black we pulled ourselves up the steep slope to the tent. Cobblestones dislodged by our feet rolled out of sight and plunked into the inky Ashuanipi.

The following day was better. The rain let up and the clouds parted briefly. Toward evening we navigated our first bad rapid. A tossing run of white water—the icing on any canoeing cake—tumbled us into Sandgirt Lake at sunset. . . .

Route Unknown Even to Guides

The all-water route between Sandgirt Lake and Unknown Falls was as new to our guides as to us.

Caching most of our outfit on an island, we ascended the Atikonak and were caught up in a battle with racing current and wind-lashed lakes.

Often we seemed to ride a watery treadmill; no matter how hard we dug at the stream, trees on shore crawled astern in slow motion.

John and Leslie never spoke of a river's current; it was always "tide." "There's less tide behind that island," they'd say, or "We'll have fair tide today."

Three miles up the Atikonak we reached a wild rapid. Here, and at a rough place a few miles above, we had to track the canoes through. . . .

Six days out, we reached the upper end of Gabbro Lake and couldn't find the inlet. . . .

After miles of futile searching for an inflowing river, we ran out of water at the head of the bay. No channel there! Next day we found the inlet—a broad stream, at that—not two miles from where we had read the compass! Moral? If you won't believe your maps and compass, stay home.

In Ossokmanuan Lake we got lost twice more, pushing to the heads of dead-end leads. . . .

Beyond "Ossok's" island-girt midsection we knew by the map we were drawing close to Unknown Falls, though the exact route was uncertain. But when we detected the first slow eddies of Unknown River slipping blackly out of Ossokmanuan, each of us felt his pulse step up a few beats.

Few Eyes Have Seen Unknown Falls

Unknown Falls were not completely unknown, but even on latest maps Unknown River's course is only a dotted line.

Prior to 1929, only three parties had fought their way to Unknown Falls. Each group saw one pair of falls and departed, unaware that another existed. . . .

Drifting down Unknown River, we were alert for surprises. Below a heavy rapid the stream swept the flanks of a high hill we had sighted from Ossokmanuan Lake.

We moored our canoes and climbed up a nearly vertical slope through incredibly tangled woods to the barren summit. The country unrolled like a map.

Ghostly wreaths of vapor marking Unknown Falls

lay 10 airline miles away, just beyond a fine-looking lake Watkins had identified as "Lake E." The falls were twice that far off by the river's roundabout course. . . .

Modern Packing Allowed Varied Diet

The wetter the weather, the bigger our fires—and the more Lucullan our repasts!

We did our buying for the trip on the premise that a wilderness menu can list something more than a tiresome succession of beans, pork, hardtack, and pemmican. We wanted good food, but had to keep the total weight down because of the canoe's limited capacity.

So our grub stores featured solid foods of high nutritive value. We stocked up liberally on canned meats—boned chicken, bacon, ham, Spam, corned beef and tuna. There was plenty of sugar and peanut butter—but not enough jam. We slathered jam on everything from cereal and biscuits to crackers and cake.

Dates and raisins, dried prunes and apricots were our fruits. We never could serve enough mashed potatoes (we just added the powdered tuber to hot milk or water) to satisfy the guides. Favorites also were hot bouillon from cubes, and vegetable stew (dehydrated) mixed either with ham or chicken.

For grain foods we took oatmeal, rice, corn meal, and flour mixes—pancake, biscuit, and cake. Cake mix, too, was in short supply before the trip was half done. . . .

Butter and dried eggs came in cans; we had powdered whole milk and tinned evaporated milk. Tea and powdered coffee rounded out the list of staples.

Not far below Lake E, past two more rapids, we came into an expansion at whose foot plumes of vapor hung above tossing breakers. There was the thunder of falling water. We had reached Unknown Falls! . . .

Upper Cataract Resembles Victoria Falls

The majestic Upper Unknown Falls suggested to us a lesser Victoria Falls; in half a dozen spouts the river tumbled 90 feet over an escarpment into a wild gorge running nearly at right angles to the face of the falls.

An island divided the cataract into two sections. The western fall was the greater. . . .

A half hour later we stood in admiration of the right-bank Lower Falls. Funneled into a single channel, the river fell more than 100 feet, straight and sheer. Spray billowed up from the foot. Swirling mists dimmed the caldron from which the stream, a mass of foam, surged down a sheer-walled canyon. . . .

That night we stumbled into camp long after sunset. Heaping plates of hot chicken and vegetables (from dehydrated stock) revived our strength.

Next morning we canoed across the river to the western shore and bushwhacked to the left-bank side of the Upper Falls, a race of frothing water. Eddying mists alternately obscured and revealed the snowy face of its two 90-foot chutes.

The sun still shone bright, so we hustled downriver, jumping brooks and striding across burned-over lands.

The map showed a tributary flowing into Unknown River from the west, above the left-bank Lower Falls. Anticipating that the stream might be too deep to wade, we had brought with us an ax and some rope to build a raft. We could not have portaged the canoe five miles across that rough country.

Sure enough, the tributary soon blocked our way. It was a moat between us and the fourth Unknown Falls. . . .

Raft River Imposes a Barrier

Fortunately, the tributary—which we dubbed Raft River—flowed with slackened current through a pool just before dropping into Unknown River.

John and Leslie cut six or eight dead trees and bound the trim logs together.

"Looks O.K.," said Ralph, but when he and Leslie stepped aboard, the raft sank to the bottom! The men quickly cut and tied another layer of logs.

We poled to the head of the pool. Away from shore even 12-foot poles failed to touch bottom. Leslie, viewing our flimsy vessel askance, volunteered to stay behind. Ralph and Andy were determined to cross. John thought the voyage worth a try.

Leslie cut two paddles. They were heavy, awkward, and narrow, but better than poles that wouldn't reach bottom.

Pushing off into the welter of the in-flowing rapid, we caught the current. At first, the heavy raft scarcely responded to our paddle thrusts.

"Let's go back and start higher up," John shouted, glancing at the approaching crest of the outlet rapid.

"We're all right now," Andy said, as the raft lurched heavily toward shore. We landed halfway down the pool.

It was a short walk to the left-bank lower Falls. Here again an islet split the flood into two thunderous sluiceways. This chute was more broken up than the others. The creamy spate of water surged with terrifying force through the corkscrew canyon that received it.

We returned to our jerry-built raft, stepped aboard, and shoved off. Suddenly one of John's legs dropped through the logs right up to his thigh.

"Paddle back!" he called out. "I'm stuck. We'll go over the rapid!"

With a frantic tug, John retrieved his leg, but a moment later Andy's foot slipped through. The raft was loosening up. Grunting with the effort, we leaned to paddles and poles—and presently the eddy caught us. We swung safely in to shore.

Leslie helped us to relax with a cup of hot tea.

Well, we thought, our persistence paid off, despite the chance taken. We were the first, we were quite sure, ever to reach and photograph both pairs of Unknown Falls in summer.

Below its two foaming steps down from the plateau, Unknown River is unnavigable to its junction with Hamilton River below Grand Falls and Bowdoin Canyon.

So we had to retrace our route to Sandgirt Lake.

Stalking a Stag Caribou

We set backs and shoulders against Unknown River rapids to reach Ossokmanuan Lake again. Threading islands just below the lake, we heard a loud whisper from Andy: "Look there, on the beach! A caribou!"

A magnificent stag with a spreading rack of antlers was browsing on willows at the water's edge. John ordered us to paddle quietly. We might slip close enough for a picture.

We were 100 yards from the caribou when he came stiffly to the alert, nose lifted to sniff the air. He cantered up the beach, toward John and Andy. But out of camera range the animal took alarm, shook his antlers, and plunged into the woods.

The second rapid below Gabbro Lake, scene of tough tracking on the upstream leg, gave us a thrilling run on the way back to Sandgirt. . . .

Wave crests around visible boulders, or below submerged ones, stayed in place. We twisted through, facing each hazard as we met it. Responding to John's steering, *Loon* slipped past one rock on the left, barely grazed two more on the right.

A hard bump over a shoal at the bottom, and the rapid was behind us! *Trout* followed close on our heels. "A good run!" observed Andy. John's face, now relaxed, was wreathed in smiles.

Began Finished No. words: 2333

_____ × 60 = _____ W.P.M.

_____ _____ No. seconds:

Preview Test

Complete the statements below by writing in the missing words.

1. This is an adventure story which took place in _____.

2. The men who took the trip were accompanied by _____.

3. They traveled in _____.

4. This was called a "_____-paddle-stroke journey."

5. The word which you supplied in the phrase above indicated to you that it was a _____ trip.

6. The country was unsettled. It was a _____.

7. Much of this country was unknown even to the _____.

8. Sometimes they had difficulty in finding a landing place wide enough to build a _____.

9. The falls called "Unknown Falls" had been seen by only a _____ people.

10. The food of the adventurers allowed _____ diet.

11. The Upper Cataract which they saw resembled _____.

12. They ran into a river that was a barrier to them. They named it _____ _____.

13. There must have been wild game in the wilderness, for among other thrills they stalked a _____ _____.

14. The article will probably be fairly easy reading, since the paragraphs are _____.

Correct your answers by referring to the article itself. Did you realize that you could get so much information by simply previewing an article and not taking time actually to read it?

Reading the article. Perhaps you have become sufficiently interested in the adventure of these two men so that you would like to find out more about the experiences they had. Try reading the article as fast as you can just for entertainment. Jot down your beginning and ending times and compute your rate as usual. Then take the test.

Checking Comprehension

Write the letter which indicates the correct answer for each statement in the appropriate space at the end of the test.

1. When people in Burnt Creek saw the men's canoes, this is how they felt about the possibility of the canoes' carrying the men on their trip: (a) confident, (b) hopeful, (c) assured, (d) pessimistic.

2. The land in which the adventurers traveled (a) had been inhabited at one time, (b) was partially cultivated, (c) had been settled by iron miners, (d) was a rarely-visited wilderness.

3. The upper Hamilton basin encompasses (a) some old iron-ore pits, (b) newly-discovered uranium mines, (c) newly-explored iron deposit, (d) abandoned silver mines.

4. When the men were ready to sleep, they (a) crawled into sleeping bags, (b) pitched tents, (c) looked for an abandoned hut, (d) lay down under a thick pine tree.

5. On their trip from Sandgirt Lake to Unknown Falls, the men (a) found smooth sailing, (b) had to walk most of the way, (c) encountered a racing current and wind-lashed lakes, (d) were attacked by wild animals.

6. The diet of the travelers included (a) meat, vegetables, cereals, fruits, milk, and butter, (b) meat, vegetables, and cereals only, (c) meat and fruits only, (d) meat, milk, bread, and butter only.

7. Unknown Falls are divided by (a) a mountain, (b) an island, (c) a boulder, (d) a canyon.

8. These men were the first to (a) build a bridge over Unknown Falls, (b) see all of the cataracts, (c) photograph all of the cataracts, (d) visit Unknown Falls on foot.

9. When they tried to photograph the caribou it (a) stayed long enough for a picture, (b) charged at them, (c) reared up on his hind legs, (d) plunged into the woods.

10. On their way back from Unknown Falls, the men encountered (a) stiff winds, (b) boulders in the rapids, (c) logs in the rapids, (d) heavy fog.

Answers: 1)——, 2)——, 3)——, 4)——, 5)——, 6)——, 7)——, 8)——, 9)——, 10)——.

Check your answers with the Answer Key on page 278. Allow yourself 10 for each correct answer. Record your score below:

Rate: W.P.M. ———— Comprehension Score: ————

Making the preview. In making your preview of the following article, read all the instructions below, then carry them out from memory. Jot down your beginning and ending time for the preview. You should be able to do this preview in just a few seconds. After completing it, take the short true-false test following the article.

1. Glance at the title to find out the topic discussed.

2. Now quickly read the subheadings and abstract as much information as you can from them.

3. Jot down your finishing time.

4. Take the previous test.

Time of beginning preview   Min___ Sec___
Time of ending preview   ___   ___
Total time for preview   ___   ___

Reading the article. After you have completed the preview and taken your preview test, read the article, under timed conditions, for the purpose of finding more information about the topic mentioned in each subheading.

Selection 2

BEGINNING TIME:_____
HR._____ MIN._____

TODAY ON THE DELAWARE, PENN'S GLORIOUS RIVER[2]

Trickling from mountain spring and duck pond, the Delaware grows—as the Nation has grown—from small beginnings to a mighty role in our busy industrial world.

Latest act in the drama of the river is the rise of one of the world's greatest steelworks, 3800 acres of vast, towering structures, amid the somewhat surprised artists, writers, and farmers of Pennsylvania's placid Bucks County.

In today's closely interconnected world, a mountain in Venezuela and deepening holes in Minnesota can cause a steel plant to spring from broccoli fields on the Delaware. For the Venezuelan mountain is mostly iron ore, and the holes are the rust-red pits where power shovels are nearing the bottom of the richest United States iron ranges.

To meet the South American ore, steelmakers turn to the Delaware, wide, deep, majestic bearer of burdens in its lower reaches. "A glorious river," William Penn, the founder of Philadelphia, called it.

Might Have Been Called the Hudson

Seeking a passage to the Orient, Henry Hudson probed the river's broad bay in 1609. Shoals turned back his *Half Moon*, and he sailed on north; otherwise the Delaware instead of the Hudson might bear his name.

[a] Albert W. Atwood, *The National Geographic Magazine*, July 1952, pp. 1-40.

Such lordly streams later determined the location of many of our major cities. Rivers like the Hudson and Delaware, which met the simple needs of early settlers, are equally essential to the teeming millions of today. . . .

River Born as Puny Twins

Both branches of the Delaware begin humbly, a few miles apart, on the western slopes of New York's Catskill Mountains.

A spring on a hill near the resort town of Stamford gives rise to the west branch.

Outside Grand Gorge, in a small marshy pond close to a creamery, the east branch is born. Although so insignificant here, it is potentially fecund enough 40 miles to the south to warrant thirsty New York City spending more than a hundred million dollars to impound and tap its waters. . . .

For some 60 miles the two branches parallel each other, zigzagging along from 8 to 15 miles apart. They come together at Hancock, New York, to form the Delaware. Both branches and the main stream as far south as Trenton, New Jersey, have an almost primitive, unspoiled beauty early recognized by the artist George Inness and the naturalist John Burroughs. . . .

Canals Carried the Region's Coal

On a trip down the Delaware, abandoned ditches show that canals once figured importantly in the life of the New York-Pennsylvania-New Jersey region. When anthracite coal was discovered in the Pennsylvania hills, canals were built to carry it to the market in New York and Philadelphia.

At Minisink Ford, New York, one of the first bridges erected by John A. Roebling, designer of the Brooklyn Bridge, is still in active use after 103 years of service.

As a pedestrian, I crossed this suspension bridge for two cents to Lackawaxen, Pennsylvania. If I had ridden a bicycle, it would have cost five cents; and if I had driven my car, twenty-five.

Originally, the bridge was an aqueduct carrying coal-bearing canal boats across the river on their way from the Pennsylvania coal fields at Honesdale to Kingston, New York. Roebling built it so well that, after railroads

ended the usefulness of the Delaware and Hudson Canal,
the bed of the aqueduct was simply changed to a road-
way, now used by automobiles. . . .

Shrewd Tom Penn Gets a Bargain

Downriver I came to the first sizable cities—Easton,
Pennsylvania and adjacent Phillipsburg, New Jersey—at
what the Indians described as the "forks" of the Delaware. At Easton the Lehigh River joins the larger stream.

Treaties with the Delaware Indians were made at the
"Place of the Forks," some of them in Easton's First
Reformed Church, still standing after several remodel-
ings.

Near-by landmarks commemorate the notorious
"Walking Purchase" of 1737. The Indians promised
Thomas Penn as much land as a man could walk in a day
and a half and felt tricked when a trained walker did
66½ instead of an expected 40 miles. . . .

Art Colonies Take Over Canal District

In 1900 Philadelphia artists began to settle in and
around New Hope, Pennsylvania, 15 miles above Trenton, attracted by the canal, old stone houses, inns, and
abandoned gristmills. The little village was then a quiet
out-of-the-way backwater.

The canal ceased to operate in 1931, but the remnants
of towpath, locks, and aqueducts still make excellent
subjects for painting and the right setting for art schools
and coffee houses. . . .

Today New Hope is a tourist town and summer resort as well as an art colony. This is partly because of
the Bucks County Playhouse, which occupies an old
mill. Lillian Gish was playing when I visited it, with
"Alice in Wonderland" next on the bill.

Other summer playhouses may have as good bills, but
this is the only one I know where a waterfall must be
turned off before each performance, for there is a large
and noisy one directly outside the theatre. . . .

Washington's Christmas Surprise Party

Not only school children but many adults suppose that
Washington crossed at Trenton. Actually the crossing
took place eight miles above Trenton. Pennsylvania and
New Jersey State parks now mark the points of em-

barkation and landing. In roaring contrast to Washington's flat-bottomed boats is a Navy jet-propulsion experiment station a few miles east of the New Jersey park.

At the site of the crossing the river is only 1,000 feet wide. But one gets a thrill standing where the boats put off on their perilous journey, and it looks a long way to row through floating ice. . . .

"Trenton Makes, the World Takes"

It is a curious fact, not generally realized, that Washington as Commander in Chief spent a fourth of his time in New Jersey and moved his army across the state four times.

To this day, indeed, New Jersey is the most traveled state in the Union, being the natural corridor between the first and third largest cities. Benjamin Franklin described it as a cider barrel tapped at both ends. Crossroads of the Middle Atlantic States, it is crisscrossed by 13 major railroads and has more track per square mile than any other state.

On the main line of through travel across New Jersey stands Trenton, its capital, and each day 170 passenger trains cross the Pennsylvania Railroad bridge which spans the Delaware at this point.

Millions of passengers see a sign that reads, "Trenton Makes, the World Takes," appropriate because Trenton is among the most highly industrialized of American cities. Despite this fact, it has been singularly fortunate in being able to retain as park three miles of river frontage. In this riverside park are the Capitol Building and other state buildings. Several persons deserve credit for saving Trenton's water front, Governor Woodrow Wilson among them.

Nearby is the historic section of the city, with its old churches, its tablets and monuments, as well as banks, stores, and hotels. Perhaps the most striking relic is the Old Barracks, built for troops in the French and Indian War and later occupied by Washington's forces and by the British and Hessians who opposed him.

New Jersey is such a small state that no legislator can live more than 100 miles from Trenton or require more than three hours to reach it by rail or automobile. . . .

At Trenton the River Changes Its Character

Although the so-called "Falls" at Trenton are merely rapids, the city is on the fall line, that geological boundary where rivers pass from rocky formations to softer soils. Close to the fall line there has developed a northwest south-east axis of travel and trade, from New York through Trenton, Philadelphia, Wilmington, Baltimore, Washington, Richmond, and on through the Carolinas to Georgia.

In a number of cases ocean-going vessels can navigate rivers below the fall line, while even a canoe has difficulty above it. The Delaware Valley levels off at Trenton into a low coastal plain, and the river itself becomes an inlet of the sea, gradually widening into an estuary and merging into the broad expanse of Delaware Bay.

Thus the bay and lower river form a long, continuous navigable channel for cheap water transportation. But more than half a billion cubic yards of sand, gravel, and rock had to be dredged from the river during the past 35 years to maintain deep draft to Philadelphia.

Further dredging between Trenton and Philadelphia will create, in effect, a single port or harbor which will include many cities and towns. Among them, besides Trenton itself, are Bordentown, Burlington, Camden, and Paulsboro in New Jersey; Bristol, Philadelphia, and Chester in Pennsylvania; and Wilmington in Delaware. . . .

Philadelphia's "Scituation" Grows

William Penn planned and built the original city at the junction of the Delaware and Schuylkill Rivers. "The Scituation," he wrote, "is a Neck of Land Between two Navigable Rivers . . . whereby it has two Fronts upon the Water. . . ." Since then the city has spread out from an area 2 miles square until it now covers 135 square miles.

Some 50 years ago Henry James, novelist and essayist, wrote of Philadelphia's "admirable comprehensive flatness," of the "absence of the note of the perpetual perpendicular, the New York, the Chicago note."

Philadelphia's great abundance of flat land has resulted in a natural spreading out of population and industry alike. Thousands of workmen live near the plants where they work, in single two-story row houses, many owned by occupants, rather than in tall, rented apartments, as in New York.

Although Philadelphia was the largest seaport in the country for about a century and is now the second largest in terms of tonnage of water-borne commerce, there is very little feeling of the sea about it, no tang of salt air. A person may live in Philadelphia all his life and not even know it is a seaport.

This is natural because the city is 101 miles from the ocean. Yet 17,635 vessels arrived at and cleared from the Port of Philadelphia area in 1951, bound from and to most of the ports of the world.

$500,000 Willed for a Street

The Philadelphia water front is well worth a visit. When you get within a couple of blocks of the river, you suddenly and abruptly leave department stores and ordinary office buildings behind and come upon customs brokers, marine insurance companies, stevedoring companies, and dealers in marine and ship supplies.

Stephen Girard, early merchant, philanthropist, merchant, and banker, and founder of Girard College, dreamed of a tree-lined boulevard along the water front but did not live to see it. He left the income from a $500,000 trust fund "to lay out, regulate, curb, light, and pave a passage or street, fronting on the Delaware River, to be called Delaware Avenue."

And there it is, Delaware Avenue, not tree-lined but a fine long, broad water-front thoroughfare.

Philadelphia is not a regular passenger port like New York, but it handles a great variety and volume of merchandise. Far overtopping everything else in imports is petroleum, although large quantities of iron ore, to be greatly increased in the future, and sugar and molasses, with lesser amounts of honey and syrup, are brought in. The chief exports are manufactured goods and grain.

The Delaware has always been one of America's chief shipbuilding centers, and during the two World Wars it was a veritable American Clyde. The Sun Shipbuilding and Dry Dock Company at Chester, Pennsylvania, built some 40 percent of all United States tankers in World War II.

This company and the New York Shipbuilding Corporation at Camden, New Jersey, directly across the river from Philadelphia, together with the Philadelphia Navy Yard, are the principle builders and refitters of ships in that area, although there are several other concerns which build smaller vessels. The New York Shipbuilding Corporation occupies nearly a mile of water front in Camden.

Six major oil companies, including two with headquarters in Philadelphia, are spending several hundred million dollars to expand and modernize their refining capacities on both sides of the river at and below Philadelphia.

An oil tanker may seem an unromantic foundation on which to build a great port, but the modern world moves on oil, and Philadelphia is becoming one of the world's foremost refining centers.

No crude oil is produced near this city, but it can be brought in from the Gulf area, South America, and the Near East, and refined products shipped away, by cheap water transportation.

Began Finished No. words: 1900
$$\frac{}{} \times 60 = \underline{} \text{ W.P.M.}$$
_____ _____ No. seconds:

Preview Test
1. This article is a description of a _____.
2. Would you think from the title that the article will deal largely with the history of the river, or its present? _____
3. A famous colonial statesman is associated with this river in the title of the article. His name was _____
4. The Delaware might have been called another name. What name? _____
5. The Delaware begins as _____ small rivers.
6. In former years coal was carried in these regions over _____.
7. Who got a shrewd bargain in connection with some deal that had to do with the Delaware? _____
8. What group of people have taken over one of the old canal districts? _____ _____

9. What great American general carried on activities in connection with the Delaware? ─────────

10. What town on the Delaware is mentioned as one that makes many things that the rest of the world takes? ─────────

11. Where does the river change its character? At ─────────.

12. A street discussed in the article is unique in that someone willed a sum of money for its betterment. The amount willed for the street was ─────────.

Correct your answers by referring to the article.

Now read the article as fast as you can to find out more about the Delaware River. Time yourself and take the comprehension test as usual.

Checking Comprehension

Write the letter of each correct answer in the space below.

1. The new steel mills on the Delaware get ore from (a) Canada, (b) the Mesabi range, (c) Brazil, (d) Venezuela and Minnesota.

2. An early explorer who probably would have sailed up the Delaware had it not been for shoals was (a) Magellan, (b) De Soto, (c) Henry Hudson, (d) Balboa.

3. The two branches of the Delaware as well as the main stream as far as Trenton lie in country which is (a) highly industrialized, (b) monotonous and uninteresting, (c) wet and marshy, (d) almost primitive in its unspoiled beauty.

4. John A. Roebling was famous for building (a) skyscrapers, (b) canals, (c) bridges, (d) factories.

5. The Indians thought that Penn tricked them in a real estate deal by employing (a) an experienced broker, (b) a trained walker, (c) a good lawyer, (d) an Indian scout.

6. When the canal ceased to operate at New Hope, the town (a) died out entirely, (b) became an industrial center, (c) became a community center for farmers, (d) became a tourist town and summer resort.

7. Washington crossed the Delaware at (a) Wilmington, (b) Trenton, (c) 8 miles above Trenton, (d) Philadelphia.

8. The most traveled state in America is (a) New Jersey, (b) Delaware, (c) New York, (d) Pennsylvania.

9. Ocean-going vessels can in time navigate all the way to the fall line of the river. This fall line is at (a) Philadelphia, (b) Trenton, (c) Camden, (d) Bristol.

10. Philadelphia doesn't have the usual characteristics of a (a) large city, (b) industrial center, (c) city of fame in colonial days, (d) a seaport.

Answers: 1)____, 2)____, 3)____, 4)____, 5)____, 6)____, 7)____, 8)____, 9)____, 10)____.

Check your answers with the Answer Key on page 278. Allow yourself 10 for each correct answer.

Rate: W.P.M. _____   Comprehension Score: _____

Vocabulary Study

Here is a list of words taken from the selections you have just read. In the sentences that follow, one word, or sometimes a pair of words synonymous with a word in the list, has been italicized. Write in the blank space the word that can be substituted without changing the meaning of the sentence.

bushwhack	estuary	lichen	wraith
myriad	vulnerable	vindication	spate
chute	shoals	encompass	escarpment
muskeg	fecund	bend	veritable
tributary	domain	portage	pessimistic

1. At one point in their journey the canoeists were troubled with *shallow water*. _____

2. The rocks were covered with a *parasitic plant*. _____

3. The birds in the forest were *innumerable*. _____

4. Australia's most *fruitful* producer is the rabbit. _____

5. The men had to *cut away* the bushes. _____

6. What does the suspect offer as *justification* for his action? _____

7. It will take seventy-five rods of fence to *surround* the plot of ground. _____

8. The wisp of fog which arose from the lake was like a *specter*. _____

9. An inclined *trough* of water came rushing down from a higher level. _____

10. There was a sharp *deviation* in the stream just beyond the rapids. _____

11. The wide lower part of the *tidal river* had salty water in it. _____

12. A caribou is *capable of receiving injuries* when hunters are around. _____

13. The men climbed to the top of a *steep slope*. _____

14. The canoeists were victims of a *sudden, violent rainstorm*. _____

15. The story the men told about the height of the falls was a *genuine* fact. _____

16. As the men walked on one of the islands their feet sank deep in a kind of *swamp-moss*. _____

17. Unknown River is a *branch* of the Hamilton River. _____

18. Hamilton River has long been the *province* of snowshoers and canoeists. _____

19. Natives took a *gloomy* view of the canoeists' proposed trip. _____

20. The men carried their canoes across the *land* between two rivers. _____

See page 278 for answers. Allow 5 for each correct answer.

Vocabulary Score: _____

Follow-Up Practice

Applying Preview Techniques in Your Regular Reading

Continue to practice during definite periods each evening. Try taking a preview of everything you read, both materials which you read informally as a part of your work or recreation, and materials which you read during your regular practice periods.

Concisely, these are the characteristics which you will need to observe in making your initial surveys:

1. Title
2. Subheadings
3. Visual aids
4. Length of paragraphs
5. Number of words (to make your time-of-reading estimate)

CHAPTER 6

SIGHT-SEEING AS YOU READ

Taking an Excursion

Suppose you are a stranger in New York and you decide to take a sight-seeing trip on one of the excursion boats that encircles the Island of Manhattan. As you glide past the shores of the magic city in the misty haze of a sultry August afternoon, perhaps all you see is a mass of buildings. "Huge, gray boxes piled one upon the other," you say to yourself.

Then the voice of the guide breaks into your reverie.

"Now, folks, look right between the low, yellow building on your left and the red building with a flat roof on your right, and you'll see a dark gray building with a spire on top that towers above everything else on the Island. This is the Empire State Building, the tallest building in the world. It has 102 stories above the street and two stories below ground. It houses 25,000 tenants."

Suddenly, as the guide talks, one building in this previously nondescript mass stands out as something significant. All the other buildings still remain just a heap of piled-up gray boxes as far as you're concerned, their only function being to furnish background for this one momentous piece of architecture. The sameness of the view has now been broken.

You sail on past another segment of water front. Suddenly one of the dozens of piers which you scarcely noticed before leaps out with color, shape and meaning.

The guide is saying, "Look at this light-green pier

which is more modernistic in shape than the others. This is the world's most unusual pier. It was recently built by the city and leased to the Grace Line. It has a roof parking area for 250 cars, and a huge storage basement entirely below the water surface."

As the guide talks, Pier 57 becomes the most important edifice on the landscape, and you keep thinking about it as the boat moves on.

"Now, look between that brown building with the tower and the gray one with the water tank on top," shouts the guide. "You'll see a wide and tall cream-colored building with a flat roof. This is the Whitehall Building where the Weather Bureau is located. The equipment is on that roof. Mr. Christie, the head of the Bureau, may be up there right now, studying the weather."

Once more one building stands out in the vista in front of you as being more important at the moment than all of the others.

And so the trip continues. As you pass each section of the shoreline the guide points out one feature as having some special significance. The dreary sameness disappears, and the aggregate of gray structures which you saw at first becomes colorful and meaningful and interesting.

An excursion in reading is very much like a trip around Manhattan. The successive sections of buildings may be likened to the consecutive paragraphs which you pass as you read an article or chapter. At a glance they all look alike, but if you examine them you will find one thought in each paragraph which will stand out above all the others. And the details in the paragraph fall into line to add information and interest, just as the information the guide told you about the Weather Bureau contributed to your interest in the cream-colored structure in which this Bureau is housed. In pointing out a building the guide told you one thing about it which made it distinctive. This was the main idea in his oral paragraph. Then he continued, giving you facts of lesser importance about the building. These lesser facts were the details in his paragraph. The details expanded upon the main idea, but they would have been quite meaningless without the one important sentence in which he identified the building and told the single thing for which it is most famous.

You should learn to use the sight-seeing technique as you read, grasping the one significant idea in each paragraph and letting the details fall into line. The chief difference between a sight-seeing trip around Manhattan and your own sight-seeing trips in reading is that you'll have no guide along while you're reading to point out the most significant thing in each paragraph. That you must do for yourself.

The Art of Reading Paragraphs

Perhaps no one technique will aid you more in improving your reading ability than learning to read paragraphs effectually. Every selection is made up of paragraphs. Each paragraph is a unit of thought. Quickly grasping the essence of each of these thought units enables you to cover reading materials rapidly and, at the same time, to get the most important ideas which the author is expressing. In a paragraph there is one point of fundamental importance, and the details revolve around this hub idea, expanding upon it.

When you toss a pebble into a pool of water, you immediately perceive a circular ripple at the spot where the pebble came into contact with the water. Then other concentric circles appear, one after the other until there is an entire set of circular ripples. So it is with a paragraph. Figuratively speaking, the author tosses one main idea into a paragraph which sets all the other ideas in motion. It is your job to learn how to find this pivotal idea, swiftly and surely.

In much of the reading that you do you won't care to take time to consider all of the details. You will be satisfied if you can speedily glean the main ideas in the selection. Expertness in "spotting" the basic thought in each paragraph is the skill that you need to cultivate.

On the other hand, some selections will be of such significance to you that you will want to read and consider the minor ideas carefully. Then you will find that locating the main idea in each paragraph is of major importance because the central thought provides you with a core around which you can organize the details. In Chapter Seven you will be shown how to use the "main idea" technique as a starting point in factual reading. In the meantime, whether you are doing cursory reading for the purpose of gathering the larger ideas, or whether you are doing detailed reading for exact information, you will find it to your advantage to acquire the technique of reading paragraphs. In order to do this you must develop a systematic approach to paragraph reading rather than just following along one sentence after the other without effort or thought in regard to paragraph organization.

The position of the key sentence in a paragraph varies. Often the germ idea appears in the first sentence. If so, this is a convenience to the reader because he doesn't have to search through the entire paragraph for the central thought. At other times, the important idea occurs in the middle, at the end, or somewhere else in the paragraph. Because of the variance in the location of the key sentence within a paragraph, position is not a reliable guide in finding the main idea. You must learn surer ways of locating the one basic thought.

The first thing to do is to develop a new attitude toward paragraph reading—the attitude of thinking of each paragraph as a unit. As you encounter a new paragraph, view it as if it were all the reading material you had before you at the moment. Decide what is the *one* important idea this paragraph has to impart. Ask yourself two things:

1. What is the basic thing, place, condition, or person discussed in this paragraph?
2. What does this thing, place, condition, or person do, or what is done to it, or what property does it have, or what condition is it in, which makes it worth while for the author to write about it?

Keep these questions in mind while studying the paragraph below. See if you can locate the main idea with certainty.

The calcium cycle is one of the most interesting cycles of nature. The ocean contains vast quantities of calcium salts in solution. These are withdrawn by living creatures and built into coral reefs and the shells of mollusks and are precipitated in other ways. In the course of geologic time, deposits of calcium carbonate laid down in the ocean become lifted up from limestone strata in mountain ranges. These formations are then attached by atmospheric and organic acids and slowly dissolved and carried back into the sea from which they came. Sometimes great caves are left behind as a result of this process and many secondary calcite and aragonite formations come into existence.[1]

1. What is the basic topic discussed in this paragraph?
2. What special property does it have?
3. At what position in this paragraph did you find the key sentence?

If you analyzed this paragraph correctly, you will have concluded that the main topic is "the calcium cycle," and that the special property which the calcium cycle possesses is that it "is one of the most interesting cycles of nature." All the remaining sentences in the paragraph are subordinate details which tell how the calcium cycle is interesting. In this particular paragraph, then, the main idea is contained in the first sentence.

See if you can quickly find the main idea in the paragraph below.

A fraction over two minutes is all that it takes to run the Kentucky Derby at Churchill Downs in Louisville. But the Derby packs more excitement into these two minutes than any other sporting event in the country. The Derby Day "Run for the Roses" dates back to 1875 when a little red horse named Aristides came in first. There were 12,000 spectators on hand then. More than 100,000 attend now, and millions more watch or listen

[1] W. Scott Lewis, "Cycles in Nature," *Hobbies*, August 1947, p. 138.

with breathless interest on TV and radio. The build-up of excitement increases year by year.

1. What is the basic subject of discussion in this paragraph?
2. What makes this subject distinctive?
3. In what position in the paragraph do you find this information?
4. What is the function of all of the other sentences in the paragraph as related to this topic sentence?

If you were right in your analysis, you decided that "the Derby" is the basic subject of discussion and that the distinctive thing about it is that it "packs more excitement into these two minutes than any other sporting event in the country." This information which expresses the main idea appears in the second sentence of the paragraph. All the other sentences are related to the subject of the Derby and expand upon this main idea, but no one of them is nearly so important or inclusive as the topic sentence, which really holds the essence of the entire cluster of thoughts expressed in the paragraph.

See if you can "spot" the key sentence in this paragraph:

We're intrigued by an ingenious device Chock Full O'Nuts Corp. used during the World Series. During the Series time, salesmen for Chock Full O'Nuts coffee were particularly welcomed by the grocers they visited. Reason: the salesmen carried portable radios tuned to catch the latest scores.

Check the most important idea:

(a) The writer was intrigued by an ingenious device.
(b) Salesmen for Chock Full O'Nuts were welcomed by grocers during the Series time.
(c) Salesmen carried portable radios tuned to catch the latest scores.

Number (c) is the most important idea in the paragraph. The first sentence merely tells us that there was an ingenious device; the second sentence tells us that the salesmen were particularly welcomed by grocers during Series time. Both of these sentences alert us to read on and find out what this ingenious device was which caused salesmen to be welcomed during Series time. The heart of the paragraph is found in the last sentence, which tells us what the device was and what it did. The big idea in the whole paragraph is that "salesmen carried portable radios tuned to catch the latest scores."

So far you have been studying paragraphs for the purpose of learning how to locate the main idea. You probably read very slowly during this initial work. Don't worry if you slow down while learning this new technique. Soon you will unconsciously include looking for the main idea in a paragraph as an integral part of your new streamlined reading ability. Then the skill-building in paragraph analysis which you are now doing will function significantly in increasing both your speed and comprehension.

Practice in Finding the Main Idea in a Paragraph

Exercise 1

As the next step in your skill-building program try to find the main idea in the paragraphs below. See also if you can pick up a little more speed as you apply this technique.

1. Find the noun or noun phrase that names the basic subject with which each paragraph is concerned.

2. Find the group of words that tells what this subject does, what it could or should do, what it is, what it has, or what happens to it which is sufficiently important to justify a written paragraph about it.

3. Try to read each paragraph a little faster than the one before as you apply this technique.

PARAGRAPH 1

The Far West states continue to be the most rapidly growing region in the nation, with an undiminished flow of migrants from all other regions. The population gain is more than twice as great as that of the rest of the nation. The whole economic structure of the Far West has expanded and continues to expand enormously. This is necessary both to serve the needs and to tap the labor and capital resources of the constant flow of newcomers to its labor force.[2]

Select the key idea:

a) The Far West states continue to be the most rapidly-growing region in the nation.
b) The population gain is more than twice as great as that of the rest of the nation.
c) The whole economic structure of the West continues to expand enormously.
d) This is necessary to serve the needs of the constant flow of newcomers.

PARAGRAPH 2

Most hunters have pet peeves. Jacob's pet peeve was that he detested the cat and all its wild cousins, such as the cougar, the panther, and the lynx. With unscientific zeal he threw the sneaky coyote into the same category. He stalked coyotes through the Blue Mountains of Oregon with a fanatical passion, but to no avail. They outsmarted him at every turn. He could never get them within shooting range to put a bullet through their pesky carcasses. "That's the cat of it," he would say.[3]

Select the sentence which is the "heart" of this paragraph:

a) Most hunters have pet peeves.
b) Jacob's pet peeve was that he detested the cat and all its wild cousins.
c) He stalked coyotes through the Blue Mountains of Oregon.
d) He could never get them in shooting range.

[2] "People Begin to Pour in," *Sales Management*, November 10, 1954, p. 106.
[3] Mike Revise, "They Tried It Before," *Field and Stream*, May 1954, p. 40.

Paragraph 3

Among engineers and plant operators there's a lot of talk about today's heavy oils—they're not what they used to be. Some of this is just old-fashioned griping, but we also find more than a grain of fact. Heavy oils *have* been made less easy to use. This is due to changes in refining methods. The newer methods aimed at improving yield and quality of gasoline, and light fuel oils have affected the by-product heavy oils and caused them to be less easy to use than the straight-run residuals of years past. So you see there is some substance back of all this talk.[4]

Select the sentence which completely and concisely sums up the information in this paragraph:

a) There's a lot of talk about today's heavy oils.

b) Some of this is just old-fashioned griping, but we also find more than a grain of fact.

c) Heavy oils *have* been made less easy to use.

d) So you see there is some substance back of all this talk.

Check your work by referring to the Answer Key on page 278.

Speeded Practice in Finding the Main Idea

Exercise 2

Now you have had enough practice in finding the main idea to be ready for some time pressure while applying this technique. In working with the following five paragraphs, try to find the main idea and at the same time apply the speed-reading procedures which you learned in Chapter Three.

1. Jot down the time at which you begin reading.

2. Note the time you finished in exact minutes and seconds. Subtract your beginning time from your finishing time and record your answer in minutes and seconds.

[4] A. J. Weber, "You Need to Know How and Why Study Fouls up Fuel-Oil Systems," *Power*, September 1954, p. 109.

3. Check the sentence in the list of choices which you believe represents the "heart" of each paragraph.

PARAGRAPH 1
BEGINNING TIME:————————————
HR.———— MIN.———— SEC.————

From the earliest days the conviction has been growing among the people and their leaders that the state must be responsible for seeing that its citizens have a certain quantum of education. That the state has this responsibility is shown by the state constitutions, the hundreds of school statutes in each state, and the scores of decisions of local, state, and federal courts. In brief, education has come to be universally regarded as a state function. The assumption of educational control by the state is not fortuitous; state control has come because of the early and ever growing belief that education is the buttress of a democratic government and cannot, therefore, be left too much to the whims of any individual or of any community. In a democracy the people cannot be permitted to remain ignorant although some of them might desire that status.[5]

ENDING TIME:————————————
HR.———— MIN.———— SEC.————

a) The conviction has been growing that the state should be responsible for education.
b) Education has come to be universally regarded as a state function.
c) The assumption of educational control by the state is not fortuitous.
d) In a democracy people cannot be permitted to remain ignorant.

PARAGRAPH 2
BEGINNING TIME:————————————
HR.———— MIN.———— SEC.————

The business meeting of any board may be handled efficiently and expeditiously if it is carefully planned in

[5] Ward G. Reeder, *Public School Administration*. Macmillan, 1941, p. 55.

advance. One excellent guarantee that the business will be thus handled is to see in advance that a definite routine, or order of business, is established. An order of business saves time and gives greater assurance that no item of business will be forgotten during the meeting. Such order of business should be made a part of the rules and regulations of the board. Another guarantee to an efficient and expeditious conduct of the board's business is to formulate ahead of the meeting a definite parliamentary procedure to follow. The more important phases of this procedure also should be made a part of the rules and regulations of the board. While the permanent pattern of fundamental procedures can be established in the rules and regulations, fresh planning will be necessary for each new meeting.[6]

ENDING TIME:————————

HR.———— MIN.———— SEC.————

a) An order of business saves time during the meeting.
b) Parliamentary procedure should be made a part of the rules and regulations of the board.
c) The business meeting of any board may be handled expeditiously if it is carefully planned in advance.
d) One excellent guarantee that the business will be handled is to see in advance that a definite routine is established.

PARAGRAPH 3

BEGINNING TIME:————————

HR.———— MIN.———— SEC.————

Ideas are elastic and flexible. They reach out beyond ordinary bounds and barriers. You have no right to take the sword and cross the bounds of other nations and enforce on them laws or institutions they are unwilling to receive. But there is no limit to the sphere of ideas. Your thoughts and feelings, the whole world lies open to them. You have the right to send your ideas into any latitude, and to give them sweep around the earth, to the mind of every human being.—*Henry Ward Beecher*

ENDING TIME:————————

HR.———— MIN.———— SEC.————

[6] *Ibid.,* p. 95.

a) Ideas are elastic and flexible.
b) They reach out beyond ordinary bounds and barriers.
c) There is no limit to the sphere of ideas.
d) You have the right to send your ideas into any latitude and to give them sweep around the earth.

PARAGRAPH 4

BEGINNING TIME:——————
HR.———— MIN.———— SEC.————

Advice and reprehension require the utmost delicacy; painful truths should be delivered in the softest terms and expressed no farther than is necessary to produce their due effect. A courteous man will mix what is conciliating with what is offensive; praise with censure; deference and respect with the authority of admonition, so far as can be done in consistence with probity and honor. The mind revolts against all censorian power which displays pride or pleasure in finding fault; but advice, divested of harshness and yet retaining the honest warmth of truth, is like honey just round the brim of a vessel full of wormwood. Even this, however, is sometimes insufficient to conceal the bitterness of the draught.
—*James Gates Percival*

ENDING TIME:——————
HR.———— MIN.———— SEC.————

a) The mind revolts against all censorian power which displays pride or power in finding fault.
b) Painful truths should be delivered in the softest terms.
c) Even careful handling is sometimes insufficient to conceal the bitterness of the draught.
d) Advice and reprehension require the utmost delicacy.

PARAGRAPH 5

BEGINNING TIME:——————
HR.———— MIN.———— SEC.————

A young woman working at a very modest salary in a New York office wanted some good imitation pearls. When Christmas came and she was given a $25 check by her employer, she decided to go to a good store and spend the whole sum on a string of beads. A new clerk helped her pick out some nice-looking pearls. She loved them, wore them constantly to work. One day, on the subway, the string broke and pearls flew in every direction. Kind passengers helped her pick up the beads, and she tied them in her handkerchief until she could take them to the jewelers to be restrung. She explained she had bought the string there a couple of years before. When she went to get the beads, she had the surprise of her life. She was ushered into the manager's office. The new clerk two years before had sold this woman a $2,500 necklace for $25.[7]

ENDING TIME:————————
HR.———— MIN.———— SEC.————

a) A young woman working at a very modest salary wanted some good imitation pearls.

b) When Christmas came and she was given a $25 check she decided to spend the whole sum on beads.

c) She was ushered into the manager's office.

d) The clerk two years before had sold this woman a $2,500 necklace for $25.

Checking Speed

Compute the time it took you to read each paragraph. Add the items of time for the five paragraphs and record your total reading time below.

Total Time No. words: 660

$$\frac{}{\text{No. seconds:}} \times 60 = \underline{\hspace{2cm}} \text{W.P.M.}$$

Checking Comprehension

Check your accuracy in finding the main idea in each of the paragraphs by referring to the Answer Key on

[7] Artemisia B. Bryson, "A String of Necklace," *Hobbies*, August 1947, p. 42.

page 278. You may allow a score of 5 for each correct answer. Multiply 20 by the number of answers you had correct. This will be your Comprehension Score.

Rate: W.P.M. ——— Comprehension Score: ———

What About Exceptions?

"This paragraph doesn't have any main idea in it" is the first comment an instructor hears when he begins to teach the technique of finding the main idea in a paragraph. It is true that occasionally you will run across a paragraph in which one "hub" idea is not stated. This, however, is the exception rather than the rule.

Furthermore there *are* techniques which can be employed in dealing with the unusual types of paragraphs.

The simplest of the exceptions is the paragraph which is made up of just one sentence, such as:

The broken-hearted scientist fell ill under the strain, and died shortly afterward with the laughter of the scientific world ringing in his ears.[8]

In such cases the reader who is searching for main ideas, should gather up the one basic import of the paragraph. The basic idea in this case is that the scientist died shortly. Scientist is the subject, and the thing that happened to him was that he died shortly.

Another type of paragraph which is more puzzling than the one-sentence paragraph is the type which enumerates several items of equal importance. For example:

The Old Testament speaks familiarly of fishhooks, and compares a woman's eyes to fish pools. The paintings on Egyptian tombs show fishermen at work using dragnets, hooks, and lines, and also bronze harpoons. The Red Sea, the Nile, and the artificial lakes gave employment to a host of dark-skinned fishermen, and supplied sea food for all the tribes of Egypt. For the trick of drying and curing fish—something not evolved in Europe until

[8] Leon Augustus Hausman, "The Famous Fossil Hoax," *The Mentor*, February 1922, p. 42.

the fourteenth century—was known to these remarkable narrow-headed Africans some six thousand years ago.[9]

Since all the ideas in this paragraph are of about equal significance, the most expedient thing for the reader to do is to formulate his own topic sentence. It might be shaped up something like this: "Fishing was practiced in Egypt six thousand years ago."

Another exception is the type of paragraph which has two ideas of considerable weight, when it is difficult to tell which is more important.

What the whole undertaking revealed to me most was the interest there is in the history of paper-making and watermarking. I have been so absorbed with these subjects since my experimenting in paper-making that I am writing a book, in two volumes, on the history of paper.[10]

Which sentence expresses the more important thought? The writer states that the most important outcome of his experience was the development of an interest in paper-making and watermarking. It is equally important that he is now writing two volumes on the history of paper. Instead of trying to decide which of these two thoughts is the main idea, it would be better to consider them together and sum them up in some such fashion as this: Because of the great interest which he developed in the history of paper-making, he is now writing a two-volume book on the subject.

Occasionally one will run across a paragraph that is just a mass of details with seemingly no outstanding idea in it. Such a paragraph is usually sandwiched in between two other paragraphs that do have main ideas. So waste no time puzzling. Forge ahead with those paragraphs that do have something important to say.

[9] John D. Whiting, "Fishing and Fisher-Folk," *The Mentor*, July 1923, p. 3.
[10] Dard Hunter, "A Maker of One-Man Books," *The Mentor*, March 1922, p. 31.

Applying Paragraph Techniques in Reading an Entire Selection

Read the next selection as rapidly as you can. Apply the techniques you have already learned for rapid reading and direction words. In addition, try to locate the main idea in each paragraph as you go along. Pass the details lightly, but try to absorb the main idea. If you encounter a paragraph which doesn't seem to contain a basic idea, use the appropriate techniques discussed on the preceding pages.

Time yourself, and take the comprehension test after the reading.

Selection 1

BEGINNING TIME:——————
HR.———— MIN.———— SEC.————

MUSIC AND LIFE[11]

Life begins and ends with music. It envelopes and permeates the world we live in. Land, water, and sky are full of elemental music of many kinds and degrees of intensity. The wind sings through the responsive leaves and plays on the harp strings of the waving reeds by the rivers; birds pour forth their lyric tunes to charm the waking morn; and the ocean waves swell in rhythmic chorus as if at the command of a master conductor.

The potency of music has been acknowledged in all ages and by all races. And it was so from the beginning of time. It is said that long, long ago Orpheus charmed all things animate and inanimate with the strains of his lyre. He even went down to Pluto's domain, Hades, and coaxed back the soul of his dead and lost love Eurydice with his music. And everyone knows of the Sirens who bewitched sailors with their songs in the Grecian Isles, and the Lorelei maiden on the rock above the Rhine.

Good and Bad Music

This suggests the thought, often stated, that good music ennobles and bad music degrades. It seems clear

[11] Fritz Kreisler, *The Mentor*, December 1921, pp. 5-12.

to me, however, that there is only one kind of music, and that is GOOD music. When music can be called bad, it ceases to be music. It simply becomes rhythmic noise. I do not think that music, in itself, produces good or bad effects, but rather that it enhances and intensifies existing ideas and instincts, good or bad. To a man in love, music may deepen the feeling of romance; a man suffering from melancholia may have his sorrows dyed a shade deeper; a warrior may have a heightened feeling of war fever. In this connection music may be compared to HASHEESH. That powerful drug produces good or bad dreams in keeping with the mental condition and environment of the drug-taker. In a room furnished in good taste, he dreams of things beautiful, but in ghastly surroundings he dreams frightful dreams. That alluring composition, HUMORESQUE, to a religious man may mean devotional ecstasy; to the frivolous, a sensuous dance. I have even been told that some highway robbers once were heard whistling it before they started on a daring escapade.

Music Is Relative

I do not think that there is such a thing as ABSO-LUTE religious or sacred music. What is true of other things in life is true of music. It is relative. What is true in art today may be deemed quite untrue by the next generation. Take, for example, the musical consonance and discord once recognized as essential elements in music. Modern composers and musicians do not recognize the old order of things. The Gregorian chant has been associated in Christian nations with religion for hundreds of years, so it invokes within us religious feeling. In a non-Christian land the same chant might rouse martial sentiment, if it had been used there for that purpose TRADITIONALLY. Play the Gregorian chant to an Australian bushman and it may not affect him devotionally at all—but a certain crude melody of his own will; at the same time, his wild music may inspire feelings of a quite different nature in others in a different environment.

The same is true of the music of different musical instruments. The horn has been associated with the chase. When we think of the chase we instinctively think of the horn. The guitar is associated with romance—a gondola under the Rialto in Venice, or a young man under a window in Seville. Nowadays, we associate war with trumpet and drum—the instruments of fire and fury. But in ancient Greece the bards were wont to lash the country into feverish martial activities by singing and playing on the lyre. The Gaelic bards did the same. Now, the lyre is to us an instrument of tender tones and romantic feeling.

During the exciting days of the French Revolution the singing of the Marseillaise was thought more dangerous by those in power than incendiary speeches or weapons of war. It inspired people to make sacrifices, it roused them to fight and to die fighting. I am certain that, in a country that knows nothing about the French Revolution or of this great song of France, the Marseillaise could be effectively used for religious revival.

Art, then, is influenced by environment, education, and association of ideas. Art, like love, is a state of mind and heart, and the art of music more so than other arts. The arts of poetry, painting, and sculpture have tangible forms. But music is formless—it is all feeling. For that reason it is the more dynamic, and produces a deeper emotional effect.

Music Helps and Heals

A beneficial act, like healing, is quite often accomplished by the art of music. The world is destined to hear more and more of this practical side of music. I shall not be surprised if a book on musical therapeutics, written by a scientist, shall have, before long, a place on the shelves of the medical libraries of the world. In the ancient scriptures of the Hindus, the Christians, the Egyptians, and the Chinese, there are references to the healing power of music. Thus we read in the Bible: "When the evil spirit from God was upon Saul, then David took an harp, and played with his hand. So Saul was refreshed, and was well, and the evil spirit departed from him."

My father was a physician, and I studied medicine for about two years—so I know a little about medical science. I do not think it is unscientific to say that, in certain instances, music can be effectively used as a healing agency. Scientists have just begun to investigate this matter. Healing is largely a normal adjustment of the maladjusted molecules of the body. Recently a case was brought to my notice. A young lady was sick with high fever in her home on a ranch in one of the western states of the Union. The doctor's home was far away and he could not be summoned readily. A friend asked the mother to give her daughter a "music cure." A certain record was played on the phonograph a few times. The young lady's temperature came down, and, I am informed, she was soon on her way to recovery. A case has been cited recently of a young woman, suffering from sleeping sickness, who was brought to consciousness and health through the ministration of music. . . .

The effect of music not only upon the ill, but also upon the insane, has been noted and considered by physicians. For my own part, I believe in the soothing, comforting, and healing effect of music. We all know how thought affects the human body. An embarrassing remark causes a rush of blood to a woman's face, and she blushes. If you look at something sour your mouth waters, or if at something tragic, tears rise in your eyes. Think of your absent beloved and your body and mind ache with the bitter pangs of separation. Happy thoughts make the body buoyant, and melancholy thoughts depress it. If the mind is "low," if the nerves are weak, the power sent to the muscles is diminished. Now every musical note is a living thought current. If electrical waves in air can carry a wireless message over thousands of miles, a musical wave may also find a response in the physical and mental being. The musical waves no doubt act and react on our nervous system. And surely they do adjust or maladjust, disturb or harmonize, the atoms and IONS of our natures.

I found my musical ear of value in war service. I soon got accustomed to the sound of deadly missiles—in fact, I quickly began to make observations of their peculiarities. My ear, accustomed to differentiate sounds of all kinds, had noted a remarkable discrepancy in the whine produced by different shells as they passed overhead, some sounding shrill, with a rising cadence, and others rather dull, with a falling cadence. Every shell describes in its course a parabolic line, with the first half of the curve ascending, and the second one descending. Apparently, in the first half of its curve, while ascending, the shell produced a dull whine, accompanied by a falling cadence, which changed to a rising shrill as soon as the acme was reached, and the curve turned down. I was told that shells sounded different when going up than when coming down, but that this knowledge was not of value for practical purposes. I found that I could, with a trained musical ear, mark the spot where shells reached their acme, and so could give the almost exact range of guns.

Music and Animals

Music affects even the animal world. The flute pleases and thrills the horse. The drum and trumpet awaken the spirit in this noble animal so that he plunges headlong on to the battlefield. The Hindu snake charmer plays on his POONGI flute, and deadly cobras crawl out and weave their sinuous way toward their seductive charmers. Not long ago a musical experiment was tried out at the New York Zoological Park. The animals were tested on the "jazz music" that so many modern human beings seem to fancy. The animals did not like it. The monkeys, in particular, went wild in anguished revolt.

National Music

It is passing strange that some would like to nationalize music. Music belongs to no nation. The spell of music is the same whether it is sung and played in America or England, in France or Italy, in India or China, in Russia or South Africa. Music, like art and literature, is universal; it transcends all national boundaries. Rodin belongs just as much to Russia as to France; Shakespeare just as much to Europe and America as to England; Kalidasa just as much to England as to India; and Brahms just as much to Paris as to Vienna. As from the mountain top the world below is bereft of all national distinctions, so, viewed from the peak of higher understanding, nationality in art disappears.

It is cultural background, intellectual training, specialization, and execution that make the difference in the appreciation of music. If badly played, even Beethoven's symphonies would be a deadly drag. From my earliest days I have been interested in music, and music is my life; and yet, if I do not like the music of a Negro in Darkest Africa, that does not make that music less vital, less real to the African. It is my own fault that I do not appreciate such music. The first time I heard Chinese music I did not like it at all. But later on, when I heard a Chinese scholar sing, the deeper and inner message of Chinese music was revealed to me. To understand music of this sort we must study national background and tradition.

In examining the cubist and futurist arts of to-day, one may fail to understand the meaning of lines and surfaces. One may scorn a picture and call it grotesque, but to the artist it is real. Adherents to the traditional laws of pictorial art scoff at him, but he does not care. He looks at the picture he has produced from the angle of a highly accentuated imagination.

The same is true of music. The last movement of Beethoven's Fifth Symphony, played to an untutored listener, may be no more than a crude march, but to one trained in music it is sublime revelation—as though the soul of a mortal had burst through the shell of egotism to stand face to face with the Infinite. When I hear Beethoven's symphonies, I think I know why he became deaf. It seems to me that he must have been so saturated with exalted music feeling that a little more would have devastated him physically. It seems almost as if he HAD TO BECOME deaf, to be shut in, in order to gain an intensified hearing of the musical inspiration within him. No sound from outside could help him any more. The sonatas that he wrote while deaf are the very essence of music.

Here it may be mentioned, by the way, that with the growing complexity of music, really great compositions are growing less in number. Haydn wrote one hundred and fifty symphonies, Mozart over forty, Beethoven nine, Tschaikovsky six, Schumann only four, and Brahms four.

The international animosities of the past few years have retarded the progress of music in the world. But in the task of reconstruction, of the regeneration of the human race, music will play a prominent part. I have, however, somewhat modified my views in this matter. Before the war I was enough of a dreamer to exaggerate the importance of music for the elevation of society. But I know Europe to-day, and I have seen things with my own eyes. Now I hold that when men, women, and children actually die of starvation, or eke out an existence of lingering death, music, even the very best of it, cannot help them! The artist himself cannot sing or play on an empty stomach. Give the hungry musician a slice of bread and a glass of water, if a cup of sugarless coffee is too much to expect—then his spirits will rise and he will produce good music. Give the hungry lover of music a bite of food—then he will enjoy music and smile. Music glorifies life but cannot preserve it. Music is the dome, a very beautiful dome, but not the foundation of the edifice of humanity.

As in music some notes mingle, so in life some vibrations are in accord. The underlying principle of this accord in life may be called love. Music and love are like twin sisters. Like flames of fire they both burn into the very core of our being. Music has often been defined as "the language of emotions," and the profoundest of all emotions is love. The dominant note of most of the beautiful songs is love. Most of the grand operas strive to unfold this glowing principle in life. Love invigorates art. One who cannot love greatly and unselfishly cannot accomplish great things in life. "Music," says von Weber, "is the purest, most ethereal language of passion." "I can grasp the spirit of music," says Wagner, "in no other manner than in love."

Most of the great musicians have been great lovers, for music creates love; it deepens and sanctifies love. Love has been the rudder to guide the ship of their lives.

In spite of all human thoughts and theories, life is still a mystery, love is a mystery, music is a mystery. No one can really define them. It is a supremely happy thing, nevertheless, that we can realize love and music in life. Both music and love blend with life as does color in a rainbow.

Began Finished No. words: 2500

―――― × 60 = ―――― W.P.M.

―――― ―――― No. seconds:

Checking Comprehension

1. The writer thinks that the potency of music (a) has always been recognized, (b) is something we have only recently realized, (c) is still not realized by most people, (d) has been greatly exaggerated.

2. The writer believes that (a) music in itself produces both good and bad effects, (b) that some music degrades, (c) that there is such a thing as bad music, (d) that music enhances and intensifies existing ideas and instincts, good or bad.

3. The writer explains the effect of music waves on the ill by saying that (a) they help patients to get their illness off their minds, (b) they remind the sick of days when they were well, (c) they adjust or maladjust the atoms and ions of our natures, (d) electrical waves are produced by music which definitely cure certain diseases.

4. The author found his musical ear was valuable during his war service for (a) giving the almost exact range of guns, (b) entertaining troops, (c) teaching proper voice control to officers, (d) improving military bands.

5. The author claims that music is the property of (a) the nation in which it was written, (b) no nation, (c) the nations that speak the same language as that of the composer, (d) the nations with the same cultural background as that of the composer.

6. The writer says that the differences in various peoples' appreciation of music are the result of (a) physical differences between peoples, (b) geographical and climatic factors, (c) early training in music, (d) cultural, intellectual, specialization, and execution factors.

7. The writer believes that Beethoven became deaf because (a) of a hearing defect that developed when he was very young, (b) he listened to loud music continuously for too many years, (c) the vibrations from his symphonies were of a type which affected the tympanum, (d) he had to be shut in, in order to gain an intensified hearing of the musical inspiration within him.

8. Really great compositions are (a) becoming greater in number, (b) less in number, (c) remaining about the same, (d) have promise of increasing greatly in the near future.

9. The writer states that international animosities of the past few years have (a) stimulated greater creative efforts on the part of a few individuals, (b) heightened musical progress within certain nations, (c) retarded the

progress of music in the world, (d) retarded the progress of music specifically in the United States.

10. The writer believes that (a) music and love are like twins, (b) music and art are twins, (c) love and art are twins, (d) appreciation of music and appreciation of art are synonymous.

Answers: 1)——, 2)——, 3)——, 4)——, 5)——, 6)——, 7)——, 8)——, 9)——, 10)——.

See Answer Key on page 278. Allow a score of 10 for each correct answer.

Rate: W.P.M. ——— Comprehension Score: ———

Vocabulary Study

Here is a list of words from the selections you have just read. Familiarize yourself with their meanings by looking them up in a dictionary if necessary. Then, write one of the words in the blank space in each of the following sentences to complete its meaning.

permeates	incendiary	accentuated
enhances	dynamic	animosities
consonance	therapeutic	ethereal
	regeneration	

1. Many people think that salt ——————— the flavor of a melon.

2. The governor was forceful and energetic. He was said to be a ——————— person.

3. The ——————— cloud wafted lightly up into the heavens.

4. Officers were quite sure that the fire had been set by an ———————.

5. The mayor ——————— the need for giving food to the flood victims.

6. When onions are cooking the odor ——————— the entire house.

7. Many people harbor ——————— against people who have harmed them.

8. Certain herbs have ———— values in treating sickness.

9. Vegetation undergoes ———— every spring.

10. As the two violinists played, their renditions were in perfect ————.

See Answer Key, page 278. Allow 10 for each correct answer.

Vocabulary Score: ————

Follow-Up Suggestions

Applying the main-idea technique in your daily reading. You have been given some basic instruction and practice in the art of reading paragraphs. You have been launched on the technique of finding the main idea accurately and quickly. The extent to which you perfect this skill depends on you. You may sharpen this tool to a very fine point by continuing to use it every time you have occasion to read. Special practice periods are of course highly desirable as well.

From this time on, in all your reading, both informal and special practice, do three things:

a) force your speed;
b) take advantage of the signpost words;
c) apply paragraph-reading techniques.

Continue to keep a record of your speed and comprehension in each of your practice periods. You should begin to note substantial gains.

Chapter 7

Mining for Details

Can You Strike Pay Dirt?

Now you have learned the technique of gathering "bright and shining nuggets" which are more or less apparent on the surface. There will be many times when this technique of gathering the larger basic ideas will serve your purpose. There will be other times, however, when you will be obliged laboriously to "sift the sands for the gold dust," or mine for details.

As Bacon has so aptly said, "Some books are to be tasted, others to be swallowed, and some few to be chewed and digested." The concern of this chapter is with reading materials that have to be "chewed and digested." This is the kind in which you must carefully study every sentence, such as in the printed instructions which accompany income-tax forms. No speed reading for main ideas in this situation!

Most of us find it necessary to do reading of this type every day. Businessmen, especially, have to do a great deal of careful factual reading as a part of their daily routine. There are financial reports which grow out of the company's activities or which have a close bearing on them. There are letters, memos, ads which tell about new processes or machines. There are directions for conducting the business which must be followed exactly. There are explanations of policies and plans in which every word is important. And so it is that the businessman *must* give attention to details.

139

The same is true of those who are in professional work. The attorney and the physician must do exact and detailed reading; engineers have to read much technical material; the chemist, the physicist, and the biologist must read material in which every word is important. This is an age of technology and scientific advancement in every field. Each business or profession has its own flood of technical articles published weekly or monthly. Thousands of people find it necessary and desirable to read these periodicals in order to keep abreast of developments in their respective fields.

There is no question about the need for detailed reading, but there is a question in the minds of many people, it seems, as to the possibility of increasing speed and understanding in this kind of reading.

One man says, "I'm an engineer. My reading is *all* technical. I have to grasp every detail. Would it be possible for me to learn to read faster?"

Another says, "I'm a lawyer. Believe me, every word is important in a legal paper. Could I learn to do this kind of reading more rapidly?"

"My work is editing. I have to do meticulous reading of manuscripts all day long. I guess there is no chance for me to speed up this kind of reading, is there?"

"I work for stockbrokers. Three fourths of my time is devoted to research in which I have to read and digest financial reports. Would the modern techniques help me to cover this material more rapidly?"

The answer "Yes" was given to every one of these questions. Each of these persons took a course under the writer's supervision, and each one markedly improved his ability to do the particular kind of reading he had to do. Furthermore, each one reported at the end of the course that he could accomplish much more work in a day with greater ease and less fatigue.

One *can* improve the ability to do detailed, factual reading. Yes, you *can* strike "pay dirt" while mining for details, if you practice the suggestions given in this chapter.

Techniques for Grasping Details

Using old skills. The ability to do detailed reading rapidly and well is a very complex act requiring the combination and application of many different reading skills. That is why instruction in and practice on this type of reading was delayed in this book until you had already mastered several of the elementary skills.

In effective reading for details you need to know how to make use of preview so that you can decide whether the material is of sufficient interest to be read for details. You need to know how to pick out the main idea in paragraphs so that you will be in a position to see details as related to this idea. And of course you need the skill which you have already acquired in learning to read fast, in order to increase your tempo in reading for details.

Learning new skills. You need also to learn two very important new skills: first, learning to discriminate between main ideas and details; second, learning to organize details around the main ideas to which they are related. After considerable practice in analyzing paragraphs and organizing details, you will reach a point at which you will read factual material in groups of meanings rather than in isolated scraps.

As you read, think of the main idea as a magnet drawing the particles toward it—the "particles" being the smaller, detailed ideas. Then think of this main idea together with its cluster of sub-ideas as a unit. These are the basic processes which will enable you to grasp a series of minor details quickly and accurately.

The necessary written work may seem laborious and time-consuming, for you must thoughtfully read all the explanations and directions and write all the answers requested. As you practice, however, you will gradually abandon written work and detailed analyses and will mentally apply the new techniques as you read. Then you will be able to grasp details more speedily, as well as with greater effectiveness. So don't be discouraged with the length of time the ensuing exercises take. Once the foundation is thoroughly laid, a new house goes up rapidly. So it is with skill development in learning to read factual material. When you become adept at grasping clusters of details in their right relationships you will have become a skillful reader.

Diagraming major details. There are major details and minor details in most paragraphs. At first we shall concern ourselves only with major details. The simple paragraph below will be used in illustrating the procedures for noting the main idea together with its major details. Read this paragraph quickly and see if you can "spot" the main idea.

In a growing number of hotels and skyscrapers across the nation, façades of steel have replaced the foot-thick brick and mortar walls once used. Tests show that a steel wall four inches thick has better insulating qualities than a 12-inch thickness of masonry. In addition, steel-curtain wall panels save both time and labor. And the floor space conserved by use of the thin wall as against the thick wall in a big office building can mean a couple of hundred dollars a year in rentals.[1]

No doubt you discovered at once that the main idea is *A growing number of hotels and skyscrapers use steel instead of brick or mortar walls.*

Now find three details that are *related* to this main idea and sum them up in as few words as possible.

Your summary should be something like this: (1) a steel wall has better insulating qualities, (2) steel wall panels save time and labor, (3) a steel wall conserves floor space.

Now think of this whole mass of ideas as one related cluster of meanings, as in the diagram.

No doubt the three details are very easy for you to grasp. If so, they are easy to grasp because you sorted them from the main idea and related them to this main idea.

Now that you see what this beginning work is like you may be saying, "This will take a terribly long time."

[1] "Steel Framing in Houses," *Science Digest*, February 1955, p. 95.

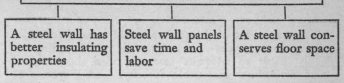

> A growing number of hotels and skyscrapers use steel façades instead of brick-and-mortar walls.

A steel wall has better insulating properties	Steel wall panels save time and labor	A steel wall conserves floor space

Please bear in mind, however, that through repeated use of these techniques you will eventually be able to apply them mentally without diagraming. Then you'll read details with speed!

No time limit is placed on the reading of the following practice paragraphs. In working with them you will be developing your skill to analyze paragraphs and to perceive relationships of their component parts. You should, however, work as fast as you can. Don't dawdle. Work at an energetic pace.

PARAGRAPH 1

Tropical fish are becoming increasingly popular. Varied in color, they are decorative for homes, offices, and even store windows. The raising of such fish is recommended as a relaxing hobby for people in jobs involving much tension. Many hobbyists have made money by breeding tropical fish varieties for which there is a special demand.[2]

Complete the diagram:

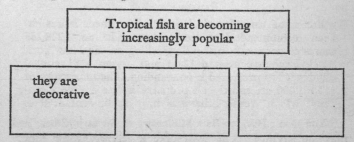

> Tropical fish are becoming increasingly popular

they are decorative		

[2] Max F. Baer, "Basement Farming Can Pay," *Journal of Living*, December 1953, p. 17.

Check your work with the Answer Key on page 279. The wording doesn't have to be exactly the same as that in the Answer Key, so long as the ideas are comparable.

PARAGRAPH 2

There are a lot of things that should come before investing in securities—particularly if you're raising a family. First, an adequate insurance plan should give your dependents reasonable security. And if you are paying for a home, you will probably want to direct all your surplus dollars into paying off the real estate mortgage. Finally, you'll want to be sure of enough money for the children's education, and have a reserve fund of cash for emergencies like unexpected medical bills.[8]

Complete the diagram:

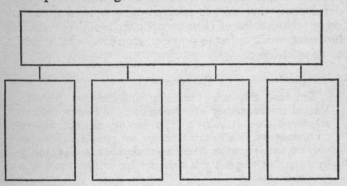

Check your work with the Answer Key on page 279.

PARAGRAPH 3

For some time Jones' chain of department stores has been recommended to stock buyers. It has 1,228,183 shares of common outstanding, selling on the New York Stock Exchange around 12-13 and paying a $1 annual dividend. No preferred is outstanding. The mortgages of $10,183,000 are mostly on property in use by the Company, which would otherwise have to be rented. It is

[8] "You Don't Have to Be a Millionaire to Invest in Stocks and Bonds," *Putting Your Money to Work*, Merrill Lynch, Pierce, Fenner and Beane, New York, 1953.

reasonably immune to bombing, and should benefit from the "tidal wave" of young people who will need clothing during the next few years.

Complete the diagram:

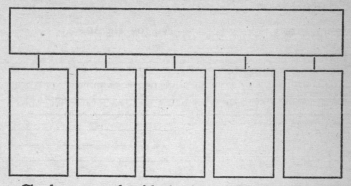

Check your work with the Answer Key on page 279.

Listing major details. Now you may use a different format for stating the main idea and grouping the major details. Follow the plan suggested by the headings and lines beneath each following paragraph. Remember you are to list only *major* details. For the moment don't bother with all the tiny sub-details under the major details.

PARAGRAPH 4

Among recent developments in the shoe industry is a specially processed leather sole said to possess the wearing qualities of composition soles. This outsole is unique in that it has been developed by a shoe manufacturer rather than a tanner. *It contains all the desirable features of an orthodox leather sole, including a high-porosity value.* In addition, it contains many of the comfortable, "cushiony" characteristics of synthetic or composition-type soles. Ordinary chrome-tanned leather is processed in a special manner in order to produce this new sole substance. The leather is leavened or plumped to loosen and spread its fibers so as to create numerous air cells in the material. It is claimed that the leather is strengthened, rather than weakened, by this process in which no grease or oil is used. Laboratory and field tests indicate that the new sole actually wears better than orthodox leather soles and is extremely light—*about half the weight of an ordinary sole.*[4]

MAIN IDEA   MAJOR DETAILS

_____   _____

_____   _____

                           _____

                           _____

                           _____

                           _____

                           _____

                           _____

Check your work with the Answer Key on page 280.

PARAGRAPH 5

The history of production is easily sketched. Early primitive man doubtless "manufactured" little, himself, but merely appropriated what nature provided—fish, game, and wild fruits. Slowly, through the centuries, however, he learned to work over the products of nature more and more, to make fishhooks from bones, to make spears, bows and arrows from trees, mallets from stones, clothing from hides. Such production was carried on by the labor of man alone, and on a very small scale. Later, animals were tamed and used in certain operations, especially in carrying burdens and in cultivating the soil, and this increase in the power of man's disposal caused a great expansion of production. Much later still, various natural forces were harnessed to production—wind, water, power, steam, and in very recent years the explosive power of gases, as in the automobile and tractor. At the present time it is estimated that the United States has available more than a billion horsepower of energy.[5]

[4] "News of the New," *Babson's Reports*, December 1, 1954, p. 256.
[5] John Ise, "The Laws of Production," *Economics, Harper*, 1946, p. 16.

MAIN IDEA   MAJOR DETAILS

_____   _____
_____   _____
                                   _____
                                   _____
                                   _____
                                   _____

Check your work with the Answer Key on page 280.

PARAGRAPH 6

The essence of Cambridge is in its surroundings. It is in the crocuses beside the walks promising an end to the long winter, and then in the daffodils declaring it has ended. It is in the roses and lupines and the tumbled gravestones of St. Botolph's little churchyard. It is in the sound of the bells of Great St. Mary's Church, though academicians in rooms hard by curse bells and bell ringers vehemently. It is in the swifts flying into lovely Nevile's Court about May tenth to set about their expected building. It is on the meadows up the river to Grantchester, where all good lovers go for strolls.[6]

Complete the blanks below to show an outline of the paragraph.

MAIN IDEA   MAJOR DETAILS

_____   A. _____
_____   B. _____
_____   C. _____
                                   D. _____
                                   E. _____

Check your work with the Answer Key on page 280.

Identifying minor details. In some of your reading the grasping of major details which expand upon main ideas will serve your purpose. There may be other times, however, in which you will wish to concern yourself with the minor details which usually cluster about a

[6] J. Frank Dobie, "Cambridge," *Holiday*, June 1950, p. 155. (Slightly revised.)

major detail in much the same way as major details cluster about the main idea. If the content of what you are reading is so important to you that you want to get *all* details in a page of text, then try to grasp clusters of major details together with their minor details, keeping in mind the relationship of these clusters to the main idea.

PARAGRAPH 7

In the paragraph below there are: (1) a main idea, (2) one major detail, and (3) several minor details related to the major detail. Read the paragraph and see if you can detect these three types of ideas.

Increased production, reduced scrap, better quality control, easier scheduling, happier workers, and lower costs are benefits which appeal to management in any industry. This is doubly so in high-volume, close-margin candy making. Few industries are so dependent upon the rigid control of temperature and humidity as to avoid losses in production and maintain product quality. Often the difference between profit and loss may be a few temperature degrees or a slight change in the relative humidity. Thus, candy makers were among the first to realize the advantages to be derived from air conditioning. As a result many plants have complete integrated systems, serving all their manufacturing, packaging, and storage areas.[7]

The relationships between ideas in the paragraph above may be represented diagrammatically as shown on page 149.

In this example it is evident that there are four minor details all closely related to the one major detail.

PARAGRAPH 8

In the paragraph below the diagram on page 149 there is a main idea as usual. Then there are three major details, each of which has its own related minor ideas. See if you can find these clusters of major and minor ideas, then complete the diagram on page 150.

[7] Charles W. Vaughan, "How Welch's Profits from Humidity Control," *The Manufacturing Confectioner*, September 1954, p. 29.

Increased production, reduced scrap, better quality control, easier scheduling, happy workers, lower costs are benefits in industry.

Doubly so in candy making

Few industries are so dependent upon control of temperature and humidity.	Often difference between profit and loss may be due to slight change in temperature or humidity.	Thus candy makers were first to recognize advantages of air conditioning.	As a result many plants have air conditioning in all departments.

In the past few months a number of commercial meat tenderizers have hit the market, aimed particularly at cost-conscious Mrs. Housewife. Largely responsible for making this little dream come true is Lloyd A. Hall of the Griffith Laboratories, Chicago, who has come up with a new tenderizer containing papain. Papain is an enzyme, or organic substance, obtained from papaya, the edible fruit of a tropical American tree. Manufacturers of the domestic product are compounding Griffith's basic composition with flavoring materials, and obtaining a variety of distinctive individual products.[8]

PARAGRAPH 9

There is a boom in pharmaceuticals in Spain, and the newer drugs which have been found effective in the United States, Britain, France, and the other more advanced Western countries enjoy active sales. Sulfa drugs, antibiotics, and many of the "mycins" are produced under license by Spanish concerns. An entire building in Madrid is devoted to Pfizer products. The directors report that their business is rapidly expanding with the

[8] "Tough Meat Made Tender," *Science Digest*, March 1952, p. 53. (Condensed from *Industrial and Engineering Chemistry*, December 1951.)

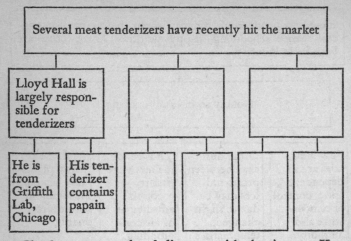

Check your completed diagram with the Answer Key on page 381.

technical guidance of an American chemical engineer loaned by Pfizer to supervise plant construction and production controls, and to train the personnel in the high standards required by the food and drug laws in the United States.[9]

Complete the diagram on page 151.

PARAGRAPH 10

You should now be ready to progress from a diagram to an outline. In the somewhat more difficult paragraph below, find the main idea. Find two other ideas of next relative importance which are used in expanding upon the main idea. Each of these two sub-ideas has several detailed facts which cluster under it. Group these details in relationship to the larger sub-idea to which it is related, and also in relationship to the total topic.

If you read for the purpose of discerning the above pattern, you should have no difficulty in filling in the outline, although you may have to refer back to the paragraph for some of the details.

[9] "Spain," *The Atlantic Monthly*, April 1955, p. 21.

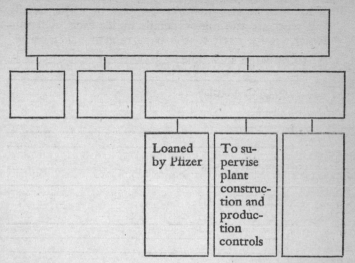

Check your work with the Answer Key on page 281.

Public industries are much less important in the United States than in some other countries. In many countries the government runs industries. In several European countries, and in Australia, New Zealand, and Canada, the government, national or state, operates some or all of the railroads; in France and several other countries the government conducts the tobacco industry as a state monopoly; and various cities throughout the world operate some or all of the public utilities. Our federal government has no important industries except the post office, certain types of banks, and a few giant hydro-electric plants, including Tennessee Valley Authority and the Boulder and Grand Coulee Dams. None of these was established for the purpose of securing revenues; in fact, most of them were unattractive to private enterprise—a common reason for government operations.[10]

Write answers in as few words as possible.

I What is the main idea? _____

_____

_____

[10] John Ise, *Economics*, Harper, 1946, p. 482.

II What are the two major sub-topics or major details, and what are the minor details under each such sub-topic? (Refer back to the paragraph if necessary.)

A. (First large sub-topic) _____

_____

   (Related details)

   a. _____
   b. _____
   c. _____

B. (Second large sub-topic) _____

_____

   (Related details)

   a. _____
   b. _____
   c. _____
   d. _____

Check your answers with the Answer Key on page 281.

PARAGRAPH 11

In working with this paragraph you will be more or less on your own, with only a few directions. Fill in the outline. Check your completed outline with the key on page 282. Correct your outline if necessary.

Gradually men have learned by experimenting that air is a real substance, that it has weight, that it exerts pressure, and that it is compressible. They have learned that it expands when heated and contracts when cooled. They have also learned that air has inertia. It offers resistance to being moved. This knowledge of the air has made possible the invention of instruments to measure air pressure and pumps to compress it. It has made possible the invention of pneumatic tires, air engines, blast furnaces, vacuum tanks, balloons, dirigibles, airplanes, and a great many other appliances. While we know a great deal about the atmosphere, many possibilities remain, and there is much still to be learned about air.[11]

[11] Ira C. Davis and Richard W. Sharpe, *Science*, Holt, 1943, p. 45.

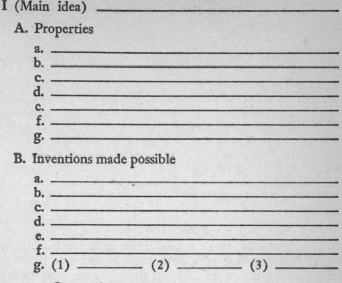

I (Main idea) _____

  A. Properties

    a. _____

    b. _____

    c. _____

    d. _____

    e. _____

    f. _____

    g. _____

  B. Inventions made possible

    a. _____

    b. _____

    c. _____

    d. _____

    e. _____

    f. _____

    g. (1) _____ (2) _____ (3) _____

        Group three together

PARAGRAPH 12

Now outline a paragraph by yourself with no help at all.

1. Read and decide upon relationships of ideas.
2. Make your own outline.
3. Correct it by referring to the Answer Key on page 282.

A knowledge of the forces and resources of nature around you enables you to appreciate and understand your environment. It is science that has changed waste places into gardens; it has conquered many germ diseases; it enables man to control sources of power in nature; it enables him to travel under water and through air; it enables him to illuminate cities by the power of a distant waterfall; it has improved the quality of fruits, root crops, cattle, horses and sheep.[12]

[12] *Ibid.*, p. 15.

Space For Your Outline

PARAGRAPH 13

You probably won't need further practice in actually writing the outline of a paragraph in order to perceive the relationships of its different parts. As an intermediary step between writing outlines and mentally grasping the "stripped-down structure" as you go along, write the numbers and figures which indicate different parts of an outline right into the text of the paragraph, thus:

I. The traditional procedure, so far as the investigation of the American financial institutions is concerned, has been to sit down and wait patiently until the symptoms have moved in orderly sequence from disturbing to alarming, to critical to fatal. (A) Then there would be an investigation. And (B) the principal object of the inquest, all too frequently, would be to find not the facts but a culprit.

Can you grasp all detailed facts in this paragraph as a whole by thinking in terms of relationships of ideas as expressed by the outline symbols?

PARAGRAPH 14

Try writing your own outline symbols into the text of the following paragraph. Use Roman numeral I for the main idea, capital letters such as A and B for important subordinate ideas, and Arabic numerals, such as 1, 2, 3, for details under subordinate ideas.

Characteristics which make automobiles the generally comfortable, smooth-running vehicles they are—as distinct from simple conveyances providing places to sit and engines to move them around—are built into every American passenger car today in varying degrees. They are the end-products of many things: a great amount of research, expert experience, technological know-how, management prejudices, consumer studies, dumb luck, and shrewd guesswork. As a result, the various brands of cars are notably unlike each other in their handling, economy, ease of repair, power and speed, riding qualities, noise level, driver vision, and safety.[13]

Check your work with the Answer Key on page 283.

PARAGRAPH 15

Another good technique to use when working directly with the text of detailed factual material is that of underlining. A single underline is used to denote the main idea; two underlines to denote the major details, and three underlines to denote the minor details.

Gardeners who have been waging losing fights against birds may find an electric snake just the thing to scare away the feathered seed-eaters. The imitation snake has a 12-foot cross-striped bamboo pole for a body and a heart-shaped aluminum head painted white with glaring black eyes. Balanced on the top of an upright, it rotates continuously driven by an electric motor.[14]

The main idea is that gardeners may find an electric snake just the thing to scare away feathered seed-eaters. The first major detail tells us that it is an imitation snake, and two minor details tell us how the imitation is accomplished: (1) it has a 12-foot, cross-striped bam-

[13] Consumer's Reports, May 1953, p. 182.
[14] "Inventions, Patents, Processes," Science Digest, March 1952, p. 95.

boo pole for a body, and (2) a heart-shaped aluminum head. The second major detail is that it rotates continuously, and three minor details tell more about this rotation: (1) it is balanced, (2) on top of an upright, and (3) it is driven by an electric motor.

PARAGRAPH 16

Try underlining the paragraph below in the same way.

In the Hudson, opposite West Point, is a famous little island that recalls heroic days of the Revolutionary War. From one end of the island a great chain was stretched across the river to the cliffs below West Point, to keep back the British fleet. The links of the chain were forged in a blacksmith shop at New Windsor, New York, and were carried down the river on a log boom. A part of the chain is today on view at Washington's Headquarters, Newburgh, New York. Another section of the chain is to be seen at West Point.[15]

Check your work with the Answer Key on page 283.

PARAGRAPH 17

Now find out how well you can read and grasp details without the aid of "crutches" such as diagraming or outlining; just concentrate on a specific cluster of ideas in terms of a specific purpose.

Make a quick preview of the material in order to locate the cluster or clusters of details in which you have a special interest. It is unwise to attempt to grasp every little detail at once. Decide instead which group of details is of special interest to you, and then read carefully for a vivid impression of this particular cluster.

With your knowledge of paragraph structure and your practice in skimming, you should now be able to make this preview in from five to ten seconds.

After previewing, read the paragraph carefully, concentrating on special clusters of details.

The geckos lay their eggs in all manner of places, and most species seem to deposit two. When first laid they

[15] Charles H. Dorr, "Constitution Island," *The Mentor*, September 1924, p. 53.

are soft-shelled and dent readily, hardening only after several hours of exposure. Within the eggs there are the usual albumin and yolk. The embryonic lizard takes on a recognizable form in about two weeks' time. The head is extremely large, and the eyes are well developed and prominent. The eggs hatch in about thirty days, although weather is a controlling factor. Most egg-laying reptiles in the United States carefully place their eggs where they will get just the right amount of moisture and heat. The geckos of Hawaii, however, seem to drop theirs wherever they will not be readily seen. Auger holes in two by four ceiling rafters are usually jammed full. In such a position, rainfall and dew cannot reach them. Others are often found at the base of long-leaved plants. In this site the leaves act as funnels and the eggs are constantly drenched with water. But still they hatch! One of the favorite situations is within the iron framework of the common recessed lock. Climbing in the keyhole the females will first start filling the far corners, and each succeeding female is forced to lay closer to the opening until the chamber is eventually crammed to overflowing.[16]

Name three special places in which geckos lay eggs:

1. _____

2. _____

3. _____

Check your answers by referring to the paragraph.

PARAGRAPH 18

Preview the paragraph below, allowing yourself a maximum of five seconds.

Then read for the purpose of grasping details in regard to each of two processes: (1) mediation, and (2) arbitration.

Strikes and labor wars are expensive to workers, employers, and the general public; and the government has tried in various ways to help preserve industrial peace— through mediation, arbitration, and, in a few cases,

[16] Lewis Wayne Walker, "Mo'o, Spirit of Hawaii," *Nature Magazine*, November 1945, p. 469.

through prohibition of strikes. In the process of *mediation*, an impartial third party, known as the mediator or impartial chairman, is called in; he confers with the employer and labor representatives in a friendly, informal way, and tries tactfully to get them together. If he is unable to do this, he is not expected to render any decision in the dispute. In the process of *arbitration*, an arbitrator or board of arbitrators is chosen, and after hearing the two sides it renders a decision which the disputants have agreed to accept; if either party is not satisfied with the decision, the dispute may come up for further action later. Both mediation and arbitration have achieved some success in promoting industrial peace.[17]

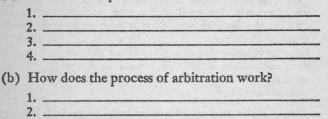

(a) How does the process of mediation work?

1. _____
2. _____
3. _____
4. _____

(b) How does the process of arbitration work?

1. _____
2. _____
3. _____

Correct your answers by referring to the paragraph.

PARAGRAPH 19

Now read for the purpose of concentrating on three different groups of details.

First: preview the paragraph for five seconds, and locate the main idea.

Second: Read carefully to grasp all details: (1) in the group that tells things that can be done with plastics, (2) in the group that tells what plastics are formed by nature, and, (3) in the group that tells what substances have been combined by different people to produce synthetic plastics.

Don't bother about dates, involved chemical terms, or other details. Just read for the details that you want to grasp for these three purposes.

[17] John Ise, *Economics*, Harper, 1946, p. 417.

Plastics are substances that can be molded, bent, or carved into various forms. Rubber and resins are plastics formed in nature, but synthetic plastics are of recent development. Carbolic acid entered the picture in 1872 when Professor Bayer discovered that carbolic acid and formaldehyde could be united to form a strong, hard, resinous material. This was merely a curiosity until 1909, when Dr. Leo H. Backeland developed a commercial process for producing this resin and fashioning it into various forms. His product is called Bakelite, after its inventor, or, chemically, "polymerized oxybenzyl-methylene glycol anhydride." Bakelite and closely-related plastics are products of the union of phenols and aldehydes.[18]

Checking Comprehension

Write one word in answer to each question or part of a question.

1. What is the main topic of this paragraph?
   _____

2. Mention three of the things which can be done with the substance discussed.
   (a) _____
   (b) _____
   (c) _____

3. What plastics have been formed by nature?
   (a) _____
   (b) _____

4. What substances have been combined by the different people mentioned below to produce synthetic plastics?
   (a) Professor Bayer
      1.
      2.
   (b) Dr. Backeland
      1.
      2.

Check your answers with the Answer Key on page 283. Allow a score of 10 for each correct response, re-

[18] Emmett James Cable, Robert Ward Getchell, and William Henry Kadesch, *The Physical Sciences*, Prentice-Hall, 1946, p. 429.

gardless of whether it is designated with a capital letter, lower-case letter, or arabic numeral.

Speeded reading of details. Building groundwork techniques is the first consideration in improving one's ability to grasp details readily, but once you have perfected the basic techniques, it is safe to begin practice designed to increase your speed.

The excellent reader has not just one speed but many. He has an extremely rapid speed which he uses when he skims material for a definite purpose; he has a lesser but still *very* fast speed for reading narrative or nontechnical material; and he has a slower speed when reading factual material in which he wishes to grasp details. The skillful reader "shifts his gears" when reading for different purposes. Of his several rates of speed, all can be improved.

Your speed in reading factual material for details will never equal your speed in reading easy narrative material for general ideas. You can, however, increase your speed greatly even in reading content that is heavy with detailed facts. Once you acquire the basic skills of seeing relationships and fixing details in your mind, then you can practice the same speed-reading techniques with factual material as suggested in Chapter Three for the easier material.

Selection 1

Try a timed exercise in reading for details in a series of paragraphs.

Preview first; find the main ideas; then read to grasp groups of details. Do not include the time it takes for your preview in the time recorded.

BEGINNING TIME:_____
HR._____ MIN._____

THE ARTS IN AMERICA[19]

Obviously, there is a difference between the cultural background of the New Englanders of the late seven-

[19] Frederick P. Keppel, and R. L. Duffus, *The Arts in American Life*, McGraw-Hill, 1933, pp. 205-207.

teenth and early eighteenth centuries, who wove, embroidered, made furniture, carved wood, and built houses which are still admired; and that of the nineteenth-century settlers in the Mississippi Valley and beyond, whose handicraft period was abbreviated by the swift spread of manufactured goods, with a resulting scantiness of creative tradition. Or if a creative tradition existed it was of a kind which could not survive the early primitive conditions. The modes of life changed too rapidly. And the Puritan tradition, the country over, though its influence has probably been exaggerated, operated for a long time to prevent any conscious and determined reaching out for aesthetic expression.

That the American people were, on the whole, unaesthetic rather than anti-aesthetic may be conjectured. When artistic stirrings began in the country they led inevitably, in the absence of national patterns, to importations from abroad; in most of our arts we have not yet ceased to import from abroad. The first really American paintings, for example, were American in subject matter rather than in method. First London, then Paris and Rome educated our artists. The growth away from this tutelage has naturally been slow. There is no reason to believe that it has been slower than might have been expected of any people under like circumstances. No permanent factors can be demonstrated in American life which deny us artistic parity with other nations. We are, and have been, going through a process of normal evolution.

At certain points this evolution has been more rapid than at others. This statement may certainly be made of architecture, though with special reference to the skyscraper; our homes, schools, churches, and public buildings are less individualistic; and a lay visitor to a modern architectural exhibition finds it hard to determine without looking at the signatures which combination of cement, steel, and glass is American and which foreign. In painting we are by no means independent of Parisian influences. Our development has, however, gone far enough to indicate that a genuinely American expression is possible. In music we have contributed some new motifs, though not yet an internationally recognized composer of the first rank. In drama we have achieved a degree of individuality and independence. In motion pictures we have set world standards, though they cannot yet be said to be high standards. In motion-picture photography, as an art by itself, we have probably gone further than any other country except Germany. Indeed, it may be said that in the cinema we have displayed both our best and our worst.

In commercial and industrial design it cannot be denied that we have had an awakening, and that whatever may be the merits of our tastes as displayed in those fields we are at least aware of taste as a factor in them. Indeed, we may set this awareness down as the most significant feature of the present situation. Art education, direct and indirect; the appeal of advertising; higher incomes and shorter working days, as they had developed down to 1930; the need for leisure-time activities—all these have led to a turning toward the aesthetic satisfactions. We cannot escape the impact of such instrumentalities as the radio and advertising—we have to look and to listen, and we cannot avoid in the long run trying to improve the quality of these experiences.

Began Finished No. words: 466

———— × 60 = ———— W.P.M.

———— ———— No. seconds:

1. Name three (any three) artistic expressions of the early New Englanders which disappeared with the spread of manufactured goods:
   (a)
   (b)
   (c)

2. What three cities educated our early American artists?
   (a)
   (b)
   (c)

3. What progress have we made in regard to:
   (a) Architecture ————————————————————

   ————————————————————————————————

(b) Painting _____

(c) Music _____

(d) Drama _____

(e) Motion pictures _____

4. What influences have led toward aesthetic satisfactions in America?
   (a)
   (b)
   (c)
   (d)
   (e)

5. Does the present development in painting indicate that
   (a) we shall develop an original art? (Underline *Yes* or *No*)
   (b) we shall develop an imitative art? (Underline *Yes* or *No*)

6. In what two types of design have we definitely had an awakening?
   (a)
   (b)

Check your answers with the Answer Key on page 284. Allow a score of 5 for each detail which is correct. Multiply the total number of correct answers by 20.

Rate: W.P.M._____ Comprehension Score:_____

Diagnosing your needs. If you read the last selection unaided by pencil work, your score on the comprehension check will afford some indication of your need for further practice. In this chapter you are not expected to do so well as you will do in the following chapter. For the moment, the following relatively low scores are set up for your reference in checking your comprehension status in reading for details.

	TIME	COMPREHENSION SCORE
Excellent	4 to 5 min.	75-100
Good	5 to 6 "	60-80
Poor	6 to 7 "	50-70
Very poor	7 to 8 "	40-60

If your scores fell within the "Excellent" group, it isn't necessary for you to make further use of supplementary aids. You are ready to go ahead "on your own," reading and mentally grasping details in paragraphs as you follow the lines of print in entire articles.

If your scores fell within the "Good" group, you would profit by working more carefully with paragraphs, placing outline numbers in the text, or underlining parts to show relationships.

If your score was within the limits of the "Poor" or "Very poor" groups, it would be well for you to continue practice in making written outlines or diagrams. When you have gained additional facility in reading for details, then proceed to work through the remaining exercises in this chapter.

Selection 2

Read to find, first, the main idea in each paragraph, and, second, the cluster of details that expand that main idea. In the test main ideas or main topics will be stated and you will be asked to identify one of the details related to the main idea.

BEGINNING TIME:_____
HR._____ MIN._____

MR. SEWARD'S BARGAIN[20]

Always the Americans have been fond of looking ahead to a grandiose future. The history of their development as a people has incessantly fed their faith in progress; and progress they identified with their own continued growth. The unconditional surrender of the South in 1865 dispelled the threat of disunity, and the

[20] Oscar Handlin, *The Atlantic Monthly*, April 1955, pp. 63-68.

aspirations of the veterans lately returned from war looked ahead to the prospect of a constantly-expanding destiny. They differed only as to the form and direction they supposed that expansion would take.

Few, however, attached their hopes to the continent's northernmost extremity. Those little-known, desolate spaces, lost beneath the snow of almost-continuous winter, seemed doomed to perpetual emptiness. Little had come of the Russian attempts to plant settlements there. And, indeed, no sober statesman, reckoning the balance of possibilities, could foresee the future wealth of Alaska—the outpouring of gold and oil, of furs and fish, of gas, timber, pulp, and tin, with which it was ultimately to enrich the nation.

No more could such a man have guessed at the immense strategic significance of this corner of the North Pacific. True enough, the visionary Tocqueville had once predicted that the United States would someday face the Russian Empire in opposition. But to the Americans who noted it, that prophetic observation referred only to the rivalry between their system of government and the Czarist despotism. No one, of course, conceived that a shift of interests in the Pacific and a new geography of flight would give this region crucial value at a moment when the United States was locked in massive competition with Russia, with the outcome certain to determine the fate of the whole world. No one, therefore, was then concerned about what the disposition of power might be were Russia established in North America, only four hundred miles away from the borders of the United States. . . .

In the 1580's Yermak Timofeiev, a Cossack fleeing the consequences of his brigandage, pushed across the Ural Mountains and defeated the Tartars. Some fifty years later, the Russians had edged across the half-empty plains of Siberia to the Pacific at Okhotsk. Into the nomadic tribes, white traders and hunters and an occasional retinue of tax collectors insinuated themselves. In the 1720's Peter the Great occasionally turned his attention to the unexploited empire in the East, and it was he who formulated the plans to extend it to America.

At this time no one yet knew whether or not America was joined to Asia. Vitus Bering, a Dane in the service of

Peter's new navy, was directed to find out. . . . His mission was to cover the six thousand miles from St. Petersburg to farthest Siberia, taking with him the necessary supplies to build his ships at the ocean's edge and then to map the uncharted seas beyond.

He left the Russian capital on his first journey in February, 1725; and three and a half years later, having built his own ships at the mouth of the Kamchatka River, he traced the northern outlines of the eastern Asiatic coast. At latitude 67° north, he satisfied himself that America and Asia were not connected, and turned back out of fear of the threatening ice floes. Returning to St. Petersburg, he persuaded the government to sponsor a second exploration. He set off again in February, 1734, at the head of a far more elaborate expedition. More than seven years of strenuous preparation and struggle with recalcitrant Czarist officials followed before his ships at last set sail from Avacha Bay in Siberia in June, 1741. This time his course was directly eastward and, before his death on an unknown island, he had chartered the Aleutians and the Gulf of Alaska and made the whole area Russian. . . .

For more than a century the Czars directed their energies in a drive toward the Balkans and the Black Sea. Now their advances toward Constantinople were a threat to the British. Were they to secure access to the Mediterranean, England's supremacy in this part of the world would be challenged. For almost forty years after Waterloo a series of parries and thrusts had occupied the statesmen of the two nations; and in 1854 the Crimean War had brought the issue into the open.

Russia's defeat in this war led to a time of reckoning. The massive incompetence of the Czarist administration called for a succession of internal reforms, and military failure called for a reassessment of the strategic situation. On the first score the government was attracted by the liberal economic policies that had succeeded so remarkably in Britain. To some Russians in the court such monopolistic companies as the Russian-American were relics of the past to be eliminated as quickly as possible, and strategically Alaska was in an exposed position, difficult to defend. During the war English sea power had dominated the Pacific. In any future conflict the British Navy could hardly be prevented from taking Alaska at will. Thus, in the 1850s, the question was increasingly debated in St. Petersburg whether the American territory was worth keeping at all. . . .

The events of the next five years made the Americans desirable purchasers from the Russian point of view. The Czar had no love for the western republic, nor any desire to strengthen or extend it. But Anglo-American tensions during the Civil War and the unsettled problems that continued to trouble the relations of Washington with London convinced him that the transfer of Alaska to the United States would weaken England or at least create an additional source of dissension. In 1865 the Russian government had signified its willingness to sell Alaska to the United States.

It was by no means certain, however, that the United States was willing to buy. Earlier suggestions looking toward the acquisition of this northernmost region of the continent had evoked no enthusiasm in Washington. Many Americans saw no necessity for further expansion while great areas of the country were still unsettled; and those who did thought that the proper direction of our growth was southeastward toward Cuba and the Caribbean. To almost everyone, Alaska seemed likely to be a useless encumbrance.

Only one statesman, nursing stale dreams as his career drew to a close, was convinced that Alaska was destined to be American.

William H. Seward also had been marked for assassination when Booth's bullet put an end to Lincoln's life; for the mad conspiracy had been directed at the Secretary of State as well as at the President. But Seward, wounded, had lived, while Lincoln died.

At the war's end, Seward was almost sixty-five and knew his active political career had not much further to go. He had largely put aside his personal ambitions. The presidency, for which he felt he was far better qualified than Lincoln, was now beyond his grasp; new and younger politicians were crowding onto the scene and would give but small regard to his earlier achievements. In the conflict between President Johnson and the Radical Republicans, principle led him to side with the Chief Executive—and that had cost him considerable public and party popularity. He would serve out his term as Secretary of State until 1869 and then retire. Yet Seward longed to leave behind him some enduring accomplishment that would fulfill the promise of his youthful career. . . .

Back in the 1840s Seward and most other Americans had believed it was their country's manifest destiny to occupy the whole continent. The advantages of their system of government and social order were so clear, they thought, that people everywhere would rush to adopt them once the opportunity was presented them. Indeed, it was only the obstruction of corrupt and undemocratic governments that prevented them from doing so. When the opportunity presented itself, the United States would brush aside those regimes, and the people would voluntarily adhere to the Union. In due course the whole continent would become the United States of America.

After 1846 the doctrine of "manifest destiny" seemed to Seward to have become entangled in the slaveholders' conspiracy to extend the area of servitude southward. Now that that danger had been averted, it was once more possible to extend the boundaries of the country outward in the interests of human liberty. The power of Spain was deteriorating and would not persist for long in the Western Hemisphere. The French had withdrawn from Mexico. Only the British and the Russians remained.

The English would be a problem, the Secretary of State knew. There was no likelihood that they would voluntarily relinquish their hold on Canada or on Central America, and powerful forces in the United States were interested in maintaining the peace that had prevailed since the establishment of the Oregon boundary in 1846.

Yet Seward was convinced that the day would come when we would move north. In 1861 he had been willing to provoke war with England and Spain in the rash hope that the shock treatment of trouble abroad would draw the seceded states back in to the Union and, perhaps, add Canada to it as well. After 1865, when it was no longer necessary to keep England neutral, the day of reckoning seemed closer than ever.

For Seward, the acquisition of Alaska would eliminate one more alien power from the continent, it would extend American holdings, and it would threaten Canada from the north. Alaska was worth buying because it would open the way to expansion over the whole continent.

When the Russian ambassador returned from a visit to St. Petersburg in the early spring of 1867, the Secretary of State leaped at his suggestion that a sale might be made. The terms were quickly agreed upon, and the next year the ratification of the purchase was pushed through an apathetic Senate and a dubious House. The utmost political pressure and personal cajolery were necessary to get Congress to agree to the consummation of "Seward's folly."

Seward himself retired, and the new territory attracted little public attention thereafter. Even later, when discoveries of gold and iron more than repaid the cost of $7,200,000, Alaska excited only momentary interest among Americans, and then receded from their consciousness, taken for granted.

Yet, had this opportunity been passed up, the Russians might never have been dislodged. By the end of the century the whole situation had changed. The discovery of gold and other mineral resources suddenly gave the territory a new and unexpected value. Furthermore, the Czar was now acquiring the means to defend it. For the construction of the Trans-Siberian Railroad, which was completed at the turn of the century, narrowed the distance between St. Petersburg and the Pacific, and allowed the Russians to establish naval bases at Port Arthur and Vladivostok, which soon became important centers of power in the area. Not many years after 1867, the Russians might have been far from willing to give up Alaska.

In that event, the bases that today flank the northern ocean would not be American, pointing toward Asia, but Russian, pointing toward the United States. If our citizens, in the air age, still feel that distance from the potential enemy gives some security to their national borders, it is in no small measure due to Mr. Seward's bargain.

Began Finished No. words: 1860

—— × 60 = —— W.P.M.

———— ———— No. seconds:

Checking Comprehension

1. Americans have always had faith in the progress of our country. They have differed only in their decisions as to (a) how much progress should be made each decade, (b) how much money should be spent to promote progress, (c) form and direction of expansion, (d) who should be responsible for progress.

2. Men in the 1800's could not have guessed the strategic importance of Alaska because (a) they didn't realize how much gold there was in Alaska, (b) they didn't envision the advantage of extending American territory, (c) they were not concerned about what the disposition of power might be were Russia established in America, (d) they visualized Alaska as a land of perpetual winter.

3. Vitus Bering made two explorations of northern lands. On the second exploration he (a) sailed around Iceland and discovered a new island in the northern Atlantic Ocean, (b) charted the Aleutians and the Gulf of Alaska, and claimed the whole area for Russia, (c) traced the northern outlines of Russia and explored Kamchatka River, (d) discovered and claimed the New Siberian Islands for Russia.

4. Russia's defeat in the Crimean War led to a time of reckoning. As one result of this reckoning the Russians (a) decided to adopt the liberal economic policies which had succeeded in Britain, (b) decided to continue their advance toward the Balkans and the Black Sea, (c) debated whether North American territory was worth keeping at all, (d) decided to conquer the British.

5. Americans became desirable purchasers of Alaska from the Russian point of view because (a) the Czar wanted to help America extend its boundaries, (b) the Czar thought the transfer of Alaska to America would weaken England, (c) the Russian Empire needed the money for reconstruction purposes, (d) the Czar held America in high esteem and wanted to cooperate with this nation.

6. One reason the prospect of purchasing Alaska evoked no enthusiasm in Washington was that (a)

America couldn't afford to spend the amount of money needed, (b) Americans didn't want to deal with Russia, (c) busy Congress didn't want to be bothered with the Alaskan proposition, (d) Americans saw no necessity for further expansion while great areas of the country were still unsettled.

7. At the end of the Civil War Seward knew that his active political career was about ended. One of the reasons he realized this was that (a) he had lost considerable public and party popularity, (b) he had lost interest in politics, (c) his health was failing, (d) he had been told that he must soon retire.

8. After the Civil War was over, Seward again saw the possibilities of extending the boundaries of the United States over the entire continent. One of his reasons was that (a) Congress was developing more interest in expansion, (b) the power of Spain was deteriorating, (c) Mexico wanted to be taken into the United States, (d) England was not doing much to develop Canada.

9. Seward had several reasons for wanting to purchase Alaska. One of them was (a) to provide an outpost for defense of America, (b) to capitalize on Alaska's wealth in minerals and furs, (c) to threaten Canada from the North, (d) to have a United States territory named after himself.

10. Had the opportunity of buying Alaska been passed up, the Russians might never have been dislodged. One reason for this conclusion is that soon after its purchase (a) the Russians learned that the fur-bearing seals in Alaskan waters were valuable, (b) the Czar was acquiring means to defend Alaska, (c) the Czar realized the strategic importance of Alaska in America's defense, (d) Russia needed Alaska as a base from which to make Arctic explorations.

Answers: 1)——, 2)——, 3)——, 4)——, 5)——, 6)——, 7)——, 8)——, 9)——, 10)——.

See the Answer Key on page 284. Allow a score of 10 for each correct answer.

Rate: W.P.M. ———— Comprehension Score: ————

Selection 3

This is a maintenance selection provided for your practice in reading easy material. You have been doing the most difficult type of reading. Now "try your wings" again on light material.

Adjust your speed to a much more rapid rate than you were able to use in working with the detailed factual selections. Try to exceed the rate and comprehension scores which you made previously in Chapters Four, Five, and Six. Your comprehension check will not be based on details. It will be concerned with main ideas and large units of thought.

BEGINNING TIME: _____
HR. _____ MIN. _____

SOME QUEER THINGS BIG BIRDS DO[21]

There are over 20,000 kinds of birds. They differ in their ways as much as in form and color—and some of their habits are very queer.

Penguins are the most devoted parents of all. The Penguins inhabit the Southern Hemisphere, and the largest species, the "emperor," lives south of the antarctic circle. In July, during the depth of the long antarctic night, when the ice is firmest, the mother penguin lays her single egg. She makes a platform of her stumpy legs and feet, on which to cradle her treasure, and warms it with a soft flap of down-covered skin. When the mother finds it necessary to enter the water for a meal she passes the egg to one of an eager company that is always ready. For it seems that, while emperor penguins are inordinately fond of brooding, few females of a flock produce eggs.

The emperor penguin stands nearly four feet in height and weighs close to ninety pounds. Its relative, the king penguin, is slightly smaller and lives farther north, where there is a firm land, though its nesting habits are essentially the same.

A king penguin, the acquaintance of which I once made, in the Zoological Gardens of London, was a magnificent bird and brilliantly colored. He had also a most charming personality, and would turn his beak skyward with a musical whistle of ecstasy when one scratched his glossy black throat.

Mammals frequently carry their young about from place to place, but this is rarely done by birds. Some ducks, such as the hooded merganser and the wood duck, nest in hollow trees, often at some distance above the ground. Just how the young get down has long been in dispute. Many observers have maintained that the mother carries them down in her bill or even on her back, but the truth seems to be that, in most cases at least, they scramble or leap to earth or water as best they can without assistance. . . .

However, birds do sometimes carry their young. The white mute swan of Europe often takes the cygnets on its back, either when they become tired or when danger is near. Some years ago I saw a splendid pair of South American black-necked swans on an estate in Holland. They had just brought off a brood of youngsters, and the family made a striking picture as they swam in a little slough covered with duckweed. When I approached the female gave some subtle signal which was readily understood, for the cygnets promptly scrambled upon her back and were rapidly borne away. Like most male swans with families to guard, the father was inclined to be pugnacious. He moved slowly toward me, wings raised and neck arched, throwing the brilliant blue and scarlet of his beak into sharp relief against the black—a picture of defiance.

There is a great diversity in the feeding habits of birds and some birds secure their food in strange ways. The flamingo, for instance, eats with his head upside down. The long, spindly legs, bare of feathers almost to the body, enable him to wade in fairly deep water; the grace-fully-curved neck allows the head to reach the mud at the bottom, where he finds his food. When feeding, the bird inverts his head, so that the upper surface of the angular beak rests on the bottom. Then, paddling alternately with his webbed feet, he stirs up the mud, draws in a mouthful, and forces it out again by raising his tongue. The sides of the beak are furnished with a row of narrow plates, which act as strainers, and sift out the tiny animal life on which the bird lives. . . .

As far as I know, parrots are uniformly vegetarians by

nature, but one kind, the "kea" of New Zealand, has developed carnivorous habits. The kea has an unusually long and pointed bill, as parrots go, well adapted to use in exhuming roots and tubers. When sheep were introduced into New Zealand the birds formed the unpleasant habit of alighting on the backs of these helpless creatures and excavating there for the fatty capsule of the kidneys. . . . So severe did the ravages of the keas become that the government offered a bounty for their heads.

Most birds work hard for a living and ply their trades with industry. But pirate birds have developed among them and live largely by robbing their more diligent fellows. The man-o'-war, or frigate, bird, a relative of the pelicans, is an expert fisherman in his own right, but when times are dull and food scarce he charges upon the smaller gulls and terns and forces them to disgorge the catch that they have stored for their own use.

Friendship among birds usually is the result of a mutual benefit. Species that have flocking instincts band together for protection, to make use of restricted nesting sites or often simply because food is available in a given locality. Unselfish attachment between individuals seldom exists among wild birds, but in captivity, where social barriers are more or less broken down, curious and thoroughly-platonic friendships are sometimes formed. . . .

Feathers are of as much importance to birds as clothes are to us. In most cases the plumage is fully renewed but once a year, and therefore the bird owner takes the greatest pains to keep his raiment in good condition until it is replaced. Special plumes and decorations, of course, are the most difficult to care for, but often these are required only during the breeding season, which is comparatively short. Particular as birds are about their plumage, I know of only one that goes so far as to provide its own decorations. The motmots are a brightly-colored South American group, with no close relatives and living in the depths of the tropical forests. The two central tail feathers are considerably longer than the others, and when they are renewed a portion of the web, just below the tip, is very lightly attached to the quill. As they grow, the bird constantly draws them through his bill, until finally the weakened web breaks away, leaving the shaft bare for a distance of an inch or more, with a little tab on the end. Thus the motmot secures the "racket" decoration, for which he is famed. . . .

The nesting customs of birds range from almost complete indifference to infinite solicitude on the part of the parents. In the East Indies there is a species related to the Australian brush turkey which merely deposits its eggs in the warm sand of the seashore and leaves them to be incubated by the sun's rays.

Originally the stork made its nest in trees, but now it almost invariably builds on the tops of buildings. In Denmark, Holland, and Germany, householders are delighted to have a stork guest nesting on the roof, as there is a well-grounded belief that the long-legged visitor is "a bringer of good." The wooing manners of the stork are extremely grotesque. With wings outspread it performs a kind of leaping dance, at the same time setting up a harsh chattering with the upper and lower parts of the beak. Storks commonly spend their summers in Europe and their winters farther east.

Began Finished No. words: 1500

$$\frac{\qquad}{\text{No. seconds:}} \times 60 = \underline{\qquad} \text{W.P.M.}$$

Checking Comprehension

1. There are over (a) 2,000 kinds of birds, (b) 1,000,-000 kinds of birds, (c) 20,000 kinds of birds, (d) 60,000 kinds of birds.

2. Penguins (a) neglect their young, (b) lay more eggs than they can hatch, (c) are not interested in brooding, (d) are devoted parents.

3. Birds (a) carry their young in their bills, (b) carry their young on their backs, (c) carry them under their wings, (d) rarely carry them at all.

4. As an illustration of the strange feeding habits of birds the author discusses those of the (a) flamingo, (b) penguin, (c) wood duck, (d) swan.

5. All parrots are (a) vegetarians, (b) carnivorous, (c) both vegetarian and carnivorous, (d) vegetarian with one exception.

6. Most birds are (a) pirates, (b) work hard for their

living, (c) are always expecting "handouts" (d) will "sing for their supper."

7. Friendship among birds usually results (a) when two flocks belonging to the same general family meet, (b) when birds get lost at migration time, (c) when they are nesting, (d) when it is to their mutual benefit to be friends.

8. As a general rule birds (a) depend upon wind and rain to take care of their feathers, (b) take good care of their feathers themselves, (c) pay no attention to their feathers, (d) try to pull out their feathers.

9. Birds are (a) always solicitous about building their nests, (b) range from indifference to solicitude, (c) are never indifferent, (d) are nearly always indifferent.

10. Originally storks made their nests (a) on the tops of buildings, (b) in trees, (c) in barns, (d) in low bushes.

Answers: 1)——, 2)——, 3)——, 4)——, 5)——, 6)——, 7)——, 8)——, 9)——, 10)——.

See Answer Key, page 284.

Rate: W.P.M. ——— Comprehension Score: ———

Vocabulary Study

The italicized words in the following phrases are taken from the selections you have just read. Underline the synonym or phrase beneath each italicized word which best defines that word. Check your answers with the Answer Key on page 284.

1. *Carnivorous* habits
    a) ferocious
    b) cannibalistic
    c) flesh-eating

2. White *cygnets*
    a) a constellation
    b) young swans
    c) flowers

3. *Inordinately* fond of fish
    a) occasionally
    b) excessively
    c) rarely

4. Bright *raiment*
    a) metal
    b) clothing
    c) sunshine

5. Fleeing from *brigandage*
    a) capture
    b) war
    c) robbers

6. *Nomadic* tribes
    a) dark-skinned
    b) roaming
    c) savage

7. *Recalcitrant* officials
   a) rebellious
   b) obliging
   c) reluctant
8. A *grandiose* future
   a) extensive
   b) famous
   c) impressive
9. A *manifest* destiny
   a) discouraging
   b) magnificent
   c) obvious
10. A *pugnacious* dog
    a) momentous
    b) animated
    c) inclined to fight
11. Followed by a *retinue*
    a) parade
    b) attendants
    c) well-wishers
12. A useless *encumbrance*
    a) bother
    b) task
    c) hindrance
13. Artful *cajolery*
    a) embroidery work
    b) delusive entice-
       ments
    c) pointillist painting
14. A familiar *motif*
    a) reason

b) pattern
c) fantasy
15. With expert *tutelage*
    a) instruction
    b) technicians
    c) adviser
16. An *apathetic* audience
    a) sympathetic
    b) impassive
    c) demilitaristic
17. A series of *parries*
    a) defensive move
       ments
    b) obstinate activities
    c) refractive interfer-
       ence
18. *Consummation* of the
    plan
    a) initiation
    b) execution
    c) completion
19. A long *regime*
    a) system of govern-
       ment
    b) life
    c) scientific treatise
20. *Ravages* of wild beasts
    a) savageness
    b) destructiveness
    c) revelations

Vocabulary Score: _____

Follow-Up Suggestions

This is necessarily a longer chapter than the others. Learning to read details rapidly is the most difficult type of reading that a person has to do, and as such it requires more development and practice than some of the simpler skills.

Using Materials of Your Selection

If you did not do well in your test of Selection 2, page

164, then continue practice with individual paragraphs which you find in your trade or professional journals or books. Outline related ideas on a separate piece of paper or within the paragraph itself; or make notes on the margin of the page; or underline main ideas and major and minor details with one, two, and three lines, respectively. Continue to use these helps as long as necessary. As soon as you can, however, try to get away from the use of such "crutches," for they slow up speed.

When you have achieved a high degree of skill in working with separate paragraphs, proceed to carry out the following suggestions.

Set aside at least one fifteen-minute period each evening for practice on reading detailed, factual articles. In each of your practice periods, select an article of this type and apply the techniques which you have learned. Work with one paragraph and try to envision that as a whole. Then go on to the next paragraph and proceed as if it were a new unit. Stop frequently to sum up what you've gotten out of two or three paragraphs. You will soon be able to make an easy transition from one paragraph to another and to grasp details in increasing numbers of paragraphs.

As soon as you can read two or three paragraphs without stopping, make a new entry in your notebook: "Speed Record—Detailed Reading." Enter the date and the number of words per minute which you were able to cover in reading material packed with facts. Continue to keep this record each night until you read detailed material as fast as you want to. You should make regular rate increases in this kind of reading—but remember this rate will never be so high as your speed in reading easy, narrative material.

Check your grasp of facts after each reading by one of these methods: have someone ask you detailed questions; make an outline from your "mental picture"; write a summary of facts; or tell yourself the important thoughts, together with the cluster or clusters of details that belong with each one. You can of course check your responses by referring to the text. Continue to force your speed in reading this type of material, as you have been forcing it in reading selections of easier content.

You should also continue your speed and comprehension practice in reading easy nontechnical material, making regular records of your speed. Don't let your detailed reading slow down your very rapid rate of reading easy material.

Chapter 8

Riding Along with an Author

Purposes and Patterns

In reading it is very important that you identify yourself closely with the author. Regardless of the chapter or article you choose to read you may be sure that it was written with a specific purpose, and the author proceeded toward his destination until his writing journey was completed. True, he may occasionally have taken detours, and here and there he may have driven rather deeply into a forest of details which he considered especially important or interesting, and at other points he may have speeded over open spaces which he considered unappealing or of little consequence. Regardless of the variations in route, the author always has a purpose for his writing journey; he always has a reason for taking the trip. If you will mount the saddle and travel right along with him toward the destination that he has in mind, your reading journey will be much more swift and sure than if you travel with a goal of your own which differs from his.

Authors' purposes for writing vary. The purpose determines the pattern into which the writing falls. If you learn to identify the pattern, you will be able quickly to recognize the author's purpose. With this information you will be able to adjust to the pattern, whatever it may be.

To use another analogy, when a tailor makes a suit coat

he lays a certain pattern on the cloth and cuts a piece of material in the shape of that pattern with as little waste as possible. He lays a different pattern on the cloth if he is going to make a pair of slacks, and he uses still a different pattern if the goal of his efforts is to be a top-coat.

So does each author "lay a different pattern on the cloth" for each of his purposes. If you can decide on the garment he wishes to turn out, and will "lay the same pattern on the cloth" that he uses, you too will have less waste material left in the way of time and lack of comprehension.

Sharing-Experience Pattern

Perhaps the pattern most frequently met is the one in which the author wishes to tell about some personal experience. This experience is so interesting, unusual, or worthwhile in his opinion that he would like to share it with others, at the same time entertaining his readers.

To identify the sharing-experience pattern ask yourself, "Is he telling some actual, first-hand experience?" Additional clues are the use of the personal pronouns *I*, *we*, *our*, or *us*.

The sharing-experience pattern is easy to identify as well as easy to read. When you start to read such a selection, you may know that it is safe to proceed at the highest speed you can command. Usually comprehension difficulties are at their minimum in such an article. There are no detailed facts that you will have to recall. All you have to do is to enjoy the author's experience in the way you would if he were telling it to you orally.

Our largest catch, a 50-pound yellow, was caught near the close of the day. A group of grabblers flushed him in open water fifty yards above us. He lunged and butted his way through another group and appeared in our midst. Our first notice of his appearance among us was when he butted Charlie Cox squarely in the stomach. We closed in and undertook to corner him. He thundered, blustered, butted and chewed fingers until we finally managed to pen him against a log. With shouts of triumph we hoisted him ashore, and thus ended our day.[1]

Question-Answer Pattern

The Question-Answer pattern, as its name implies, is one in which the author states a question, then proceeds to answer it. The question may be stated as the title of an article, as a subheading within the article, or at the beginning of a paragraph.

The question-answer style can be used in writing technical material, but usually it isn't. It more often appears as an "interest tickler."

The author may make one of two uses of the question-answer technique in his writing. He may use the question to excite curiosity so that you will be interested in reading what he has to say. On the other hand, he may use this technique in order to indicate his intentions in a concise and clear-cut form. This "sharpening" up of the subject by couching it in the form of a question may be his way of helping you understand his purpose at once.

The question-answer pattern has many advantages for the reader. For one thing, it states the reader's purpose for him. He doesn't have to formulate his own motive for reading the article. Second, it is easier to hold in mind a question than a topic sentence, for the question stands out sharply throughout the reading of the text that follows. Thus it furnishes a compelling and constant frame of reference with which details can be associated.

The question-answer pattern also has the advantage of easy identification. A glance reveals the question. When you encounter a question in a title, subdivision, or paragraph you know immediately that the author is going to answer the question.

The question-answer pattern also facilitates speed. If the content is of such a nature that you don't care about

[1] Ewart A. Autry, "Acres of Catfish," *Field and Stream*, May 1954, p. 121.

the details, simply read the question, glance through the text until you find the answer—and let it go at that.

Try this technique in reading the sample paragraph below.

> What is time?—The shadow on the dial, the striking of the clock, the running of the sand, day and night, summer and winter, months, years, centuries—these are but the arbitrary and outward signs—the measure of time, not time itself. Time is the life of the soul.
>
> —Henry Wadsworth Longfellow

Imparting-Information Pattern

This pattern also is easy to identify, but it is often difficult to read. Frequently this pattern contains many factual details. If you wish to remember these details you must use the very careful techniques already taught. Usually one quick glance at a selection will tell you if the author's purpose was to give information. If so, be prepared to adjust your speed to careful, detailed reading.

A sample of the "Imparting-Information" pattern is given below. Put yourself in a state of mind for reading a paragraph packed heavily with informative details.

> The radioactivity of uranium minerals may be detected by use of Geiger and scintillation counters (Wright, 1953, 1954a; Brownell, 1950; Wilson and others, 1954). Their use gives the prospector an unusual advantage, for these instruments can detect the presence of radioactive minerals even if they are concealed from sight by a few inches or so of soil or rock. Geiger counters and scintillation counters have been developed in various shapes and sizes, suitable for use by the prospector on the ground, for carborne (Nelson, 1954) and airborne (Stead, 1950; Stead and Davis, 1952) reconnaissance, and for drill-hole logging (Faul and Tittle, 1951; DiGiovanni, and others, 1953). The scintillation counter is much more sensitive than the Geiger counter and therefore will detect much less intense radioactivity. For this reason, scintillation counters have now largely displaced Geiger counters in airborne reconnaissance. Light planes,

such as those used by the Atomic Energy Commission, are used to search for specific deposits in broadly favorable areas (Tavelli, 1951; Foote, 1954). They fly at an altitude of about 50 feet and are equipped with scintillation counters that detect almost all abnormal radioactivity that field Geiger counters detect on the ground. Larger planes, like the Geological Survey's DC-3, are used for quick reconnaisance of large regions (Stead, 1950; Balsley, 1952). The Survey's plane is flown at an elevation of about 500 feet along traverse lines about a quarter of a mile apart, and records both radioactivity and magnetic measurements.[2]

Opinion-Reason Pattern

The writer uses this pattern in order to state an opinion and give his reason for it. You may have to read two or three paragraphs before you can determine whether the author is expressing his opinion and also whether he intends to give reasons supporting it. Some clues are such phrases as "I think," "I believe," "I prefer," "I judge," "I am sure," "in my opinion," "as I see it," "according to my viewpoint," "I regard," etc. If you find statements such as these and the reasons follow, then all you need to do is to get a concise understanding of the author's opinion, then find his reason or reasons for believing as he does. Synchronize your purpose and techniques to the author's style, and there will be no lost time or effort.

Try adjusting yourself to the opinion-reason pattern while reading the paragraph below.

From my earliest youth I have regarded slavery as a great moral and political evil.—I think it unjust, repugnant to the natural equality of mankind, founded only in superior power; a standing and permanent conquest by the stronger over the weaker.—All pretence of defending it on the ground of different races, I have ever condemned, and have even said that if the black race is weaker, that is a reason against and not for its

[2] U.S. Atomic Energy Commission, *Search for Uranium in the United States*, U.S. Gov. Printing Office, 1955, pp. 20-21.

subjection and oppression.—In a religious point of view, I have ever regarded and spoken of it, not as a subject of any express denunciation, either in the Old Testament or the New, but as opposed to the whole spirit of the gospel, and to the teachings of Jesus Christ.—The religion of Christ is a religion of kindness, justice, and brotherly love;—but slavery is not kindly affectionate; it seeks another's and not its own; it does not let the oppressed go free; it is but a continual act of oppression.

—Daniel Webster

Substantiated-Facts Pattern

This pattern usually begins with a conclusion and is followed by facts to prove this conclusion. The conclusion, however, sometimes comes at the end. This pattern is most frequently found in technical or scientific content, although occasionally in a popular article. This is the most convincing type of pattern an author can use in making his point.

In identifying this pattern, look for a definite statement in the form of a conclusion. Unlike the opinion-reason pattern, this statement will contain no personal pronouns, nor will it contain such verbs as "think" or "believe." It usually is a terse statement of fact. The series of statements which follows the conclusion offers substantiation in the form of data, scientific observations, experiments, or quotations.

This pattern usually must be read far more carefully and slowly than the experience pattern or question-and-answer type of material.

The meaning of every word must be grasped in order to understand the evidence presented. If you wish to remember the proofs, then you need to employ all your techniques for reading and recalling detailed facts. The conclusion stated by the author will of course be the topic sentence, and all the subsequent proving sentences will be related to this statement as reinforcing details.

Try out these suggestions in reading the substantiated-facts sample that is presented below.

1) Make certain that you comprehend the significance

of the author's conclusion; 2) then mentally challenge him to prove it to you; 3) read on to see if his proof is convincing.

There are many visible evidences that the moon has little or no atmosphere. The illuminated portion of its surface is always visible. No haze, clouds, or dust storms have ever been observed. When the moon passes between the earth and the sun, no luminous atmospheric ring is visible. The moon's margin is sharp and black. When the moon passes between the earth and a star, the light of the star is cut off sharply and suddenly, not gradually. It is quite certain that if it ever possessed an atmosphere, it has lost it now.[3]

Applying What You've Learned

Following are selections which represent each of these patterns. Identify the author's pattern of writing, then try quickly to adjust to this pattern as you read. You will be rated on your accuracy in identifying the patterns, on your comprehension of each selection, and on your speed of reading.

The selections are assembled in three groups in order that you may obtain a check of your rate in reading different types of material: 1) easy short selections, 2) more difficult short selections, 3) long selections.

Practice Section I

Easy Short Selections

All five of these selections are easy to read and are of such a nature that you probably won't care to linger over details. Your test at the end will check your identification of the pattern and general comprehension in each selection. You will also be checked on the time it takes you to read all five paragraphs.

As you start to read each selection, quickly identify the pattern of writing and synchronize your reading pattern with the author's writing pattern. This will contribute much both to your speed and comprehension.

BEGINNING TIME: _____
HR._____ MIN._____

Selection 1

No Hollywood Star could be so temperamental, so hilarious, so touching, or so frightening as some of the actors that have performed their roles before my camera.

As a member of the Walt Disney wildlife camera crew, I spent two seasons filming the spectacular true-life adventure, *The Vanishing Prairie*. We followed and found our animal and bird actors in remote sections of the West—in the last retreats of the native wildlife of the Great Plains.

This was my greatest camera adventure.

My "actors" were unpredictable. They misbehaved continually. Small ones disappeared down burrows just when I was ready to start my camera. Of course they ran from me whenever I inadvertently revealed myself. They hid from me much more easily than I from them. Larger ones often charged me angrily when I got too close.

Yet all this was to be expected.

The story for this film was their story—the everyday adventures of the animals and birds of the vast American prairie. They wrote the script with nature as their director. My camera was merely the "invisible" intruder.[4]

Selection 2

Why, then, do doctors prescribe, and parents often demand the expensive formulations put out under the fancy labels? For the doctor, it is often the easy way out: the formula pad is handy, the infant is doing well under its hospital-prescribed mixture, and the parents will be satisfied to continue the "official" routine the hospital started. For the parents, the expensive product with the fancy label gives the satisfaction that they are not stinting, but giving their new child "the best."

But there are signs of change. Some hospitals have

[4] Tom McHugh, "Animals Are Like People," *Field and Stream*, September 1954, p. 113.

started to use sugar and milk—any brand—and to forego the free offers of the companies. Some pediatricians are following the same progressive technique. And some parents, even some whose babies started out on traditional and expensive formulas, are asking questions of their doctors, and beginning to realize that the most expensive course is not necessarily the best one.[5]

Selection 3

The tropical rainstorm had stopped as suddenly as it had begun. Long shafts of yellow sunlight were lancing down through the dripping trees as I stepped from the porch of the trading station at Sietevaca, a tiny native village in eastern Honduras. At the end of the long boardwalk that stretched out into the murky, sullen water of the Patuca River a half dozen curious Hondurans were assembled to watch the rapid approach of a huge pitpan, or native dugout canoe.

Under normal conditions, the arrival of one cargo canoe would have been no cause for interest. But this pitpan was not filled with cargo. There were three men in the boat. One of them was lying motionless in the bottom, and the other two were excitedly calling to the onlookers to find the doctor. Stepping back up to the door, I called to Doc McGuartney, the only man within a radius of fifty miles who was qualified to call himself a physician, and waited while he heaved his ponderous bulk out of the wicker chair and lumbered toward the door.[6]

Selection 4

What can be done about emotionally-caused overeating?

To break the conditioned reflex of eating under stress, you must first recognize the wide prevalence of emotional conflict. Everyone has weaknesses, though we express them differently. Some people lose their appetite under stress; others overeat. Still others take to alcohol, or develop stomach pains, diarrhea, cardiac palpitation, or migraine headaches.

[5] "Infant Formulas," *Consumer Reports*, October 1952, pp. 484.
[6] William Thomas Helm III, "Spotted Killer," *Field and Stream*, September 1954, p. 43.

Breaking food reflexes must start with a conscious deliberate setting up of *different* reflexes. This takes time. A few days or weeks of dieting is not enough. Be prepared to allow months for the job, because only then can results become permanent.

Overeating is a habit. It can be broken, like all habits, by the substitution of other routines. Once you remove the need for overeating through self-understanding and tolerance, you can give yourself the motivation to carry through to a permanent goal.[7]

Selection 5

What is the reason for the existence of this great glacial system on this mountain? It is not simply the altitude of Mount Rainier, for there are other mountains which are slightly higher above the level of the sea. Both Mount Whitney in California and Mount Elbert in Colorado may boast of greater elevation, but neither possesses glacial systems. The reason is snow. Upon the broad flanks of this huge volcano, due to the great amount of moisture that is swept inland from the Pacific in the prevailing winds, occurs one of the heaviest snowfalls on record in our country. At Paradise Valley (5557 feet), which is widely known for its wild flowers during the summer season, it is not unusual for twenty-five feet of snow to be found upon the ground in midwinter, while unquestionably a great deal more snow falls at the higher levels where most of the glaciers are born. This snow, in packing down is transformed into glacial ice and keeps alive these remnants of the "ice age." Each winter it partly repairs the damage of the warm summer sun, but the glaciers are fighting a losing battle. Eventually, perhaps, at some time in the distant future these great glaciers, some of which are more than four or five miles long today, may be mere traces of their former magnificence.[8]

Began Finished No. words: 880

——— × 60 = ——— W.P.M.

——— ——— No. seconds:

[7] Wilfred Dorfman, "How to Stop Overeating," *Journal of Living*, December 1953, p. 70.

[8] C. Frank Brackman, "The Wonders of Mount Rainier," *Natural History*, March 1936, p. 257.

Checking Comprehension

If necessary you may refer back to the selections in answering the first five questions about patterns, but do not refer back while answering the last five questions which check comprehension of content.

1. What pattern of writing was used in Selection 1? _____

2. What pattern was used in Selection 2? _____

3. What pattern was used in Selection 3? _____

4. What pattern was used in Selection 4? _____

5. What pattern was used in Selection 5? _____

6. The photographing of animals was discussed in one selection. Where was this photography done? ____
_____

7. In one selection "formulas" are discussed. What kind of formulas are under consideration in this article? _____

8. What was the object of excitement in the selection with a setting in Honduras? _____

9. What is the cause of overeating as discussed in one selection? _____

10. The glacial system on Mount Rainer was discussed. What is the reason this glacial system exists? _____
_____

The Answer Key is on page 284.

Rate: W.P.M. _____ Comprehension Score: _____

Practice Section II

More Difficult Short Selections

In this section you will again have practice in reading selections in different patterns. Unlike the selections in Practice Section I, however, these as a whole are of the detailed factual type. You will therefore need to read them at a slower rate.

You will be checked on the patterns of writing and also

on some of the details in each selection. In addition, you will have an opportunity to check your speed.

When you are ready to start, jot down your beginning time, and when you have finished reading all five selections record your ending time.

Identify the pattern of writing in each selection and "read to the pattern." Force your speed as much as you can while still grasping the information. Don't feel frustrated, however, because you cannot read at such a high speed as in the preceding section. These selections are more difficult to read, and you will have to "shift your gears."

BEGINNING TIME:————————
HR.———————— MIN.————————

Selection 6

Improvement in machines has been the result of many factors, one of which has been the rapid advance in the science of metallurgy. There are now some 5000 different metal alloys, some of them much better than the metals formerly used. It has been claimed that the steel produced today wears nearly twice as long as most of the steel made fifty years ago. The advance has been phenomenal in some of the hard cutting metals. A new material is now available which consists of a mixture of tungsten and titanium carbides cemented with cobalt. This is perfectly satisfactory for cutting steel, and it has been found to have 60 times the life in operation that the original cemented tungsten carbide had. Through chromium plating the life of various tools and parts has been extended from 3 to 20 times. By the use of tungsten carbide, Carboloy tools have been formed which operate in some cases 300 to 400 times as efficiently as the old steel tools. On a brass-plug job the number of finished pieces produced by old tools was 200; through the substitution of Carboloy tools this was increased to 15,000. Great improvements have been made in some articles through the use of the lighter metals and alloys, some of which are extremely strong as well as light. Scientists say that we are entering a new era in which steel will to some extent be displaced by these materials.[9]

[9] John Ise, *Economics*, Harper, 1946, p. 509.

Selection 7

Let me state at once my theme and my deep personal conviction: that, by not lifting the Language Curtain which she has lowered on her shores since the time of World War I, America persists in imperiling her international commitments and weakening her influence as a promoter of world peace and understanding. By indulging our linguistic and cultural isolationism long after we have abandoned political isolationism, we seem to others a nation of good intentions paving the road to an atomic hell. I am using the phrase "Language Curtain" deliberately to invite comparison with another more familiar and more metallic screen. Is it pure coincidence, one of the forgivable synchronisms, that the rise of the Soviet Union and the decline of foreign language study in this country began at precisely the same moment in history and have continued to do global damage together? This sounds like a charge of "guilt by association" against those responsible for the decline of foreign languages, but I reject the inference. It would be more accurate to call it guilt by dissociation, or going to another equally unfortunate extreme. There have been too many Americans whose smug answer to the problems of a shrinking, suspicion-ridden world has been "Let 'em learn English!" [10]

Selection 8

The rare 1913 nickel is not the Buffalo type but is the Liberty-head type. Shortly after their coining (only six were made), a then well-known coin dealer was detailed by the late Colonel Green to approach the mint regarding the sale. After negotiating for a short time, four of the six 1913 Liberty-head nickels were sold to him for $500 each, $2000 for the four. All were in brilliant uncirculated condition, and the fifth was kept for the United States Mint collection. No one knows what became of the sixth nickel, and this mysterious nickel is probably the reason so many non-collectors have been acquainted with the rarity of the 1913 Liberty nickel.

For years a well-known dealer advertised very exten-

[10] William R. Parker, "The Language Curtain," *School and Society*, October 31, 1953, p. 129.

sively throughout the United States that he would pay $50 for a 1913 Liberty-head nickel, but this coin has never been found and probably never will be. The chances of anyone finding it are practically nil, for we must remember that the average life of a nickel in circulation is not over twenty years. There have been hundreds of millions of nickels coined since 1913, and millions are in circulation all the time. Our population is in excess of 160,000,000 people, anyone of whom might have that poor nickel, so you can figure what odds there are against your ever finding it, or its still being in existence.[11]

Selection 9

Only an all-out war against the virus itself, if successful, would eradicate colds. Medical science now has a new weapon which could accomplish this.

"Ultraviolet 2537" has already been used in hospitals, clinics and other institutions, where it has proved itself an efficient germ killer. At the University of Toronto's Hospital for Sick Children, twice as many children suffered infections where the lamps were not installed as where the lamps were used. At the U. S. Naval Training Center, Sampson, N.Y., respiratory diseases, including colds, were reduced by one fourth by installing the lamps in the sleeping quarters, although mess halls and classrooms were unprotected. The Cradle Society, Evanston, Ill., reported a 90% reduction in the spread of upper respiratory infection among infants in cubicles equipped with "2537" as compared with those in untreated cubicles.[12]

Selection 10

When I speak of freedom, I believe that I approach a subject which is of interest to you not only in general but which must be definitely in your minds as you approach the matter of security, for I presume that we should all be ready to admit that the person who is truly free in this world is the most secure. He has the needed

[11] Charles French, "Money of Yesteryear," *Hobbies*, October 1953, p. 120.
[12] John D. Murphy, "New Cure for Colds," *Strange Medical Facts*, November 1954, p. 6.

flexibility; he does not need to become a slave of any particular age and therefore unable to meet the revolutionary changes which inevitably come as we move from age to age.

Do you recall that in the passage on the grand inquisitor in Dostoevski's *Brothers Karamazov* he says, "I tell thee that man is tormented by no greater anxiety than to find someone quickly to whom he can hand over that gift of freedom with which he, ill-gaited creature, is born?" [13]

Began Finished No. words: 970

$$\frac{\qquad}{\qquad} \times 60 = \underline{\qquad} \text{ W.P.M.}$$

_____ _____ No. seconds:

Compare your rate for reading easy, narrative material with that for reading detailed factual material. Is the latter rate lower than the former? If so, that is what you should expect. You should, however, show an increase in speed in reading both types of content.

Checking Comprehension

Write a brief answer to each question.

You may refer to the selections in answering the first five questions, but do not refer back in answering the last five questions.

1. What pattern was represented in Selection 6? _____
2. What pattern was represented in Selection 7? _____
3. What pattern was represented in Selection 8? _____
4. What pattern was represented in Selection 9? _____
5. What pattern was represented in Selection 10? _____
6. How many different metal alloys are there now?

_____

7. According to one of the articles, the decline of foreign-language study in this country began at the same time in history as a certain foreign development. What was this foreign development? _____
8. What is the date and name of the nickel which is so rare? _____

[13] Douglas Horton, "Slaves to Freedom," *Education for National Security*, American Assoc. of School Administrators, 1953, p. 5.

9. The effectiveness of Ultraviolet 2537 was reported from three centers: University of Toronto's Hospital, U.S. Naval Training Center in Sampson, N.Y., and where else? Name the institution and its location. ─────────────

10. Can you complete this sentence? ". . . the person who is truly free in this world is the most ─────── ─────────────────."

The Answer Key is on page 285. Allow yourself a score of 10 for each completely correct answer. In questions 8 and 9 you may allow yourself a score of 5 for each correct part.

Rate: W.P.M. ─────── Comprehension Score: ───────

Practice Section III

Long Selections

The short selections with which you have been working should have afforded you sufficient practice in identifying different patterns of writing and adjusting to them.

In each of the selections that follow, first of all identify the pattern of writing. If it is in the Question-Answer pattern, concentrate on the question or questions and then read for the purpose of finding the answer or answers. If the pattern is that of personal experience, probably all you will need to do is to live with the writer vicariously as he tells what happened. Should the giving-information pattern be used, then read carefully to find out what information the writer wishes to impart. If the pattern is of the opinion-reason type, focus sharply on the opinions expressed and then read to find out the author's reasons for holding them. Finally, if you encounter the substantiated-fact pattern, first look for the conclusions, and then find the facts which support each conclusion.

Read as fast as you can in terms of the pattern at hand.

Selection 1

BEGINNING TIME: _____
HR. _____ MIN. _____

HOUSES, SIGNS AND PORTRAITS PAINTED! [14]

In the early part of the eighteenth century the *South Carolina Gazette* carried a notice "to gentlemen AND OTHERS" that portraits, engraving, heraldry, and house painting would be undertaken and performed by a native artist "at the lowest rate." This was the usual rather than the unusual thing in the days before and just after the Revolution. Only a fashionable painter could make a living by painting portraits, even though, in those pre-photographic days, that was the only means whereby a man might preserve his image for posterity. Nor could an artist hope to make a living in any one place, because commissions were too rare and competition too keen. He had to go from place to place, painting likenesses at a furious rate, working eight or ten hours a day, and resorting to every kind of time-saving device in order to keep the wolf from the door. If he were not a well-known artist his lot was even harder. He dared not even hope to make a living by his brush, but must eke out his livelihood in more practical fields of endeavor.

A painter whose services were in demand usually received about twenty-five dollars for a portrait; and it is recorded as an evidence of phenomenal success that one artist painted a hundred likenesses at this price in six months. A modern photographer would close up shop if business were as poor as that. The usual rate, however, was even lower, as the following advertisement from a Boston paper of 1790 shows:

"The public are respectfully informed that the artists who took the most correct likeness of the President of the United States and executed a medal of him are at the house of John Coburn in State Street and will continue for one month only to make the most correct likenesses in two minutes' sitting and finish them for one dollar to three."

Samuel B. Morse, inventor of the telegraph, made his

[14] J. Pennington, *The Mentor*, October 1924, pp. 45-47.

living in his youth painting miniatures. His price was five dollars if the sitter provided his own ivory; the rate for profile drawings was one dollar. Morse afterward made several full-size likenesses, among them a well-known portrait of General Lafayette. John Wesley Jarvis, nephew of John Wesley, the founder of Methodism, devised two ingenious schemes for saving time in making likenesses. In his early days he invented a machine for drawing profiles on glass, the reverse then being blacked in very quickly. Later on, when he became more successful, he spent his winters in New Orleans executing commissions for portraits, and took with him a lesser light named Inman. Jarvis would paint the head and face and then turn the canvas over to have the background and drapery completed by Inman.

Sometimes the artist survived the struggle, and sometimes he did not. The scarcity of orders, the low prices paid, and the keenness of competition were not the only obstacles in the path of the artist. Puritan prejudice against him was strong. In the "Records of the Selectman of the Towne of Boston," this entry appears: "Lawrence Brown, a Limner, asks admittance to be an Inhabitant of this Towne, which is granted on Condition that he gives Security to Save the Towne Harmless."

There was also the difficulty of securing the materials of one's craft, which had to be imported and were therefore expensive. Benjamin West, called the father of American portrait painting, secured his colors and brushes in this way: The Indians taught him to make the reds and yellows they used for painting themselves, and his mother gave him some indigo. He had never seen a camel's-hair brush, but it had been described to him; so he took a goose quill and fastened to it some hairs from the cat's tail. Another ambitious youth who lived in the backwoods fashioned a palette from a piece of board in which was arranged a row of thimbles filled with various colors.

There was one unfailing expedient to which the Colonial artist could resort, and that was the painting of signs. In the days when shops and houses were not numbered, every business street presented a succession of golden balls, blue gloves, crowns and scepters, dogs, elephants, and horses. These signs very often had no relation to the nature of the business they represented. In Philadelphia, particularly famous for its signs, there was a representation of a cock in a barnyard "which for many years graced a beer garden in Spruce Street. The execution of this was so fine and the expression of nature so exactly copied that it was evident to the most casual observer that it was painted by the hand of a master."

The master whose hand had painted this sign, and many others in Philadelphia, was Matthew Pratt. From childhood Pratt had been interested in painting, and so he was apprenticed to his uncle to learn all branches of the business—that is, sign, house, and portrait painting. His first known portrait is one of Benjamin Franklin. After some months of study under Benjamin West in London, Pratt returned to Philadelphia. In spite of a reasonable number of commissions he was compelled to resort to sign painting as a means of supporting his family. Pratt's signs were a source of great pride to his fellow citizens. He painted the Federal Convention, showing "a group of personages engaged in public discussion," with the venerable head of Dr. Franklin conspicuously displayed in the foreground. Under it was the following rhyme:

These thirty-eight great men have signed a powerful deed
That better times to us shall very soon succeed.

Citizens crowded about busily engaged in identifying the figures in the group. Pratt's portraits were often excellently done. At his best he was the equal of Benjamin West, and a number of his paintings have been attributed to Copley. His picture "The London School" shows West's studio. In it the master is criticizing a picture held by Pratt, and in the foreground is a picture of Delanoy, the artist son of a Philadelphia oysterman.

There were other interesting figures among the early American painters. Charles Willson Peale was apprenticed to a saddler and subsequently worked as a coach builder, a clock- and watchmaker, and a silversmith. When a portrait painter came to town Peale decided to try his hand at the same craft; so he went to Philadelphia and purchased the materials he needed and a book of instructions.

While studying, unaided, Peale also learned to model

in wax and to cast in plaster. He painted miniatures, engraved plates, and taught his brothers the art of painting—even as he was learning it himself. Peale was a soldier in the Revolution, founded a museum of natural history, and then went on a lecture tour. As he began to lose his teeth he found speaking difficult, so he gave up lecturing and began making dental plates—at first a set in ivory for himself, and then porcelain teeth for his friends. Among his clients was Washington, and in several of his portraits the Father of our Country wears a strained expression around the mouth due to an ill-fitting set of teeth made by Peale. Peale had many children, all named for famous painters. One of them, Rembrandt Peale became a good painter in his own right. The elder Peale founded the Pennsylvania Academy of Fine Arts in Philadelphia.

Another man to achieve unusual things was William Dunlap, one of the first to paint Washington and his wife. In addition to the vocation of portrait painter, Dunlap was a theatrical manager and playwright, an editor, author, poet, soldier, and farmer. He had only one eye, but his infirmity did not prevent his painting some large canvases of historical and Biblical scenes, in imitation of those of Benjamin West. The public paid twenty-five cents to see them when they were sent on exhibition.

Chester Harding was one of the most romantic figures of the period. A giant well over six feet tall, until he was twenty-one he lived the rough life of a pioneer. When the ambition to paint first struck him he left his father's farm, floated down the Allegheny on a flatboat, and set up shop as a sign painter in Pittsburgh. Finally, encouraged by Gilbert Stuart, Harding opened a studio in Boston. The backwoodsman-artist received so many commissions that even Stuart became envious.

There are countless others who deserve mention, who suffered for the sake of art and pursued it at all costs. Edward G. Malbone, the famous miniaturist, at one time painted theatrical scenery. Bass Otis, a scythemaker's apprentice, painted many portraits and made the first lithograph ever printed in this country. Robert Fulton, inventor of the steamboat, painted portraits, landscapes, and miniatures in his early manhood.

The work of these early American portrait painters

had "power and serenity." As a whole, their art may be summed up by a phrase used to describe the worthy Matthew Pratt's signs: "Here is no niggling in style or touch."

Began Finished· No. words: 1400

$$\frac{}{\rule{3cm}{0.4pt}\ \ \rule{3cm}{0.4pt}} \times 60 = \rule{2cm}{0.4pt}\ \text{W.P.M.}$$

———— ———— No. seconds:

Checking Comprehension

1. Before and just after the Revolution most artists (a) had enough portrait painting to do to earn a good living, (b) were very famous, (c) were very well paid, (d) often had to do other kinds of work to earn a living.

2. An artist of early times (a) set up a studio of his own in one town and stayed there, (b) usually worked with a group of artists in one studio, (c) traveled about from place to place, (d) settled in Boston to become a part of an art center.

3. In colonial times an artist usually received for painting a portrait: (a) about ten dollars, (b) about fifty dollars, (c) about one hundred dollars, (d) about twenty-five dollars.

4. The following inventor was an artist as a young man: (a) Eli Whitney, (b) Samuel B. Morse, (c) Cyrus McCormick, (d) Alexander Bell.

5. Benjamin West, one of the colonial painters, solved the problem of obtaining expensive red and yellow paints by (a) importing paints, (b) using materials from his own fields, (c) having the Indians teach him how to make red and yellow, (d) using water colors.

6. The most common work by which artists supplemented their income was (a) farming, (b) selling landscape paintings, (c) teaching art, (d) painting signs.

7. The artist most famous for sign painting was (a) Matthew Pratt, (b) Benjamin West, (c) John Coburn, (d) John Wesley Jarvis.

8. One of the things which made William Dunlap famous was (a) modeling in wax, (b) being one of the

first to paint Washington and his wife, (c) engraving plates, (d) painting signs.

9. Charles Willson Peale, in addition to painting, made: (a) ship models, (b) furniture, (c) houses, (d) dental plates.

10. Chester Harding set up his first shop as a sign painter in (a) Boston, (b) New York, (c) Philadelphia, (d) Pittsburgh.

Answers: 1)——, 2)——, 3)——, 4)——, 5)——, 6)——, 7)——, 8)——, 9)——, 10)——.

See the Answer Key on page 285.

Rate: W.P.M. ———— Comprehension Score: ————

Selection 2

BEGINNING TIME:————
HR.———— MIN.————

STATEMENT OF DONALD B. WOODWARD[15]

Your letter of September 22 asks for a statement of what I believe to be "the specific implications and long-run effects on Government finances and on stability of the economy in following at this time a policy of allowing interest rates on short-term Treasury issues to rise."

1. *The question's setting.*—My response is necessarily conditioned by my concept of the environment and the Relationship the incidents you mention have to it. My reply may be clearer if those concepts are very briefly made explicit.

The American political economy of our age seems to me to be marked by two transcending imperatives: First, that freedom must be protected from tremendous exogenous threats; and second, that the economy must be protected from the disequilibration, indeed, the disintegration, of major depression and major inflation. (At the moment the greater danger seems to be major inflation, but emphasis on it alone could cause us to go to extremes; the major preoccupation of analysis with

[15] Donald B. Woodward, *General Credit Control, Debt Management, and Economic Mobilization,* U.S. Govt. Printing Office, 1951, pp. 77-79.

combatting depression between 1929 and 1941 so inhibited balanced thinking as to produce extensive antidepression policies when inflation was the problem.) And major depressions and inflations are occurrences involving credit and money in a great degree, if, indeed, they are not really essentially monetary phenomena.

These two imperatives are intimately interrelated at various levels. They can have and have had major consequences upon each other. Both major inflation and depression have weakened the country's power and consequently its ability to protect freedom, while the struggle to protect freedom has brought about conditions inducing at different times major inflation and depression. In view of these interrelationships, it is important to avoid partial views when these matters are considered.

During the course of national efforts according with the two great imperatives, two major developments have occurred during the past two decades which, in my opinion, bear with great force on your question. First, the public debt has grown enormously. Second, the value of the dollar as commonly measured by price indexes has fallen by only a little less than half.

The existence of the two imperatives, and the developments resulting from them, have greatly broadened the horizons and increased the depth of the question you ask.

I turn now to your question, which deals both with governmental finances and economic stability. Let me first consider the two parts separately.

2. *Government finances.*—The purpose of "following at this time a policy of allowing interest on short-term Treasury issues to rise" (to use your terminology and emphasis) is to curb the inflation manifested for some weeks in rising bank loans, commodity prices, and the like. "The specific implications and long-run effects on government finances" of such a policy depend preponderantly upon whether inflation is likely to be curbed by the policy followed.

It is traditional central bank and orthodox economic theory that rising interest rates penalize and dissuade those considering expansion of their businesses and also result in increasing saving and curtailed consumer demand; all this is supposed to operate in part directly from rising short-term rates, and in part from the effects of rising short rates on long-term rates (and the opposite effects are had from declining rates). This inhibiting effect supposedly is felt on the private sector of the economy and presumably, though this has been less clearly developed, on the public sector as well. This view of the functioning of rising (or falling) rates has long been and still is vigorously challenged as unrealistic and contrary to much available evidence; on the other hand, it has been supported by arguments of marginal economics and an array of evidence of the association of rising interest rates and the ending of booms. The evidence does not appear to validate either point of view conclusively.

But there is another consideration. The policy of raising interest rates to curtail inflation is now being followed in a new environment; the public debt has grown large. When Mary's little lamb grows to a size far surpassing an elephant, can it appropriately be treated any longer as a little lamb? If Mary does so, may she not be endangering the house she lives in, the school house, the lives of her schoolmates, the teacher and herself? Rising short-term interest rates produce rising medium-term and longer-term rates, and rising rates mean declining prices of Government securities. Many holders of government securities have been encouraged to believe that no one could take a loss on these issues; though, of course, no contract or commitment exists that prices will never go down. There is a risk that falling government security prices, with below-par quotations for a number of issues, may make for dissatisfaction among holders, with consequent sales (or presentation to the Treasury for redemption of demand issues) and declining willingness to invest in such issues in the future.

The present is a very unhappy time for such a question to be raised. The present is just on the eve of a period of years in which the vast amount of 10-year securities sold to finance World War II must be refinanced, when the volume of short-term debt is large, and when international conditions might require new and sizable deficit financing. During the next few years the Treasury must find buyers for literally many hundred billions of dollars of government issues. If prospective buyers question the attractiveness of the paper, then the banking system, including the Federal Reserve, will of necessity become the buyers, because it is inconceivable that the Treasury would be left without necessary funds. In that event, the money supply would be substantially increased, and this would be inflationary. The possibility, therefore, exists that very much of a rise in interest rates at this time might prove to be inflationary rather than anti-inflationary as intended, because of the change in the environment from the times when traditional central banking and orthodox economic theory were formulated.

But there is another aspect to the matter. Inflation, i.e., loss of purchasing power by the dollar, may also cause a diminution in willingness to hold promises to pay dollars in the future. Inflation already has raised questions about the desirability of holding government securities, and the further inflation proceeds, the greater may be the Treasury's difficulty in doing the refunding and financing it has to do in the next several years. And, in addition, inflation increases the cost of goods and labor.

Viewing these various aspects of the matter, I conclude that the most important consideration to government finance is that inflation be halted. If it is not, I judge that the Treasury is likely to experience considerable trouble during the next several years. This conclusion can be reached with confidence, however one may feel about the efficacy of changing interest rates as an anti-inflationary technique. I shall return to the question of technique later. But it should also be noted that serious deflation, which does not now seem likely for a long time to come, would also be quite harmful to the Treasury, and its prevention, as well as that of inflation, should be part of the continuing objective.

For purposes of completeness, I should add two points to these comments on government finances. First, higher interest rates mean that the Treasury will have to pay a higher interest cost than would otherwise be the case. Second, rising short-term rates mean that longer term issues are made less attractive to buyers relatively, so that any refunding of short paper into longer paper by the Treasury is made more difficult. But these are evidently of subordinate importance to the larger question just developed; and the higher interest cost argument has been tremendously over-exaggerated.

3. *Economic stability.*—The chief "specific implications and long-run effects . . . in the stability of the

economy in following at this time a policy of allowing interest rates on short-term Treasury issues to rise" also relate to inflation control.

The time which has elapsed since the rise in rates was started has been very short, and the phenomena which have appeared can properly only be noted for consideration along with subsequent events which will provide greater perspective. Subject to this treatment are two items: (a) The Federal Reserve, in the weeks since the interest rate rise was started, has had to buy about $1.2 billion of government securities to maintain orderly market conditions; and during the period has turned from a seller of long-term issues to a buyer. (b) During this time the commercial loans of the commercial banks have continued to rise, which was under way prior to the action, and the total of such loans outstanding has reached a new high level for many years. These developments do not indicate immediate success in credit curtailment, and they raise the question whether limited increases in interest rates in the new environment of the vast public debt have any effect on the ability or willingness of the banks to accommodate their customers. Is the availability of credit significantly affected?

Yet such questions should not in any way obscure the fact that the interests of economic stability, just as the interests of government finance, require that inflation be halted, that if the decade of the 1950's is marked by any such robbery of the dollar as was the preceding decade, the United States will be harmed economically, and as well politically, internationally, socially, morally, and spiritually. And they should not mask the extremely intimate relationship between inflation (and depression) and monetary and credit developments.

4. *What conclusion?*—The territory over which we are now traveling is so new as to make evidence scanty and dogma dubious. Tentatively, and rather gingerly, I would advance the following hypotheses for consideration:

(a) Realization of this country's twin objectives of freedom and prosperity, in an environment including the large public debt and an already seriously depreciated dollar, require careful fiscal policy and operation and more extensive, skillful, and successful monetary management than ever before; and it is more true perhaps than at any previous time that "money will not manage itself."

(1) To the degree that monetary management and fiscal policy are inadequate or fail, the country probably will resort to direct price control, allocation and rationing. These deal only with the results of inflation, which they may suppress for a time; but they cannot prevent or cure inflation. While they may be necessary in a great national emergency, they cannot be used over any prolonged period of strain, and the attempt to do so would be catastrophic.

(b) The necessity for effective monetary management means that every possible technique and device should be utilized.

(1) A rigorous pay-as-you-go fiscal policy in inflationary periods, with strictest curtailment of public expenditures not absolutely essential, and a tax policy designed to stimulate production which is itself a major inflation control, is an essential procedure to prevent further aggravation of the already serious monetary problems.

(2) The central bank should be given and encouraged to seek the greatest possible latitude of operation consistent with the objective of economic stability. Developments, during the weeks since a policy of allowing interest rates on short-term and, to a degree, other Treasury securities to rise was adopted, have provided no conclusive evidence of the efficacy of that policy in halting inflation, which is its objective, and broader considerations also leave the question subject to controversy. This does not mean that the policy should be abandoned, or even that it should not be pursued further, but it does mean that the operation carries sizable risk to government finance and economic stability and should be very cautious.

(3) Because monetary management is so vital, and because the traditional techniques are so inhibited, the development of new techniques and devices is extremely urgent. Some selective credit controls have been utilized in recent years, e.g., consumer credit and stock-market credit, and now mortgage credit. And public-debt management has been utilized a little for monetary-management purposes. I believe

that both these areas could be utilized much more effectively and extensively for and by monetary management, and so deserve more attention.

The Joint Committee on the Economic Report can most appropriately and usefully pursue this subject. The committee has a great opportunity to perform a significant public service.

Began Finished No. words: 1700

$$\underline{\hspace{2cm}} \times 60 = \underline{\hspace{2cm}} \text{ W.P.M.}$$

_____ _____ No. seconds:

Checking Comprehension

1. This statement is Mr. Woodward's opinion on the advisability of (a) lowering the interest on long-term Treasury issues, (b) raising the interest on long-term Treasury issues, (c) lowering the interest on short-term Treasury issues, (d) raising the interest on short-term Treasury issues.

2. One of the "transcending imperatives" that Mr. Woodward mentions is that (a) freedom must be protected, (b) the present "boom" must be continued, (c) a more conservative government must come to power, (d) a less conservative government must come to power.

3. Two developments have occurred during the two past decades which have a bearing on the question being discussed. One is that the value of the dollar has fallen. The other is that (a) population has increased, (b) imports have decreased, (c) the public debt has grown enormously, (d) taxes are higher.

4. The question which the writer was asked to discuss consisted of two parts. One part had to do with government finances. The other part had to do with (a) interest on loans, (b) selling treasury bonds, (c) bank policies, (d) economic stability.

5. The possibility exists that a rise in interest rates at this time might be (a) anti-inflationary, (b) inflationary, (c) stabilizing, (d) not felt at all.

6. There are two viewpoints in regard to the functioning of rising or falling rates on our economy. Evidence (a) supports both of these points of view, (b) doesn't

validate either point of view conclusively, (c) supports one point of view more directly than the other, (d) has nothing to do with either point of view.

7. The most important consideration in government finance is to (a) halt inflation, (b) maintain prosperity, (c) avoid too many controls, (d) bring business techniques into government.

8. Prior to Mr. Woodward's statement, increased interest rates on short-term loans had been in effect for several weeks. It is pointed out that during this time commercial loans had (a) declined, (b) continued to rise as before, (c) remained constant, (d) continued to rise, but at a lower rate than before.

9. The policy of allowing interest rates on short-term Treasury securities to rise (a) should be intensified, (b) should be discontinued immediately, (c) should be continued with caution, (d) is neither recommended or not recommended.

10. In the field of monetary management, the author says there is a need for (a) another expert opinion, (b) a survey, (c) new techniques and devices, (d) the hiring of more experts by the government.

Answers: 1)——, 2)——, 3)——, 4)——, 5)——, 6)——, 7)——, 8)——, 9)——, 10)——.

See Answer Key on page 285.

Rate: W.P.M. ——— Comprehension Score: ———

Selection 3

BEGINNING TIME: ———
HR.——— MIN.———

GENERAL INTRODUCTION[16]

This report is prepared in response to a letter from the chairman of the Joint Committee on the Economic Report requesting a survey of foreign experience in the field of treasury-central bank relationships.

Almost all countries have central banks, and in all

[16] *General Credit Control, Debt Management, and Economic Mobilization*, U.S. Govt. Printing Office, Appendix I, p. 80.

cases these institutions are separate and distinct from the treasury departments of their governments. The function performed by central banks in all countries is to regulate the supply of money in such a way as to serve national interests. Activities of central banks, designed to influence or control the availability of loan funds, necessarily affect interest rates paid by private and governmental borrowers. Conversely, actions designed to affect interest rates have repercussions upon the supply of credit. Because of the great importance of public debts in the financial structure of most countries, the need for coordination between monetary and credit policies, on the one hand, and public-debt management and fiscal policies on the other, has been recognized in almost all countries. Methods of working out a harmoniously-functioning relationship between treasury and central bank have varied widely. There is wide diversity also in the devices adopted in foreign countries to restrict the over-all supply of credit within the framework of policies which take account of large-scale financing needs of treasuries.

This survey of foreign experience is designed to provide background material for the study of problems of monetary policy in the United States. It will be immediately apparent, however, that devices which may have worked well in foreign countries may not be suitable here. Differences in political, economic, and financial structure between the United States and foreign countries, as well as among the foreign countries themselves, are so profound that a comparison of national monetary policies serves primarily to bring into sharper focus the peculiarities of national problems.

To illustrate this point, it may be well to review briefly some of the principal differences in underlying conditions among the countries whose experiences will be described below and between them and the United States.

Differences in economic structure and development are possibly most important in accounting for the lack of comparability of treasury-central bank relationships among various countries. Thus, in countries where there are highly developed money and capital markets, issues concerning monetary and debt management policies tend to revolve around questions of the interest-rate structure, since the rate structure affects, on the one hand, demand and supply factors in the money market and, on the other, the rates at which the treasury can place its obligations with investors other than the central bank. But in countries where the central bank is the principal source of funds for financing government deficits, market rates of interest are of less importance for debt management; in these countries agreement must be reached as to the amounts that can be advanced by the central bank to the treasury in view of the unstabilizing effect of these advances on the economy. Again, in a country where hyperinflation or currency reform has virtually wiped out the public debt, monetary problems are of a different nature from those characteristic of a country where the public debt is large in relation to national income and is widely dispersed among both bank and nonbank holders.

Wide differences among the various types of banking systems must also be recognized. Credit control techniques that are adequate in a country with a highly centralized multiple-branch banking system, in which bank policies can be influenced by direct contact and suasion, may be of little help in a country whose banks are numbered in the thousands. Also, differences in banking traditions and attitudes, such as the extent to which banks are willing or reluctant to hold long-term government securities or to borrow from the central bank, may mean that policies that are effective in some countries will not work elsewhere.

Began Finished No. words: 640

—— × 60 = —— W.P.M.

———— ———— No. seconds:

Checking Comprehension

1. This report covers the relationships in foreign countries between treasuries and (a) small banks, (b) central banks, (c) commercial banks, (d) savings banks.

2. The institution of the central bank exists (a) in all foreign countries, (b) in almost all foreign countries, (c) in a few foreign countries, (d) in no foreign countries.

3. The function of the central bank is to (a) regulate

the supply of money, (b) keep smaller banks from financial difficulty, (c) handle the government's payrolls, (d) take care of the national budget.

4. The survey of foreign experience in banking was designed to (a) bring the United States into closer relationships with foreign countries, (b) find out how much these banks are aiding their government, (c) provide background for the study of monetary policy in the United States, (d) find out the average interest charged abroad.

5. Devices which have worked well in foreign countries (a) should be adopted here, (b) should be used in communist countries, (c) reveal how banks are aiding their government, (d) may not be suitable here, (e) reveal the average interest rate charged abroad.

6. The most important factor in accounting for incomparability of banks is (a) differences in the amount of money they handle, (b) differences in debts they owe, (c) differences in rate of interest charged, (d) differences in economic structure and development.

7. Another factor which must be recognized in considering differences in banks is (a) size of cities in which they are located, (b) the various types of banking systems used, (c) the climate of the country, (d) the products of the country.

8. In countries where there are highly-developed money and capital markets, policies tend to revolve around questions of the (a) interest-rate structure, (b) amounts of money advanced by the central bank, (c) administration of the national budget, (d) determination of wage and price standards.

9. In countries where the central bank is the principal source of funds for financing government deficits, agreements must be reached in regard to the (a) interest-rate structure, (b) amounts of money advanced by the central bank to the Treasury, (c) administration of the national budget, (d) determination of wage and price standards.

10. In some countries the national debt has been wiped out by (a) high taxation, (b) low government spending, (c) hyperinflation or currency reform, (d) deflation.

Answers: 1)——, 2)——, 3)——, 4)——, 5)——, 6)——, 7)——,
8)——, 9)——, 10)——.

See the Answer Key on page 285.

Rate: W.P.M. ———— Comprehension Score: ————

Selection 4

BEGINNING TIME:————————
HR.———————— MIN.————

CIGARETTES[17]

Sixteen cigarettes of each 'brand, each cigarette from
a different pack, were "smoked" in CU's laboratory tests
for nicotine and tar in cigarette smoke. Twenty-seven
brands, purchased in 19 cities throughout the United
States, were included in the tests. All kinds of cigarettes
were represented: regular-size and king-size; regular-
price, low-price, and premium; the common American
blend and Turkish and Virginia blends; low-nicotine,
denicotinized, and untreated; flavored and mentholated;
and untipped, cork-tipped, ivory-tipped, and filter-
tipped. For so great a variety, most of the differences
were, nevertheless, significant. Several positive conclusions can be drawn from the data.

The kind of tobacco

The test results indicate that the nicotine content of
the smoke from a cigarette is influenced, first of all, by
the type of tobacco used. The cigarette with the least
nicotine in its smoke was one made with tobacco especially developed for its low nicotine content. This
brand, JOHN ALDEN, had an average of only 0.4 milligrams
of nicotine per cigarette in the smoke puffed in by the
laboratory smoking apparatus. (A milligram is about
1/28,000th of an ounce.) Other cigarettes with less nicotine in their smoke than the big-selling brands were in
general those made largely of Turkish tobacco. The low-
priced YORKSHIRE cigarette was as low in nicotine as any
of the Turkish types.

[17] *Consumers Reports*, February 1953, pp. 67-70.

The "popular" brands

The most widely-advertised and widely-sold regular-length cigarettes—CAMELS, LUCKY STRIKES, CHESTERFIELDS, PHILIP MORRIS, and OLD GOLDS—were practically identical in the nicotine content of their smoke, which averaged about five times as high in nicotine per cigarette as the smoke from JOHN ALDEN.

The smoke of king-size cigarettes (about 3⅓ inches in length) generally contained about a fifth more nicotine than the smoke of regular-length American brands (about 2¾ inches in length), when both were smoked down to a butt of a little under an inch. When, however, the extra length of the king size cigarette is left unsmoked—that is, when only as much of the longer cigarette is consumed as of a shorter one—the total nicotine from the king-size cigarette is lower. The single exception found—EMBASSY—gave only about as much nicotine as a regular cigarette, even when smoked down to a butt just under an inch.

Most filter-tip cigarettes tested—contrary to the statements in the ads for them—actually had about 20% more nicotine in their smoke than regular brands—as much as that of the typical king-size brands smoked down to about a one-inch butt. Among the filter-tip brands tested, there was the single exception already noted: KENTS were second only to JOHN ALDENS in freedom from nicotine in their smoke, averaging only about one milligram of nicotine per cigarette.

As the smoke passes through it, the tobacco in the cigarette itself acts as a fairly effective filter; CU's tests included a determination of the filtering effect of the length of tobacco which is replaced by other materials in filter-tip cigarettes. Two thirds of an inch of a regular-size cigarette were cut off, and the remainder smoked to the usual extent; 16% more nicotine was found in the smoke than in the smoke of uncut cigarettes.

Some special cases

Slightly above KENT in nicotine content—but appreciably below the big-selling regular brands—were SANO, a "denicotinized" cigarette, MURAD, a Turkish brand, and YORKSHIRE, the Sears brand, which appears similar to the more-widely-sold brands. Two other Turkish cigarettes, HELMAR and MELACHRINO, also ranked between KENT and the big sellers in nicotine content of their smoke, but they were only a little below the popular regular-size American blends.

Some brands—VIRGINIA ROUNDS and CRAVEN A—had a higher nicotine content than the popular brands, probably because of their particular blends of tobacco.

KOOLS, the largest selling mentholated cigarette, are, like so many other brands, promoted as being "mild," but in nicotine content of their smoke KOOLS were about the same as the popular regular brands.

Tars are not found in unsmoked cigarettes but are produced as a result of incomplete combustion. Because of the variability between different cigarettes of the same brand, and because of inherent shortcomings in available test methods, the differences in tar content between brands can be considered only approximate; differences of a few milligrams are of no significance. The tar content of the smoke from KENT cigarettes was found, however, to be consistently low.

Comparison with previous tests

The tests on which this report is based showed a somewhat higher nicotine content for many brands than was found in the limited tests of these brands reported on in June, 1952. CU pointed out at the time that the very small number of cigarettes of each brand tested made those results only approximate. The present results reflect the greater accuracy afforded by the greater number of cigarettes tested. The large difference found in the two tests with respect to KENT cigarettes appears to be mainly the result of a change in the filter during the interval. CU noted last summer that KENTS required "considerably more effort to draw on than do other cigarettes." This characteristic appears now to have been largely corrected with a looser and, therefore, a more permeable filter.

CU's current tests were for nicotine and tar content. Blindfold tests, which have been performed many times by many groups, including CU, and which have almost uniformly shown that smokers cannot with any regularity distinguish among the popular brands by taste, were not a part of this survey. In the course of its investigation, CU did have members of its staff who were habitual smokers try out various brands, but no attempt was made to conceal the names of the cigarettes being smoked. Some of the comments were interesting. With almost no exceptions the smokers showed the same reluctance to shift from their favorite brands that some advertising surveys have shown to exist widely. Many of the smokers said they would not shift from the brand they smoked to some of the brands even if these cost appreciably less.

Filter holders

The filter holders CU tested were the DENICOTEA, in which silica is used as the filtering agent; the MEDICA, in which a roll of paper is used; the PURA-SMOKE, in which alumina is used; the WEBER, in which charcoal is used; and the ZEUS, in which a cigarette in the tube acts as the filter. Two of each brand were tested.

Cigarettes held in the filter holders were "smoked" as for the cigarette tests, and the smoke was collected and analyzed by the same methods. A typical regular-size cigarette was used. Each holder was "smoked" on a run of five cigarettes. The two brands which proved most effective on the initial run—the ZEUS and the DENICOTEA —were further tested for their effectiveness when the same filters were used without change for longer runs. The filtering action of the DENICOTEA was determined for the last five of 15 cigarettes, and the effectiveness of the ZEUS for the last five of 20. Both were found effective even after such long use. (The DENICOTEA effectiveness had decreased and the ZEUS effectiveness had increased slightly.)

In length the holders ranged from $3\frac{1}{2}$ to $4\frac{3}{4}$ inches; the long metal tube of the ZEUS holders was found to be more effective by itself in removing nicotine than some of the holders with the filters in them. When used without a cigarette inside as a filter, the ZEUS tube condensed nearly 20% of the nicotine in the smoke from the first five cigarettes smoked.

Most of the members of a panel of smokers who normally did not use cigarette filter holders found the odor of the filters after a few cigarettes extremely unpleasant.

One may have to suffer through a period of building up a tolerance to the odor in order to be able to use one of these filters regularly. Some users found the extra effort of drawing through them objectionable; others disliked the weight of the holders. One found the smoke relatively tasteless, and noted that he smoked more cigarettes when using the filter. While cigarette holders have the advantage of keeping tobacco grains out of the smoker's mouth (an advantage shared by filter-tip cigarettes), they cause the smoke to impinge on a small area of the tongue, which can cause the same "bite" that pipes cause.

One unhappy tendency of smokers who use a filter holder is to smoke cigarettes down to the very end, thus negating at least a part of the nicotine-removing effectiveness of the filter. Another tendency, which has the same effect, is to smoke deeper puffs with a holder than without.

Began Finished No. words: 1360

$$ \underline{\quad\quad} \times 60 = \underline{\quad\quad} \text{ W.P.M.} $$

_____ _____ No. seconds:

Checking Comprehension

1. According to the tests, one of the most important factors that influence the nicotine content of the smoke from a cigarette is (a) the type of tobacco, (b) the treatment of the tobacco, (c) the manner in which the tobacco is packed, (d) the type of paper used.

2. The nicotine content of the smoke of the five most widely-advertised and widely-sold regular-length cigarettes was found to be (a) variable, (b) highest in Camels, (c) lowest in Old Golds, (d) practically identical.

3. In general, the nicotine content of the smoke of king-size cigarettes was (a) about a fifth lower than that of regular-size cigarettes, (b) the same as that of regular-size cigarettes, (c) about a fifth higher than that of regular-length American brands, (d) higher than regular size in some, and lower in others.

4. The nicotine content of most filter-tip cigarettes was found to be (a) about 20% less than that of regular

cigarettes, (b) the same as that of regular cigarettes, (c) about 20% more than that of regular brands, (d) 20% higher than that of king-size cigarettes.

5. Test results for tars in cigarette smoke (a) proved the superiority of king-size cigarettes, (b) proved the superiority of filter-tip cigarettes, (c) proved the superiority of mentholated cigarettes, (d) showed Kent cigarettes to be low.

6. The report refers to a previous test made for nicotine content in 1952. It points out that the results of this test were only approximate because of (a) poor testing methods, (b) insufficient experience in testing, (c) poor equipment, (d) small number of samples used.

7. The study revealed that when a suggestion is made that a smoker change his brand of cigarette, the reaction is (a) willingness to change, (b) willingness to change if the price of the suggested brand is lower, (c) willingness to change if laboratory tests show the suggested brand to have a lower nicotine content, (d) reluctance to change.

8. Two brands of filter holders were tested initially and then were tested again for their effectiveness after long use. After the second test it was found that (a) they were both effective, (b) neither one kept its effectiveness, (c) one brand kept its effectiveness while the other did not, (d) no conclusions could be reached.

9. Smokers who did not use filter holders found that a filter (a) made the smoke taste better, (b) caused the odor to be unpleasant, (c) enhanced the aroma, (d) caused them to smoke fewer cigarettes.

10. According to the article, one unhappy tendency of smokers who use a filter holder is (a) to run out of filters, (b) to hurt their teeth by gripping the filter holder, (c) to smoke cigarettes down to the very end, (d) to smoke more than other smokers.

Answers: 1)——, 2)——, 3)——, 4)——, 5)——, 6)——, 7)——, 8)——, 9)——, 10)——.

See the Answer Key on page 285.

Rate: W.P.M. ——— Comprehension Score: ———

Selection 5

THE CURSE OF TONDO[18]

What happens when a place is cursed? Does the curse linger on through the ages, bringing evil to all who fall under its spell? Is this true of Lake Elsinore in Southern California?

This blue, mystic lake lies in an inland California valley which is teeming and steaming with hot springs. Rimmed by shaggy mountains whose forested crests are reflected in its clear waters, Lake Elsinore is the very personification of peace—but on it rests the curse of Tondo.

Lake Elsinore has had a colorful history. Much of it lies buried in legend, and it is difficult to separate fact from fiction. There have been stories of underground volcanoes on the lake bottom, erupting, killing fish and discoloring the water. There have been tales that, although portions of the lake were shallow even in wet years, other parts are bottomless abysses. There have been stories of a playful sea serpent that lived in its depths.

Long noted for its scenic beauty and health-giving waters, the lake was a famous resort in the Nineties.

But long before the first white man had set foot along the shore of the lake, this part of California had been the home of the Soboba Indians. Their chief was Tondo, a stern and unforgiving man.

He had a daughter, Morning Star, who was in love with Palo, son of the chief of the Palas, a neighboring tribe. The Sobobas and Palas were sworn enemies. For a time the lovers met secretly. Then one day they were discovered by Tondo. His rage was terrible to behold. He forbade the lovers ever to meet again.

Morning Star tried in every way to appease her father's anger, to soften his heart toward Palo. But in time she saw that it was useless; that he would never give his consent to their marriage. Vowing that they

[18] Belle C. Ewing, *The American Mercury*, July 1954, pp. 125-126.

would never be separated, the Indian maid and her lover walked hand in hand into the lake, as the dreary November sun cast long shadows on the land. They were followed by a group of orphan children whom Morning Star had befriended. All walked into the lake, singing the mournful death song of their people, while Tondo stood on the shore and cursed the lovers, cursed the blue water into which they all walked to their death.

Ever since that day it would seem that a jinx has been laid over Lake Elsinore. Old-timers tell of a great upheaval in the lake which caused water to spout into the air like a geyser and turn blood-red. Later, it became known that three hundred springs of boiling mud and water were born in the valley during that upheaval. The springs reeked with sulphur.

Shortly after this, mysterious lights were seen dancing over the water. The Indians declared that the spirits were having a powwow.

For many years after this phenomenon the lake remained peaceful. Then boats were overturned for no apparent reason, and few of their occupants ever returned to tell the story. This continued for several years. At the same time, strong swimmers dived into the lake never to reappear.

In 1833 and again in 1846, fish in the lake suddenly died.

In the spring of 1850 came the Battle of the Gnats. They bred in the water of the lake and swarmed over the land. They invaded the countryside until the harassed inhabitants called for help.

And in this century, in July 1951, the sky-blue waters of the lake vanished like mist before a noonday sun. When the bottom was laid bare there was no trace of a volcano, the bottomless pits, or the other disturbances of legend or fact.

The copious winter rains of 1951-1952 have replenished the lake. But what menace does its haunting beauty hold today? For tomorrow?

The once mighty Sobobas are few now. But the old men swear that their ancestors still haunt the lake; they claim to hear their voices in the rustle of the tules—see them walk across the water, bearing in their hands a spirit light. They nod grizzled heads and murmur that the great Tondo's curse will forever remain upon the lake. Only Time, the wise and silent one, can tell.

Began Finished No. words: 700

$$— \times 60 = —— W.P.M.$$

————— ————— No. seconds:

Checking Comprehension

1. Lake Elsinore is considered by legend to be (a) beautiful, (b) temporary, (c) full of gold, (d) cursed.

2. This lake is located (a) in a volcanic crater, (b) in the desert, (c) in a valley, (d) near the ocean.

3. During the Nineties the lake was famous (a) as a resort, (b) as the center of a mining area, (c) as a stopping place for people going West, (d) as a Pony Express station.

4. Chief Tondo was (a) a kind man, (b) a stern man, (c) a great leader who united two Indian tribes, (d) a bitter enemy of the white men.

5. Probably Chief Tondo's rage was due to the fact that (a) Palo was not wealthy enough, (b) Morning Star was too young to marry, (c) Tondo's tribe and Palo's tribe were enemies, (d) Palo had murdered Tondo's brother.

6. Morning Star and Palo finally (a) married, (b) killed Tondo, (c) killed themselves, (d) walked to their death in the lake.

7. Old-timers tell of a great upheaval in the lake. They say that at that time, the water turned (a) red, (b) blue, (c) green, (d) yellow.

8. When boats were mysteriously overturned in the lake, their occupants (a) swam ashore, (b) righted the boats, (c) had to avoid vicious fish, (d) usually never returned.

9. On two occasions, fish in the lake (a) suddenly died, (b) became plentiful, (c) developed weird shapes, (d) became very large.

10. When the lake dried up in 1951, it was found that (a) there was an old volcanic crater at the bottom, (b) there were deep trenches at the bottom, (c) there

were relics of Indians on the bottom, (d) there were no traces of disturbance on the bottom.

Answers: 1)——, 2)——, 3)——, 4)——, 5)——, 6)——, 7)——, 8)——, 9)——, 10)——.

See the Answer Key on page 285.

Rate: W.P.M. _____ Comprehension Score: _____

Vocabulary Study

Each line extending across the page below contains one word which appears in a selection in this chapter. Two other words appear which are miscellaneous in meaning. There is a fourth word in each list related in meaning to the first word. Underline the related word in each horizontal list.

1. *extempore*	unpremeditated	inadvertently	peremptorily
2. *agitation*	palpitation	instigation	commotion
3. *phenomenon*	eventuality	incontrovertible	marvel
4. *anachronism*	synchronism	simultaneousness	incongruity
5. *scrutinizer*	examiner	inquisitor	intruder
6. *nomenclature*	escutcheon	terminology	heraldry
7. *inventive*	endowment	adulatory	ingenious
8. *perceived*	received	manifested	discerned
9. *preponderantly*	precipitate	dominantly	prevalence
10. *interpolation*	insertion	diminution	abatement
11. *languish*	attenuate	curtailment	pine
12. *tentative*	indubitable	provisional	enigmatic
13. *efficacy*	puissance	omnipotence	opalescence
14. *infringe*	implicit	encroach	include
15. *transcending*	surpassing	culminate	pre-eminently

Check your answers with the Answer Key on page 285.

Follow-Up Practice

Using materials of your own selection. Continue with your regular practice periods each evening. Devote some of your practice time to improving your speed and comprehension in reading nontechnical material and some to improving your ability to read and recall detailed facts. Keep a record of your speed and comprehension in reading both types of material.

In all the reading you do in connection with your duties, continue to apply the techniques that you have learned up to this point, including the new technique of identifying patterns of writing. As soon as you pick up something to read, decide upon the pattern, then read in accordance with the author's design. The continuous application of this technique to every situation should contribute much to your skill in reading all types of material.

CHAPTER 9

THE KNACK OF SKIMMING

Swallows Skim—So Can You!

The swallow skims swiftly through the air, catching and devouring insects while simultaneously flapping his wings to propel his body. He even drinks as he skims along over brooks, ponds, and rivers, gathering drops of water in his beak with no cessation in flight. This versatile creature doesn't pause or labor over any one insect or any one pool.

The swallow's mode of skimming for food and water may be likened to the method used by skilled readers who skim over the pages of print, gathering what they want as they "fly" along. With instruction and practice a reader can become extremely adept in "catching" what he desires from reading while "on the wing." This is the type of reading in which some people cover 1,000 words per minute and are able to repeat the gist of what they have read.

What Can Skimming Do for You?

There is no reading asset of greater value to the present-day adult than this highly-developed skill. Skimming enables a person quickly to select material which he wants to read and to discard that in which he is not interested or which is inconsequential to his purpose. The ability to skim expertly makes it possible for the businessman to clear his desk rapidly. If he is skilled in skimming, just a few swift glances will enable him to segregate and organize a miscellaneous pile of papers. Quickly he can toss into the basket those materials which hold no interest for him, stack in a pile those things which he needs to read carefully, and place in another pile those pieces which he may later skim once more for main ideas. Probably two thirds of the stack on his desk (and this includes correspondence) can be disposed of through the skimming technique.

Clearing a desk quickly is not the only function of skimming. All of us find the skimming technique useful in newspaper and magazine reading. We skim to find the articles we wish to read and those which we prefer to skip. Probably almost everyone has developed some initial skill in skimming, through contacts with newspapers and magazines.

Skimming is useful also in choosing a book to read, whether it is fiction or nonfiction. It is advisable to skim through several different books for general impressions. Such a procedure yields guidance in the choice of the book which seems to hold the best promise of personal satisfaction and pleasure. In selecting a factual chapter or article, either in a book or magazine, it is helpful to be able to locate a topic of special interest by skimming.

Rarely does the person who is skillful in skimming complain that he doesn't have time to cope with the mass of reading material which confronts him.

Techniques of Skimming

While skimming is the most useful of the reading skills, it is also the most complex. Skimming is a hierarchy built upon and utilizing all other reading skills which have been discussed in this book. That is why this chapter on skimming was delayed until the other skills had been presented. There is no easy trick which will enable you immediately to become an expert in skimming. All you have done so far has built the foundation, and new techniques will be suggested in the pages that follow. A high degree of proficiency can come only as a result of stepped-up practice in applying both the old and the new techniques in the right proportions at the right times.

Some specialists use the term *scanning* to designate the process of quickly locating a particular fact or figure within a selection, while the term skimming is used for the process of quickly passing over an entire selection or passage to get a general impression of it. The difference is in the purpose rather than in the process. For this reason both are treated in this chapter under the general heading of skimming.

Applying Skills Previously Learned

A strong, leading-on purpose is absolutely essential in successful skimming. Your intent in reading must be clearly formulated and kept uppermost in your consciousness, for how can you skim unless you know what you are skimming for? Is it to find something which you may enjoy as recreational reading? Is it to find an informative article which will contribute to your business, professional, or general knowledge? Is it to find main ideas or just one specific fact? Is it to grasp the meaning of something to which you must give attention in your office communication? Whatever your reason, cleave to it throughout your skimming process.

The procedures suggested in regard to speed reading have special significance for you now. In skimming you need to force your speed, to accelerate your reading tempo far beyond that used in your fastest reading of even easy material. In skimming you really "fly" over the pages, but you should learn effective procedures for getting what you want while "flying," or the flight will be wasted effort.

Recognizing the signposts, finding main ideas, previewing, detecting patterns of writing, searching for and remembering clusters of related details are all techniques which you call into action as you skim for different purposes. You have no doubt mastered these techniques by now, and you can now integrate them into your new stepped-up super-speed skimming.

Knowing how to preview, for example, will often

serve you as the first step in your skimming process. If it is a book that you wish to skim, flash your eyes over the table of contents to get an over-all view of the material which the book contains and to decide whether you would be interested in the book as a whole or just in certain chapters. If the book doesn't have a table of contents, flick the pages through hastily for fleeting glimpses at the chapter titles. Should any of the titles intrigue you, note subheadings and visual aids, if any are provided.

If this book is factual in nature, it will probably contain an index. Suppose you are interested in finding information about just one topic. It is possible that this information can be found only in one paragraph, so consult the index for the one word that names the topic, then turn quickly to the designated page, and read.

The preview procedure not only provides you with a skimming technique for rapidly grasping information about a book, chapter, or article as a whole, but it also enables you to discard or select sections if you decide to dip into the text. So, in all of your skimming, preview first.

If, after the preview, you decide to skim a chapter, then two other techniques that you have learned will be your useful allies: 1) finding the main idea, and 2) identifying patterns of writing.

If the author has used the relating-experience or the imparting-information pattern and you wish only to get his most important ideas, quickly locate the main idea in each paragraph. Sweep your eyes straight down the middle of the page or column until you find in each paragraph the phrase that names the topic of the paragraph and tells what this subject does, what happened to it or what property it possesses which makes it worth a paragraph. Once the main idea is found, flash your eyes to the next paragraph, locate the important idea there, and so on. With practice you can become highly skilled in skimming for main ideas. Watch out for the signposts, though, as you race along. If you note the go-ahead and turn-about words, you will not have to retrace your steps.

Should the author's pattern be the question-answer, the opinion-reasons, or the conclusion-facts type, then the pattern can facilitate your skimming process in locating the important idea. Should the pattern be that of question-answer, perhaps you will wish to skim only to find the answer or answers and won't bother about the details. If the pattern is that of opinion-reasons, maybe you will wish to skim only for the opinion or opinions and will not care to read the reasons. Should the pattern be of the conclusion-facts type, possibly you will care only to grasp the conclusion as quickly as you can and will be satisfied to omit the facts that substantiate the conclusion.

Referring again to the question-answer pattern, in skimming a very good use can be made of this pattern by changing each subheading into a question and then skimming for the answer to the question.

These techniques can be used in situations in which you are interested in finding main ideas, opinions, conclusions, or answers to questions. There may be situations, however, in which you want to skim for a certain detail or cluster of details. In such cases skim until you find the section of content that deals with the detail or details in which you are interested, and then use your techniques for grasping related clusters of details. Should you find it important to remember the details, apply your techniques for recalling them.

New Skills to Learn

Developing a new attitude toward reading is a prime requisite in learning to skim at a high speed. This new attitude is a combination of resigned willingness to pass hastily over a page without reading all that it has to say and of release from a feeling of guilt because you haven't done thorough reading. For many people whose daily work requires meticulous reading, such as editors, lawyers, physicians, and scientists, considerable effort and will power is necessary to "break loose" and cover quantities of material without reading every word.

There is much reading that must be done meticulously, of course, but most people could skim through, without loss, a great deal of the material they now read carefully. To do this, one must cut all moorings with past reading habits and recklessly take a chance at merely catching snatches of printed symbols here and there. It is necessary to cultivate an attitude of abandon while engaging in the high-powered skill of skimming.

In so far as new techniques are concerned, the first is that of skimming for main ideas *only*. Ignore all content in a selection except the main idea in each paragraph. This will be your first experience in this book at skipping over large sections of content. Do this with no feeling of restraint. Be satisfied to find the main ideas only and rush on.

Another new technique is that of making use of *key words* only. Certain words are important in conveying the general meaning of a selection, and others aren't. Developing skill to read only the key words and omitting all words of lesser importance greatly facilitates skimming.

And you should use a new pattern of eye movements —the pattern in which you sweep your eyes from the top to the bottom of pages. No doubt you have developed excellent speed by this time in reading horizontally from left to right. The next step is to develop skill in making fleeting eye sweeps vertically. The old habit of reading from left to right has been ingrained in your nervous system since childhood, and it may be difficult to develop vertical eye movements to a point at which they are as facile and fleeting as your horizontal eye movements.

Normally, our eyes move from left to right across the page, and for this reason all of us are accustomed to using our *lateral* field of vision. We fixate at a point on a line and read all the words we can see at the left and right of this fixation, then move on to another fixation and repeat the perception process. But it happens that we also possess a vertical field of vision which usually lies dormant in so far as reading is concerned. It is possible to cultivate this to take in words above and below the point of fixation, as well as at the left and right of it. Undoubtedly the phenomenal skimmers who claim they can grasp 3,000 or 4,000 words per minute make use of their vertical field of vision.

The formerly-learned skills to be integrated into the new procedures are forcing your speed, heeding signposts, finding main ideas, detecting patterns of writing, grasping clusters of details, and impressing them upon your mind. The new attitude and skills which you are to develop are (a) cultivating a willingness to skip large portions of content, (b) making use of key words, (c) developing facility in using a vertical pattern of eye movements, and (d) developing ability to use your vertical field of vision.

Cultivating the habit of skipping large sections of content. In working through the two selections below, resign yourself to passing over large portions of text with no attempt to find out what is said in the parts you are skipping.

Also make a conscious effort to speed up your vertical eye movements. Try sweeping your eyes down through the print on any one page and up to the top of the next page just as fast as it is physically possible for you to do so.

Skimming for Main Ideas

In this selection skim for main ideas only and omit everything else.

1. Preview the title and subheadings.
2. Decide upon the pattern of writing.
3. Formulate your purpose for reading the article. For practice purposes let's agree that you want to read to find the answer to the question, "What was the hoax?"
4. Grasp the main idea in each paragraph as quickly as you can, then sweep your eyes with high speed straight to the next paragraph, grasp the main idea in that paragraph, and so on. Pay no attention to anything but main ideas.
5. Time yourself allowing a total of one minute. Stop at the end of one minute whether or not you have finished.

6. Take the comprehension test which is based upon main ideas only.

Selection 1

BEGINNING TIME:_____
HR._____ MIN._____

THE FAMOUS FOSSIL HOAX[1]

The hoax of the Wurzburg fossils, a far-reaching piece of foolery perpetrated two hundred years ago by German university students, ranks in ingenuity with the "Balloon Hoax," the *New York Sun* "Moon Hoax," and other celebrated practical jokes of history.

The butt of the fossil joke was a serious-minded old professor, Johann Beringer, who held an honorable position as a Doctor of Philosophy and Medicine in Wurzburg University. The doctor, highly respected for his learning and studious habits, was appointed private physician to the reigning Prince Bishop of the old university town. He was distinguished as a scholar and writer in the fields of zoology, botany, and medicine.

Of all the problems then engaging scientific minds, none had caused more contention than the origin and meaning of fossils. It was claimed by some that the creation of fossils was due to an unknown influence of the stars. Another theory explained fossils as the remains of oceanic animals and plants stranded on the land by the Flood. It was not until about 1800 that it was determined that fossils were relics of animal and vegetable life that existed in prehistoric times and had become entombed in rock, in frozen mud, in the beds of rivers, even in the soft gum of conebearing trees.

The science of paleontology, or the knowledge of fossils, attracted Professor Beringer. He advanced an original theory that fossils were merely a capricious fabrication of the Creator, placed in the earth to test human faith. He was so keen about this pet notion that some of his pupils at the university could not forbear playing a trick on the old professor.

With the connivance of some of his own colleagues, the students prankishly fashioned "fossils" out of clay

[1] Leon Augustus Hausman, *The Mentor*, February 1922, pp. 40-42.

and hid them among the rocks of a hillside where they knew Beringer used to roam around on geological exploration. It was not long before the venerable professor chanced upon the fictitious deposits during one of his walks. Completely deceived, overjoyed at his discovery, Beringer hurried back to the university and exhibited the organisms he had found.

The jokers, perceiving with glee the success of their jest, now went further and buried the most fantastic figures their imaginations could suggest. Not content with these they even buried inscriptions, worked out on "fossil" shells, one of them being the name of God himself, in Hebrew!

Professor Beringer's elation upon the discovery of these latter forms knew no bounds. He was now completely convinced of the soundness of his doctrine, and made ready to publish the results.

The semireligious fervor of the honest old scholar swept all before it. Despite the advice of level-headed friends, he hurried his ponderous work to completion.

And now for the strangest part of the story. The jesters came forward and confessed. They exposed all they had done. To their confusion, Beringer refused to listen. The hoaxers reiterated their statements that the whole thing was a colossal joke. Beringer could not be convinced. He conceived this as a base trick of his adversaries. He suspected them of trying to rob him of the glory of proclaiming his discoveries and establishing the truth of his theory. He hurried into print. His *magnum opus* appeared!

The entry of the volume into the world of learned literature was heralded by a shout of laughter! The author's name became a byword in the universities of Europe. Some declared his book was only an attempt to fool the scientific world, others set it down as the product of a mind diseased.

Copies of the weighty volume, printed in Latin, bore the title *The Figured Stones of Wurzburg*, and was illustrated with "marvelous likenesses of two hundred figures, or rather, insectiform stones." It was published in Wurzburg in 1726. The pompous dedication, full nine pages long, is to Christopher Francis, Prince Bishop of Wurzburg. After the dedication and the preface, comes the body of the work, descriptive of Beringer's discovery of the fossils, the manner of their exhumation and examination, the account of the attempt of his colleagues to dissuade him from the work, and the description and significance of the "fossils" themselves. At the end of the volume are plates. . . .

For a time there was question in some parts of the scholastic world as to whether or not Beringer's book was of value, a condition which spurred the deceived scientist to greater efforts in his own defense.

But, as the truth became generally established, Beringer himself was finally undeceived. The blow staggered him; he was overwhelmed.

From the pinnacle of learned dictatorship, which he had formerly occupied so securely, he beheld himself tumbled headlong, almost in a night.

In a frenzy he attempted to buy up all copies of his book that had been issued. His most assiduous efforts were futile, however. Finally he desisted and surrendered to despair. His life's work was treasured and exhibited by many as an object of ridicule.

The broken-hearted scientist fell ill under the strain and died shortly afterward, with the laughter of the scientific world ringing in his ears.

Even after Beringer's death there was no end to the tragic joke. A bookseller, one Hobhard of Hamburg, seeing an opportunity to make capital out of Beringer's misfortunes, bought up all available copies and not only reissued them, but compiled a second edition which achieved a large circulation!

Checking Comprehension

1. The hoax of Wurzburg (a) boomeranged on the perpetrators instead of hitting its mark, (b) ranks with the greatest practical jokes of history, (c) brought eventual fortune to the man at whom the joke was aimed, (d) was really not a hoax in the true sense of the word.

2. The butt of the joke was (a) a university student, (b) a professor, (c) a physician, (d) a minister.

3. The science of paleontology is concerned with (a) bacteria, (b) the planets, (c) medicine, (d) fossils.

4. The jokers fashioned their fossils out of (a) soap, (b) wax, (c) clay, (d) wood.

5. The hoax was perpetrated by (a) Beringer's colleagues, (b) students with the connivance of his colleagues, (c) students without the knowledge of his colleagues, (d) none of the foregoing.

6. The jokers (a) placed their most fantastic figures on the professor's desk, (b) placed them on a stairway leading to his classroom, (c) buried their second batch in a place where Beringer would discover them, (d) placed them in a glass case containing fossils.

7. When Beringer discovered the fossils he (a) was delighted, (b) ignored them, (c) returned them to whom he considered to be the rightful owner, (d) recognized them as fakes.

8. When Beringer was informed about the hoax, he (a) refused to believe it at first, (b) withdrew from the university staff, (c) wrote a public confession and apology, (d) went into seclusion.

9. After finding the fake fossils, Beringer (a) punished the jokers, (b) gave lectures on the discovery, (c) published a book, (d) sent articles to a newspaper.

10. In the end Beringer (a) convinced others that he was right, (b) received recognition from other scientists, (c) died because of the strain which accompanied his discovery of the truth about the fossils, (d) tried to capitalize financially on the sale of his books.

Answers: 1)——, 2)——, 3)——, 4)——, 5)——, 6)——, 7)——, 8)——, 9)——, 10)——.

See the Answer Key on page 285.

Comprehension Score:————

Skimming for a Cluster of Details

In this next selection you will use a technique for grasping detailed facts about some *one* item under a title, ignoring everything else in the article. Use your vertical eye movements in skimming the pages from top to bottom until you find the paragraph or paragraphs concerning the phase of the topic in which you are interested. Then use the techniques which you learned for grasping details. If you wish to remember the details, use the techniques to impress them upon your mind.

Suppose that while you are looking through a magazine you come upon this informative article, "Stalking a Hurricane." You don't care about reading details concerning hurricanes in general, but you are interested in that phenomenon called "the eye of the hurricane," and you want to obtain specific details about it.

With this purpose in mind:

1. Skim through the article, using vertical eye movements at your highest speed, until you come upon mention of "the eye of the hurricane." Don't try to read any of the text until you find this particular section. And don't worry because you skip paragraph after paragraph without knowing what they say.

2. When you find "the eye" slow down, reading and absorbing each detail about the eye of the hurricane and fitting each detail into a pattern of relationships to the main idea and to one another. Of course you should do this detailed reading as fast as you can and still be sure you are grasping all details.

3. When you reach the point in which nothing more is said about "the eye," stop reading.

4. Allow yourself no more than one minute for this exercise. If you can do it in less time, so much the better.

5. After you have read for the specified length of time, take the comprehension test which in this case is concerned *only* with details concerning the eye of a hurricane.

Selection 2

STALKING A HURRICANE[2]

Why are there fewer deaths and less property damage from hurricanes? Are the "big winds" getting weaker? Or fewer in number?

[2] E. John Long, *Science Digest*, September 1953. (Reprinted from *Nature*, August 1953.)

Not at all. The hurricane remains one of the most powerful forces on earth. During the 1952 hurricane season, six of these colossal whirlwinds roared through the American tropics with momentum enough to carry several of them on into northern areas as the worst storms of the year. But property damage set no records, and no deaths could be attributed directly to any of them.

Yet in 1935 a hurricane whiplashed across Florida and the dead totaled 400. In 1928 another Florida hurricane took 1,800 lives. At Galveston, Tex., in 1900, a hurricane killed more than 6,000, and as late as 1942 casualties from the big winds were still numbered in scores.

The explanation of reduced casualties and smaller property damage in recent years is, in three words, *better advance warning*. . . .

During the progress of a major hurricane the Miami Hurricane Warning Center, for example, issues four "advisories"—weather versions of a wartime communique—daily, based on reports received during the previous six hours. Each Weather Bureau office in the network then distributes the forecast as widely and as rapidly as possible. Precautions against hurricane damage—such as boarding up houses and shops, flying planes to safer regions, moving small craft, etc.—are expensive, so everyone wants to know: "Is it the real thing?"

In the meantime a search plane has made contact with the enemy. Far ahead through the rain squalls the pilot sees a dark, ominous-looking mass of whirling clouds, mist, and water that seems to reach up into the heavens and stretches fully 30 miles from side to side.

When the plane radios confirmation of the hurricane's existence, the first act of the Hurricane Warning Center is to give it a name. If this is the second hurricane of the season, it might be called "baker," from the International Phonetic Alphabet used in radio voice communications. The first might have been called "Able," the third might be "Charlie," etc.

Because a hurricane's safest point of entry is usually its westward side, the plane approaches from the west. And from now on, every 15 minutes information obtained from meteorological instruments and by radar will be radioed to Miami.

The pilot brings the plane down to an altitude of 800

feet—or even to 400 feet if visibility is poor. The plane shudders and shakes as it bucks the outer rings of light thunderstorms and 35-mph winds which try their hardest to drive it southward.

After nearly an hour of sampling the air on the fringes of the hurricane, the pilot heads directly into it. The heavy, four-engined ship pitches and yaws, dives and soars again, until its creaking frame seems to be tearing apart. Sea and sky dissolve in pelting rain and spray, and the shrieking wind drowns out even the roar of the engines, straining at full throttle.

An interminable quarter hour of this—and suddenly the plane breaks through the storm into the clear. All pitching and tossing ceases, the howling gale quiets as if a valve had shut it off, and bright sunshine pours through the drenched windshield. Down below, the sea shows a few whitecaps, but the whole aspect is one of peace and calm. The transition is so sudden and unexpected that it comes as a shock, even to crews who have experienced it many times.

This strange world, called "the eye of the hurricane," is one of the weirdest, most awesome sights on earth. The eye is roughly circular. Its boundary is a vertical curtain of black, reaching from the ocean far up to the open sky above. It is difficult to believe that beyond this ebony cylinder, now 10 to 15 miles in diameter, is a watery chaos, revolving furiously in a counterclockwise direction as it is driven by gales of from 180 to 200 mph.

Strange things have been observed by planes cruising "the eye." Flocks of birds sometimes take refuge there, moving along within the comparative safety of the storm's vortex, which may have a forward motion of only 10 to 15 mph. Ships sometimes seek "the eye" to ride out the worst of the storm's violence before resuming their course. One plane observed a fishing boat, with the crew on deck sunbathing, within a hurricane's eye.

As the hurricane-stalking plane cruises around the eye, the "dropsonde" operator goes into action. As the dropsonde, an instrument dropped from the plane by parachute, slowly descends it automatically records atmospheric pressure, temperature, and humidity of the air, and relays these to the plane by a self-contained radio transmitter.

But now the fuel is getting low, so the pilot plunges back into the black wall of the hurricane, choosing the western or "weak" side, where, experience has taught him, a hearty tailwind can be picked up. Fifteen minutes more of furious buffeting, and the tired crew heads for the barn, clipping through squalls that would be bypassed by ordinary pilots.

Although many hurricanes simply veer back out to sea and finally subside in the colder climate of the North Atlantic, each of them is constantly pursued by watcher planes, which radio back the vital information needed to chart its course and to warn shipping and other planes in its path.

. . . . . .

What actually causes a hurricane?

Scientists have two theories. One, the convection theory, holds that it starts when a large mass of warm air rises in the doldrums of the open Atlantic, east and south of the West Indies. Sea-level air rushes in to replace the vacuum left by the rising warm air. The rotation of the earth deflects the slowly-moving air mass into a counter-clockwise swirl. Soon a vigorous wind system is set up, and a full-blown hurricane is roaring on its way. Although it appears to take generally a westward course, the earth is really moving eastward under it.

The second theory is the counter-current theory. It explains that opposing tradewinds, warm and cold, cause the initial air lift; thereafter it is like the other theory.

Checking Comprehension

Follow the usual procedure in working with the statements below.

1. The adjectives used to describe "the eye" in the article are (a) black, very dangerous, (b) windy, strange, treacherous, (c) weirdest, most awesome, (d) powerful, terrifying.

2. The shape of "the eye" is (a) circular, (b) cylindrical, (c) eliptical, (d) conical.

3. "The eye" is bounded by (a) a black circular band, (b) horizontal black bands, (c) heavy orange lines, (d) a vertical curtain of black.

4. The diameter of "the eye" is (a) approximately 1 mile, (b) approximately 5 miles, (c) approximately 6 miles, (d) 10 to 15 miles.

5. The hurricane is driven by gales (a) 180 to 200 mph, (b) 40 to 60 mph, (c) 400 to 500 mph, (d) 10 to 20 mph.

6. "The eye" is (a) furiously active, (b) drenched with rains, (c) sometimes calm enough so that birds or ships can take refuge in it, (d) cold and snowy.

7. "The eye" (a) has no motion, (b) moves around in circles, (c) moves forward at about 100 mph, (d) may move forward with a motion of only 10 to 15 mph.

8. As the search plane cruises around "the eye" it (a) flies through it and reports its location, (b) flies into it and stays there, (c) avoids it, (d) puts the dropsonde into action.

9. The functions of the dropsonde are to (a) record the direction and velocity of the wind, (b) record the diameter and height of "the eye," (c) record the atmospheric pressure, temperature, and humidity, (d) record the size of the area which the hurricane is covering.

10. When fuel gets low the search plane leaves "the eye" on the western side because (a) the plane is facing the sun, (b) the hurricane is strongest in the west, (c) the "eye" is in the western part of the hurricane, (d) experience has taught him a hearty tailwind can be picked up there.

Answers: 1)——, 2)——, 3)——, 4)——, 5)——, 6)——, 7)——, 8)——, 9)——, 10)——.

The Answer Key is on page 286.

Comprehension Score:_____

Using Key Words in Skimming

Grasping key words is another short cut to the superspeed of skimming for general comprehension. Usually the import of a selection is carried largely through nouns, verbs, adverbs, and adjectives. Familiarity with the English language enables a person who practices the skill mentally to supply words of lesser importance, without stopping to read each one of them.

Examples of words of "lesser importance" are the articles *the*, *an*, and *a*; pronouns such as *you*, *your*, *it*, *they*, *them*, *we*, *my*, *their*, *our*, *his*, *her*; prepositions such as *in*, *of*, *with*, *to*, *by*, *at*, *for*, *from*, *on*, *over*, and *under*; and many other words which are not absolutely essential in "putting across" the stripped-down import of a sentence.

In the selection that follows, the less important words have been omitted.

1. Skim through the key words as rapidly as you can, trying to follow the trend of the author's message.
2. Allow yourself 30 seconds only to skim the article with the use of the key words.
3. Take the comprehension test after you have skimmed the article.

Selection 3

My Neighbor the Hippo[3]

_____ mud hut _____ _____ I lived _____ five years _____ British East Africa _____ situated _____ two miles _____ Lake Elmenteita. _____ remote stretch _____ water remains _____ _____ _____ undisturbed _____ white men. Except _____ _____ _____ naked savage _____ spear _____ club, no human being troubles _____ lives _____ _____ _____ waterfowl _____ scarlet flamingos.

I used _____ wander _____ _____ _____ shores because _____ knew _____ _____ depths inhabited _____ hippopotami. _____ certain seasons _____ sunrise _____ sunset _____ air would resound _____ _____ _____ _____ bellows.

_____ "zee-koes," _____ "cows of the lake," _____ Dutch pioneers call them, seldom leave _____ water _____ _____ daytime, _____ _____ _____ _____ return _____ _____ first indication _____ danger. Throughout _____ _____ _____ noons _____ lounge _____ _____ _____ _____, sometimes floating _____

[3] Llewellyn Powys, *The Mentor*, June 1922, pp. 30-31.

_____ surface, sometimes walking _____ _____ _____
_____ bottom _____ _____ lake, _____ sometimes lying
_____ _____ muddy reach _____ _____ great _____
heads resting _____ each other.

But toward sundown _____ preposterous _____ animals,
growing impatient for _____ land pastures, draw _____
toward _____ shore. _____ can catch sight _____ _____
heads appearing _____ _____ _____ _____ _____, _____
close _____ _____ _____ seem possible _____ cast _____
stone· down _____ _____ _____ mouths _____ yawn
_____ _____ _____ _____ _____ _____. _____ span
_____ _____ hippopotamus's open mouth _____ _____
_____, _____ jawbone _____ _____ _____ _____ _____
four feet.

I used _____ believe _____ _____ never wandered far
_____ _____ _____ _____ _____ midnight excursions, but
_____ _____ _____ _____ _____ _____ _____ found grass
_____ _____ _____ chewed _____ hippos _____ _____
three miles away. _____ moonlight night _____
_____ stood _____ _____ _____ hill _____ observed
_____ country _____ acres around dotted _____ _____
_____ _____ forms moving _____ forward _____ _____
lowered heads _____ enormous mouths drew in _____
_____, _____ _____ grass.

_____ every direction _____ _____ _____ _____ _____
"hippo paths"— _____, _____ _____ tracks _____ led
through _____ rushes _____ brushwood. _____ tracks
_____ distinguished from _____ of _____ rhinoceros;
_____ walking, _____ hippopotamus moves _____ front
_____ hind foot _____ two parallel lines _____ _____
_____ center ground under _____ body _____ not trod-
den _____ _____ _____, _____ so short _____ _____ legs
_____ _____ _____ rainy season, _____ _____ soil gives,
_____ _____ bodies drag _____ earth.

_____ _____ _____, for all _____ grotesque appearance _____
hippopotamus _____ _____ exquisitely designed _____
_____ unusual conditions _____ _____ existence: nature
_____ contrived _____ anatomy _____ _____ _____
_____ _____ _____ eyes, nostrils, _____ ears can remain
above water _____ _____ rest _____ _____ body _____
submerged. _____ _____ ears _____ nostrils _____ _____
fitted _____ _____ valves capable _____ shutting _____
_____ water when _____ sinks below _____ surface.
_____ specific gravity _____ hippopotami _____ such

_____ _____ sink _____ _____ greatest depth without _____ _____ trouble; _____ do not dive, _____ _____ allow themselves _____ disappear like submarines. _____ _____ also good swimmers.

One calf _____ born _____ _____ time. _____sees light first _____ _____ hidden lair _____ _____ rushes near _____ water, _____ _____ mother conducts it shortly after birth.

During _____ infancy _____ mother never remains under _____ water _____ _____ long period, _____ may be seen rising _____ _____ surface _____ _____ _____ _____ little hippo standing _____ _____ wrinkled neck. Hippopotami _____ devoted mothers.

_____ fight between full-grown hippopotami _____ _____ something _____ witness! _____ watched one _____ _____ _____ quarter _____ _____ hour. _____ took place _____ _____ rushes under _____ _____ bank. I had been attracted _____ _____ place _____ _____ succession _____ _____ _____ roars, _____ peered over _____ rocks. _____ _____ early morning. The lake _____ radiant _____ _____ _____ _____ _____ _____ sun, _____ poured down _____ _____ _____ grass, _____ rushes, _____ baboon-haunted ledges _____ _____ _____ _____ _____ amphibia below appeared _____ _____ like two prehistoric monsters, tusking _____ gnawing _____ _____ _____, struggling _____ _____ _____, _____ giving vent _____ _____ _____ _____ snorts _____ must have been heard _____ _____ _____ vultures far up _____ _____ sky.

_____ one time, during _____ _____ dry spell, _____ _____ lake water _____ _____ stagnant _____ ill-tasting, _____ hippo made _____ habit _____ drinking _____ _____ _____ farm troughs. If _____ had been content _____ drink decently _____ would not have had _____ _____ objection, but nothing _____ do him but _____ _____ place _____ _____ feet _____ _____ iron sheeting, bending _____ twisting _____ like tinfoil. _____ actually caught _____ at it one night, _____ rewarded _____ _____ _____ bullet _____ my rifle; but _____ got back _____ _____ lake, _____ _____ _____ _____ _____ three weeks later _____ _____ _____ _____ _____ _____ body came drifting _____ _____ _____ _____ shore. _____ _____ _____ _____ well _____ steer clear _____ dead floating hippopotami, because _____ _____ accumulation _____

gas puts ＿＿＿ ＿＿＿ ＿＿＿ strain ＿＿＿ ＿＿＿ wrinkled
hide ＿＿＿ ＿＿＿ ＿＿＿ explosion takes place. ＿＿＿,
＿＿＿ ＿＿＿ shot one but ＿＿＿ regret, ＿＿＿ the mis-
giving that ＿＿＿ ＿＿＿ ＿＿＿ accelerating ＿＿＿ coming ＿＿＿ ＿＿＿ day when ＿＿＿ ＿＿＿ ＿＿＿ ＿＿＿
animals ＿＿＿ ＿＿＿ extinct.

Checking Comprehension

1. The area in which the story takes place is inhabited
only by (a) civilized white men, (b) savages, (c) civilized
Indians, (d) wild animals.

2. The writer, in his wanderings (a) stayed close to
shore because the depths were inhabited by hippopotami,
(b) stayed close to shore to make certain that he would
not lose his way, (c) went out into the center of the lake
in order to observe better the shore movements of the
hippopotami, (d) went to the center of the lake occasionally to observe the hippopotami at close range.

3. The hippopotami come to shore (a) toward sundown, (b) at sunrise, (c) rarely, (d) at noon.

4. During their midnight excursions the hippopotami
(a) stay on the shore of the river, (b) never go more
than a few rods away, (c) travel 10 or 15 miles inland,
(d) have been known to chew grass three miles away.

5. Hippopotami tracks are distinctive in that they (a)
form double parallel lines in the center of the ground
under their body, (b) are heavier than those of other animals, (c) form an irregular pattern, (d) distribute their
footprints at regular intervals.

6. The writer remarks about the anatomy of the hippopotamus by saying that (a) it is most massive, (b) it
is amazingly well equipped for combat, (c) it is exquisitely designed for its mode of living, (d) it varies
from hippopotamus to hippopotamus within the species.

7. A mother hippopotamus (a) frequently abandons
her calf, (b) is sometimes cruel to her young, (c) leaves
the care of the calf to the father, (d) is a devoted mother.

8. The writer shot a hippopotamus one night because
he was (a) tearing up the writer's farm trough, (b)
drinking water at the trough, (c) scaring the farm animals, (d) frightening the writer himself.

9. Three weeks after the shooting (a) the writer discovered the animal alive, (b) the writer found the body in a thicket, (c) the body drifted up on the shore, (d) the incident was repeated with another hippopotamus.

10. After shooting the hippopotamus (a) the writer regretted having accelerated the extinction of hippopotami, (b) claimed that the hippopotamus managed to get back to the water, (c) encountered several other hippopotami to his dismay, (d) tried to help the animal.

Answers: 1)——, 2)——, 3)——, 4)——, 5)——, 6)——, 7)——, 8)   , 9)   , 10)——

The Answer Key is on page 286.

Comprehension Score:_____

Grasping Key Words Only

The unimportant words have been retained in the selection below. You are now ready to take the more advanced step of reading text with the less important words in it but ignoring these words as you skim through, grasping key words only.

1. Skim at your highest speed, reading key words only as necessary in following the trend of thought.
2. Allow yourself exactly two minutes to skim, noting key words exclusively. If you can cover the article in less than two minutes, so much the better.
3. Take the comprehension test at the end of the article.

Selection 4

THE BIRDS' BEAUTY PARLOR[4]

Nature provides no beauty specialists for birds. It is a case of every bird his own manicurist, tailor, and bath attendant.

Frequent baths are an important feature in the daily round of bird life. Anyone that has watched the family canary at his morning plunge knows how thoroughly

[4] Lee S. Crandall, *The Mentor*, May 1929, pp. 49-51.

the work is done. When the bather emerges, he spreads his feathers by means of the delicate muscles provided for the purpose, and, shaking his body with violence, invites the application of air to as much of the surface as possible. The intricate process of rearranging his disordered plumage is accomplished with his beak. When the toilet has been completed, each feather is in perfect alignment, every particle of dirt has been removed; the plumage has the sheen of lustrous silk.

If the dexterity of the canary arouses our admiration, what shall we say of a bird like the pelican? His beak, nearly eighteen inches long, is armed at the tip with a heavy pointed hook. Each feather is drawn through that mighty beak with the utmost delicacy; each crevice is searched as with the finest comb.

Every kind of bird bathes in its own particular way. Where the canary and the sparrow plunge bodily in, the barn swallow dips lightly, cutting graceful arcs over the water.

A few birds never wash in water. Turkeys, pheasants, and the common hen have a deep-seated prejudice against water. Yet they do bathe, in their own fashion, in dust or sand. Everyone has seen the humble hen engaged in the pleasant duty of dusting herself in the warm silt of a country road. Her motions are those of the canary in his tub. Clouds of powdered loam rise gently into the summer air; quantities are sifted through the plumage, suffocating tiny parasites.

Pigeons confine themselves exclusively to water. On the other hand, the "English" or house sparrow, and many of our native species, use both water and dust for cleansing purposes. Often, in crossing a dry back-country pasture, one comes upon an open space dotted with tiny hollows in the dry earth, like diminutive buffalo wallows—the dusting places of field or vesper sparrows.

Greasing the bodies of long-distance swimmers is not a new idea. Ducks have used it for generations. The phrase "like water off a duck's back" refers to the damp-proof quality of the plumage of waterfowl. All ducks seek their living in or about water.

For success in such a life it is necessary for the duck to shed water not only from its back, but from every portion of its body. A duck rises from the water as freely as a land bird from the ground; wet wings would be a serious handicap. As might be expected, the duck accomplishes this desirable result by the use of grease, and he carries his own grease pot. At the base of his tail lies an organ known as the oil gland, which secretes the necessary unguent in sufficient quantity for the purpose. Though ducks spend most of their time in the water, they nevertheless find frequent washing and dressing of the plumage a necessity. After each bath the feathers are arranged with care, and oil is spread throughout.

Birds use powder too. In many groups, notably the herons, the parrots, and some birds of prey, there occur tufts of matted feathers known as powder-down patches. These feathers grow continuously but never fully mature, because their tips constantly break off. The resulting detritus is a fine, greasy powder of much the same consistency as fuller's earth. This powder works its way through every portion of the plumage, adhering closely to the surface of the feathers.

In the herons, the powder-down patches are found in large masses on the breast or thighs, partially hidden by the surface feathers. The African gray parrot, famous for its ability as a mimic, has another point of distinction—it powders its face! This portion of the bird's anatomy is free from feathers, but is always thickly coated with the fine, white product of the powder-down patches.

Just what the full function of this powder may be is not known; in some cases it serves as waterproofing. The pigeons have no definite patches, but certain small feathers of the flanks serve the same purpose, as they slowly disintegrate. The plumage of pigeons is thoroughly saturated with powder, so much so that it remains on the hands if the bird is handled, or will soil a black cloth if it is used to wipe the feathers.

Care of the nails is another refinement practiced in the birds' beauty parlor. Daily contact with earth, sand, and rock keeps pace with the growth of nails or claws, so that they are always of the correct length. Canaries and other cage birds, as well as poultry or pigeons kept on board floors, soon demonstrate the lack of natural trimming. The nails not only become extremely long but also acquire a curious spiral formation, like an exaggerated ram's horn. They must then be manicured (or, rather, pedicured) in the human fashion, or they are likely to become entangled in cage wires with tragic result.

"Scarce as a hen's tooth" is scarce indeed, for hen's teeth are rare. Birds have no need for dentists. Yet the horny sheaths of beaks grow as persistently as do the nails and must be kept trimmed in much the same manner. Constant use in finding and eating food does much of the work, but many birds add the finishing touches by whetting their beaks on wood or stone. A piece of cuttlefish bone is a necessary item in a canary's cage, not only for the lime it supplies but also for use as a grindstone.

In the matter of clothing, birds are rather stingily treated. No bird has more than two full suits a year; some acquire an extra new coat and waistcoat in the spring, but many must make the old ones do. This is why birds are so particular in the care of their plumage. No needle mends their rents; no tailor provides new raiment. Worn or broken feathers are not replaced until the next molt. But, curiously, if a feather is lost completely, the follicle from which it grew is immediately stimulated to action and a new plume is produced, from four to six weeks being required for it to mature.

When hatched most young birds are provided with swaddling clothes of softest down, in varying amount, though some, like the great caciques or oropandulas of tropical America, come into the world quite frankly stark. With song birds, in particular, it is essential that they should be able to leave the nest and fend for themselves as quickly as possible, so the wings must make rapid growth. In from ten to fourteen days most fledglings of this group leave the nest, with the body completely clothed in the first suit of real feathers, the wings well grown, but the tail still stumpy and apologetic, since uncertain wings have little need for a balancing device.

In late summer and early autumn, the time of the great annual molt, all northern birds receive new clothes for old. Youngsters hardly more than two or three months out of the nest doff their juvenile raiment and acquire plumage that usually, though not always, resembles that of adults. Some, like the cowbird, have a complete change, including the wings and tail; others, such as the towhee, waxwing, and catbird renew the small body feathers only, the others remaining the same.

Once this annual change of clothing has been made, many birds must be content with it for a full year. Our two rather shady European immigrants, the house sparrow and the starling, are among those provided with sparse wardrobes. But both of these birds take the canny precaution of adding a suit of overalls, each feather being margined with a broad, dull edge, which hides the brighter colors underneath. During the rigors of a hard winter, these protectors gradually become weathered and worn, and by April have disappeared completely. Then the proud owner stands forth resplendent, his well-burnished spring ensemble glistening brilliantly in the warm sunshine.

Among the birds that enjoy a partial renewal of plumage in spring is the scarlet tanager. At the autumnal molt the adult male exchanges his brilliant red body plumage for a winter overcoat of somber olive, like that of his mate. In early spring the dull body feathers are replaced by the scarlet jacket that makes him the most brightly colored of North American birds.

Few indeed are the varieties of birds that are granted two complete costumes each year. Most conspicuous among these varieties is the bobolink, which leaves us in autumn clothing almost exactly like that his wife and children are wearing, but returns in spring from far Brazil, arrayed in formal bridegroom's regalia of dazzling black and white.

For the most part, birds are satisfied with Nature's allotments and accept such attire as she distributes, be it plain or gaudy. Only one group is known to attempt improvements. This comprises the motmots, tropical birds of jay-like appearance, though not related to those noisy, sagacious creatures. The two central feathers of the motmot's tail project considerably beyond their fellows. When they first appear they seem to be quite normal, except that close examination shows a portion of the web, at each side, to be lightly attached to the shaft. When these feathers have reached nearly their full length, the motmot sets to work, drawing the tips slowly through his beak and constantly picking at them. The effect of these attentions soon becomes evident, for presently the weakened web yields, leaving an inch or more of the shaft quite bare. The tip remains intact, forming a distinct spatula at the end of the feather. This ornament is obviously a source of great delight to its owner, for he sits for hours proudly swinging to and fro his newly decorated tail.

Checking Comprehension

1. Nature has created each bird (a) to be a beauty specialist for himself, (b) naturally beautiful without need of beauty treatments, (c) dependent upon man-made aids to achieve its fullest beauty, (d) dependent upon beauty specialists provided by nature.

2. Regarding bird bathing the author says that (a) some birds don't require bathing, (b) birds have a variety of ways of bathing, (c) bathing is an important daily feature in bird life, (d) some birds require more bathing than others.

3. Birds who never wash in water clean themselves by (a) pulling out soiled feathers, (b) shaking themselves, (c) fluttering in dust or sand, (d) scraping their feathers with their beaks.

4. Greasing their backs is a practice used for generations by (a) pelicans, (b) pigeons, (c) ducks, (d) all birds.

5. The powder that many birds use comes from (a) flowers, (b) certain kinds of fruit, (c) tufts of matted feathers, (d) dried leaves.

6. Manicuring of wild birds' nails is accomplished by (a) shedding the nails, (b) daily contact with earth, sand, and rock, (c) breaking off the nails, (d) doing nothing, since the nails never grow.

7. In the matter of clothing, nature treats birds (a) generously, (b) stingily, (c) a little better than most animals, (d) badly.

8. All northern birds have their great annual molt (a) in the spring, (b) in midsummer, (c) in late summer and early autumn, (d) while they are south in the winter.

9. Birds who are allowed two complete costumes a year (a) are many, (b) are few, (c) do not exist, (d) are extremely rare.

10. The motmot is distinctive in that it (a) receives

three complete sets of feathers per year, (b) has the most beautiful feathers of any bird, (c) has a huge top-knot on its head, (d) decorates its own tail feathers.

Answers: 1)——, 2)——, 3)——, 4)——, 5)——, 6)——, 7)——, 8)———, 9)——, 10——.

See the Answer Key on page 286.

Comprehension Score:———

Skimming with the Use of Vertical Field of Vision

Now you will be introduced to the highest skill in the hierarchy of skills in skimming—that of using your vertical field of vision. The development of this skill enables you to see two or three words or figures or phrases *above* and *below* the point at which your eyes are fixed, without moving the eyes up or down. In making use of this skill you simply hold your eyes in one place and take in everything within your range of vision, *vertically*.

Exercise 1

Grasping three sets of figures in a vertical column. First try to see three sets of figures in a vertical column at one glance.

1. In this vertical column look squarely at the middle figure, and read all three figures *without moving your eyes:*

    12:15
    12:30
    12:45

2. Try doing the same thing in reading the three groups of figures in the lists below that begin respectively with a) 4:00, b) 9:15, c) 11:10, d) 7:15, e) 5:05.

1:15	7:15
1:30	7:30
1:45	7:45

2:15	8:00
2:30	8:25
2:45	8:40
3:00	9:15
3:25	9:30
3:45	9:45
4:00	10:05
4:15	10:35
4:35	10:55
5:05	11:10
5:25	11:35
5:50	11:55
6:00	12:05
6:15	12:15
6:30	12:30

Exercise 2

In this exercise you are requested to use your vertical eye movements and vertical field of vision. But you will also need quickly to switch to the use of your horizontal eye movements and your horizontal field of vision as you work through the exercise. In other words, you will alternate, using your vertical eye movements and vertical field of vision, then your horizontal eye movements and horizontal field of vision. Your speed will depend upon the rapidity with which you can make these changes in your mental and visual processes.

Suppose the radio schedule shown appears in the morning newspaper. You decide you would like to hear the news while you are eating lunch between 12:15 and 12:45. What is the quickest way of finding the station which will present a news program at that time?

1. Preview to locate the heading which tells you which section is devoted to *daytime* programs.

2. Using your vertical eye movements glance down the first column, back to the top of the second column, and down again until you find 12. This should require only two or three sweeps of your eyes.

DAYTIME

7:00—WRCA: News; Bill Cullen
WOR: News Reports
WQXR: Composer Varieties
WABC: Ernie Kovacs Show
WCBS: News; Jack Sterling
WNYC: Sunrise Symphony
WQXR: N. Y. Times News
7:05—WOR: Bright and Early
7:15—WOR: John Gambling
7:25—WABC: News; Ernie Kovacs
7:30—WRCA: News Reports
WCBS: News; Jack Sterling
WQXR: Business Picture
7:35—WQXR: Breakfast Music
7:45—WRCA: Bill Cullen
WCBS: News Reports
WNYC: Weather; News
7:55—WABC: News; Ernie Kovacs
8:00—WRCA: News Reports
WOR WCBS: News
WNYC: Around New York
WQXR: N Y Times News
8:05—WQXR: Breakfast Music
8:10—WRCA: Bill Cullen
8:15—WOR: Dorothy and Dick
WCBS: Bob Haymes Show
8:25—WABC: News; Ernie Kovacs
8:30—WRCA: News; Bill Cullen
8:40—WNYC: Social Security
8:45—WNYC: Food Talks
8:55—WCBS: News Reports
9:00—WRCA: News; Bill Cullen
WABC: News Reports
WCBS: Breakfast Club
WOBS: News; Lanny Ross
WNYC: Masterwork Hour
WQXR: N. Y. Times News
9:05—WQXR: Just Music
9:15—WOR: Second Breakfast
9:30—WRCA: Pegeen Fitzgerald

WOR: McCanns at Home
WCBS: Martha Wright
WQXR: Piano Personalities
9:45—WQXR: Composer Varieties
9:55—WRCA: Visit With Josh
10:00—WRCA: Mary M. McBride
WOR: News Reports
WABC: My True Story
WCBS: Arthur Godfrey Time
WQXR: N. Y. Times News
10:05—WRCA: Dr. Norman Peale
WQXR: Morning Melodies
10:15—WRCA: Weekday; Margaret
Truman, Mike Wallace;
Harold Arlen, Guest
WOR: Martha Deane; Anna
Kross, guest
12:25—WABC: Whispering Streets
10:30—WNYC: You and Health
10:45—WABC: When a Girl Marries
WNYC: Dedication of Library
11:00—WOR: News; Story Time
WABC: Companion
★ WNYC: U. N. General
Assembly
11:05—WQXR: N. Y. Times News
11:15—WQXR: Mid-Morning Music
11:20—WABC: Paging the New
WOR: Queen for a Day
WRCA: News Reports
WNYC: Make Up Your
Mind: Denise Lor, Guest
11:35—WABC: Walt Disney's Magic
Kingdom
11:45—WCBS: Howard Miller
WQXR: Luncheon Concert
11:55—WNYC: News
WRCA: News; Al Collins
12:00—WOR: News; Your Baby
WABC: News Reports
WCBS: Wendy Warren, News

WNYC: Midday Symphony
WQXR: N. Y. Times News
12:05—WQXR: Luncheon Concert
12:10—WOR: Answer Man
12:15—WOR: McCanns at Home
WABC: Frank Farre l Show
WCBS: Backstage Wife
12:30—WOR: News Reports
WCBS: Helen Trent
12:45—WOR: Luncheon at Sardi's
WCBS: Our Gal Sunday
12:55—WABC: WNYC: News
1:00—WABC: Paul Harvey, News
WCBS: Road of Life
WNYC: Famous Artist
WQXR: N. Y. Times News
1:05—WQXR: Midday Symphony
1:15—WABC: Arthur Van Horn
WCBS: Ma Perkins
1:30—WRCA: Sydney Smith
WOR: America; Front Door
WCBS: Young Dr Malone
WNYC: Chemical Society
1:45—WCBS: The Guiding Light
WNYC: Weather; News
1:55—WABC: News Reports
2:00—WRCA: News; Weekday
WOR: Letter to
Lee Graham
WABC: Todd Lawrence
WCBS: Second Mrs. Burton
WNYC: Board of Education
Series
2:05—WQXR: N. Y. Times News
2:15—WQXR: Footlight Favorites
2:25—WABC: Perry Mason
2:25—WABC: News
2:30—WOR: Martin Starr
WABC: Martin Block
Make-Believe Ballroom
WCBS: This Is Nora Drake

WNYC: For the Ladies
WQXR: Alma Dettinger;
Other People's Business
2:35—WOR: Radio Playhouse
2:45—WCBS: The Brighter Day
3:00—WOR: News Reports
WCBS: House Party
★ WNYC: U. N. General
Assembly
WQXR: N. Y. Times News
3:05—WOR: Radio Playhouse
WQXR: Symphonic Matinee
3:30—WRCA: Hotel for Pets
WCBS: Ga-en Drake
3:45—WRCA: The Doctor's Wife
3:55—WNYC: News
4:00—WRCA: Right to Happiness
WOR: Drive East
WCBS: News; Lanny Ross
WNYC: Critics' Choice
WQXR: N. Y. Times News
4:05—WRCA: Concert Hs
4:15—WRCA: Stella Dallas
4:30—WRCA: Widder Brown
WQXR: Jacques Fray
4:45—WRCA: Pepper Young
4:55—WNYC: News
5:00—WRCA: Woman in My House
WOR: Bob and Ray
WNYC: News; John Faulk
WQXR: Adventures in Jazz
WQXR: N. Y. Times News
5:05—WQXR: Cocktail Time
5:15—WRCA: Claude Rains
5:30—WRCA: Lone Ranger
★ WNYC: A. F. L.-C. I. O.
Unity Convention
5:45—WOR: Les Paul-Mary Ford
5:50—WOR: Sports; News
5:55—WRCA: Weather Reports
WCBS: News

EVENING

6:00—WRCA, WCBS: News
WOR: Lyle Van, News
WNYC: Window on the World: Kenneth Bird
WQXR: N. Y. Times News
6:05—WRCA: Dinner Concert
6:15—WQXR: Jimmy Powers
WOR: Dorothy and Dick
WCBS: Herman Hickman
WNYC: Veterans' News
6:25—WCBS: Weather Report
6:30—WRCA: Tex and Jinx
WOR: News Reports
WCBS: Martha Wright
WNYC: Canadian News
6:45—WRCA: Three Star Extra
WOR: Stan Lomax, Sports
WABC: Sports, Bill Stern
WCBS: Lowell Thomas
WNYC: Weather Report; U.N. News
7:00—WRCA: Symphonette
WOR: Fulton Lewis Jr.
WABC: John Vandercook
WNYC: Larry LeSueur
WQXR: Masterwork Hour
WNYC: N. Y. Times News
7:05—WCBS: Tennessee Ernie Show, With Doris Drew

WQXR: To France With Music; Jacques Fray
7:15—WOR: Today's Business
WABC: Quincy Howe, News
7:20—WOR: The Answer Man
7:25—WABC: Wall Street Final
7:30—WRCA: Morgan Beatty
WOR: Gabriel Heatter
WABC: Events of the Day
WCBS: Bing Crosby
7:45—★WQXR: Hanshro and Zayde
WOR: One Man's Family
WCBS: Basil Heatter
WCBS: Edward R. Murrow
7:55—WRCA: News Reports
8:00—WRCA: News Reports
WOR: Official Detective
WABC: The World and You
WCBS: My Son, Jeep
WQXR: N. Y. Times News
WRCA: Great Gildersleeve
8:05—★WQXR: Symphony Hall
8:15—WCBS: Yours Truly, Johnny Dollar
8:25—WABC: News Reports
8:30—WRCA: This is My Story
WOR: Crime Fighters
WABC: Your Better Tomorrow
★WCBS: Arthur Godfrey Digest

★WNYC: Man's Right to Knowledge
8:55—WABC: News Reports
9:00—WRCA: News Reports
WOR: News Reports
WABC: Sound Mirror
WCBS: News Reports
★WNYC: Cooper Union Forum
WQXR: N. Y. Times News
9:05—WRCA: American Adventure
WOR: Special Edition
WCBS: Jack Carson Show
★WQXR: The Spoken Word
9:15—WOR: The Book Hunter
9:25—WABC: News Reports
9:30★WRCA: Conversation
WOR: Martha Deane
WABC: Offbeat
WCBS: Amos 'n' Andy
WQXR: Listening Booth
9:55—WCBS: News
WABC: News Personality
WNYC: News (FM to 3)
10:00—WRCA: Fibber and Molly
WCBS: Weather
WABC: Edward P. Morgan
WCBS: United Jewish Appeal
Drama: The Stowaway
WQXR: N. Y. Times News
10:05★WQXR: Panorama
10:15—WRCA: News Reports

WOR: John Gambling
WABC: How to Fix it
WRCA: News Reports
10:30—WABC: George H. Combs
10:35★WRCA: Tex and Jinx Show
10:45—WABC: Plasterbrauin
11:00—WRCA, WOR, WCBS: News
WQXR: N. Y. Times News
11:07—WQXR: Recorded Previews
WABC: Lee Griffith, News
WCBS: Record Previews
11:10—WCBS: Eric Sevareid
11:15—WRCA: Dan Peterson
WCBS: Christmas Chimes
11:20★WRCA: Tex and Jinx Show
11:30—WOR: Music
WABC: Music
★WCBS: This Is New York
12:00—WRCA: News; Tex and Jinx
WOR: News; Music
WABC: Mostly Music
WCBS: Music Till Dawn
WQXR: N. Y. Times News
12:05★WRCA: Midnight Symphony
12:15—WOR: Dance Time
12:30—WRCA: Music Through the Night, With Fleetwood
1:00—WOR: Mitch Reed Show

3. Look at the middle figure in a group of three twelve o'clock figures, and read not only this middle figure but also the one above and below it *without moving your eyes*.

4. Once you find the 12:15, 12:30, 12:45 group, glance quickly at the words to the right of these numbers in search of the one word *news*.

5. Then with one quick backward fixation, grasp the call letters of the station. All of this should take about one second.

6. Try it.

Use the same techniques in locating each of the following as fleetingly as possible:

(a) Galen Drake's program in the middle of the afternoon.
(b) A Bing Crosby program early in the evening.
(c) Edward P. Morgan's commentaries during the ten o'clock evening programs.
(d) A program called "This is New York" which appears during the eleven o'clock hour at night.

Exercise 3

In the table[5] on page 254 statistics are given in regard to the number of failures in different fields of industry during 9 months in 1954 and 1955, respectively. The table also presents the amount of liabilities for each industry during these periods. The liability figure in each case represents millions of dollars; for example: 7.8 means 7 and .8 millions of dollars.

In working with this table make use of your vertical field of vision in scanning to locate the names of certain industries for a further investigation in regard to the failures and liabilities.

Fixate in the middle of the first group of names, then in the middle of the second group, and so on, until you find the industry you are looking for. You don't have

[5] From *Dun's Review and Modern Industry*, November 1955, p. 25.

to read all the names in any one group. Look at a point in the middle of the group and, holding your eyes right there, gather a reading impression of the phrases above and below the point at which your eyes are fixated. In doing this you will be making full use of your vertical field of vision and will thus save a great deal of time which otherwise might be wasted in reading each separate line individually and horizontally.

Now, to apply the techniques you have just read about, see how quickly you can find the name of each of the following industries by making just one fixation in the

FAILURES BY DIVISIONS OF INDUSTRY

	Number 9 Months		Liabilities 9 Months	
(Current liabilities in millions of dollars)	1955	1954	1955	1954
MINING, MANUFACTURING...................	1635	1710	120.9	138.1
Mining—Coal, Oil, Misc.	41	36	3.5	7.8
Food and Kindred Products	120	131	11.8	13.9
Textile Products, Apparel.................	376	408	18.2	21.9
Lumber, Lumber Products..................	239	247	10.0	12.0
Paper, Printing, Publishing................	80	98	3.0	8.1
Chemicals, Allied Products	39	61	3.0	4.8
Leather, Leather Products.................	69	78	4.1	5.5
Stone, Clay, Glass Products...............	38	42	1.6	1.2
Iron, Steel and Products..................	89	87	10.3	9.0
Machinery................................	216	225	31.9	34.7
Transportation Equipment.................	38	40	3.8	4.7
Miscellaneous.	290	257	19.8	14.7
WHOLESALE TRADE.........................	891	857	39.3	41.6
Food and Farm Products..................	220	219	9.9	10.5
Apparel..................................	49	37	1.8	1.0
Dry Goods...............................	39	49	1.3	2.2
Lumber, Bldg. Mats, Hdwre...............	101	84	5.2	3.9
Chemicals and Drugs......................	28	32	0.9	0.6
Motor Vehicles, Equipment................	54	44	1.3	1.6
Miscellaneous.............................	400	392	18.9	21.7
RETAIL TRADE............................	4036	4174	88.6	114.7
Food and Liquor..........................	785	740	13.1	10.6
General Merchandise......................	146	141	4.3	6.1
Apparel and Accessories...................	658	629	13.0	12.2
Furniture, Furnishings....................	561	731	16.4	37.1
Lumber, Bldg. Mats, Hdwre...............	230	231	6.6	6.7
Automotive Group........................	392	459	8.9	17.6
Eating, Drinking Places...................	733	737	15.3	14.2
Drug Stores..............................	96	119	2.1	2.6
Miscellaneous.............................	435	387	8.8	7.5
CONSTRUCTION............................	999	956	57.4	39.3
General Bldg. Contractors.................	320	337	28.3	20.6
Building Subcontractors...................	624	579	22.3	16.6
Other Contractors........................	55	40	6.8	2.1
COMMERCIAL SERVICES.....................	636	668	24.0	24.8
TOTAL UNITED STATES	8197	8365	330.2	358.5

Liabilities are rounded to the nearest million; they do not necessarily add to totals.

THE FAILURE RECORD

	Sept. 1955	Aug. 1955	Sept. 1954	P.C. Chg.†
DUN'S FAILURE INDEX*				
Unadjusted	37.5	37.4	37.5	0
Adjusted, seasonally	43.6	41.6	44.1	−1
NUMBER OF FAILURES	602	666	819	+0.4
NUMBER BY SIZE OF DEBT				
Under $5,000	129	157	121	+7
$5,000–$25,000	388	431	400	−3
$25,000–$100,000	227	223	291	−2
$100,000 and over	78	77	67	+16
NUMBER BY INDUSTRY GROUPS				
Manufacturing	168	158	153	+10
Wholesale Trade	99	107	113	−12
Retail Trade	366	430	406	−10
Construction	114	134	88	+30
Commercial Service	75	59	59	+27
	(LIABILITIES in thousands)			
CURRENT	$33,120	$36,028	$36,381	−9
TOTAL	33,348	36,425	37,757	−12

* Apparent annual failures per 10,000 listed enterprises, formerly called DUN'S INSOLVENCY INDEX.
† Per cent change, September 1955 from September 1954.

BUSINESS FAILURES *include those businesses that ceased operations following assignment or bankruptcy: ceased with loss to creditors after such actions as execution, foreclosure, or attachment: voluntarily withdrew leaving unpaid obligations; were involved in court actions such as receivership, reorganisation, or arrangement; or voluntarily compromised with creditors out of court.*

CURRENT LIABILITIES, *as used in The Failure Record, have a special meaning; they include all accounts and notes payable and all obligations, whether in secured form or not, known to be held by banks, officers, affiliated companies, supplying companies, or the Government. They do not include long-term, publicly held obligations. Offsetting assets are not taken into account.*

middle of a group of names and using your *vertical* field of vision:

> *Paper, Printing, Publishing*
> *Chemicals and Drugs*
> *Automotive Group*
> *Building Subcontractors*

Did you discover that you could find these names readily with the use of your "above" and "below" field of vision, without moving your eyes from the middle point at which they were fixated? Most people could improve their scanning ability tremendously by making greater use of their vertical field of vision.

In scanning this table for information you will also

have to make some use of your horizontal field of vision. After you find the name of the industry in which you are interested, you will want to read the two numbers at the right which give comparative figures in regard to the number of failures the industry had and the two comparative figures which appear still further at your right in regard to the number of million dollars the industry lost. In finding these two bits of information make just one fixation for each of the pairs of figures. This fixation should be in the column of vacant space midway between the two groups of figures, so that you can take in both groups with the use of your horizontal field of vision and without moving your eyes. As an example, suppose you wish quickly to grasp the comparative figures showing the number of failures for Paper, Printing, and Publishing: look directly at the middle of the space between 80 and 98. As you fixate precisely in the middle of this space you should be able to see the 80 clearly at the left, and the 98 clearly at the right.

Similarly, if you wish to grasp quickly the comparative numbers which represent the number of million dollars of liabilities in this industry during the two periods look straight at a spot halfway between the 3.0 and 8.1, at which point you can see both numbers without moving your eyes.

If you proceed in this way, you will make only three fleeting fixations in locating the name of an industry in any one group and in grasping the two sets of figures concerning it. In the first of these fixations in which you are locating a name within a group of names, you use your vertical field of vision, and in the other two in which you are grasping two figures at a time you use your horizontal field of vision. You must make the switch from the vertical to the horizontal with great speed.

See how fleetingly and accurately you can complete your scanning for the different items needed in filling in the blanks below. After each hasty scanning in connection with an item, write the correct numbers in the blank spaces.

Name of industry	Number of Failures		Liabilities in million of dollars	
	1955	1954	1955	1954
Textile Products, Apparel	___	___	___	___
Stone, Clay, Glass Products	___	___	___	___
Dry Goods	___	___	___	___
Lumber, Bldg. Mats., Hardware	___	___	___	___
General Building Contractors	___	___	___	___

Check your answers with the table.

Exercise 4

Now that you have had some experience in using your vertical field of vision in scanning groups of numbers and groups of words, try using it in skimming a selection consisting of sentences and paragraphs.

Increasing numbers of magazines are using double columns these days. This practice facilitates skimming with the use of vertical eye movements and the vertical field of vision. Often it is possible to sweep the eyes straight down through the middle of one of these narrow columns, taking in the central area of two lines at a time with the use of the vertical field of vision. In the great majority of cases, this central section of the lines contains enough words to convey the information given in the selection even though the words at either side of the central section are not seen. If you find that you aren't following the thought at a certain point while using this procedure, you can always glance quickly to the left or right to catch a key word needed in completing the meaning. Even if you do have to take a side excursion now and then to catch a key word, you can still cover the selection very much more rapidly by reading the central part of two lines at a time than by moving your eyes back and forth across all the lines of print.

1. Sweep your eyes straight down through the middle of the short selection on page 258.

2. Gather all the important details you can by reading

the central portion of two lines at one fixation and without changing the position of your eyes.

3. If you lose the thought at any point, catch a necessary key word with a fleeting left or right glance.

4. Allow yourself exactly five seconds to skim the article in this way.

5. Take the comprehension test after you have finished skimming the article.

FACTS ABOUT HAMSTERS

Hamsters have been increasing in favor as laboratory animals. They're also kept as pets.

Hamsters can be bought from the same source as white mice. Price is $2.50 to $3.00 a pair. Keep your hamsters in a room with a temperature between 55° and 70° F. Keep them in metal cages, or in wooden cages protected on the inside with hardware cloth to keep them from gnawing their way out. A cage 12 x 15 x 12 inches will house a pair, while a cage 35 x 25 x 15 inches will take care of eight to ten animals. An adult hamster needs about 10 to 15 grams of food per day (⅓ to ½ ounce).

You can breed your animals throughout the year, but most litters are produced between November and May. A female will produce only five or six litters in her lifetime. The gestation period is about sixteen days. The number of young per litter averages about seven.

Hospitals, laboratories, biological supply houses, schools and certain other institutions offer the best market for the sale of hamsters. You should assure yourself of such a market before you raise many hamsters for sale.

Checking Comprehension

(Write "True" or "False" to the left of each statement.)

_____ 1. Hamsters are decreasing in favor.

_____ 2. They are bought from the same source as white mice.

_____ 3. The price of a pair of hamsters is from $5.00 to $10.00 per pair.

_____ 4. They may be kept in a metal cage protected with hardware cloth.

————— 5. One pair should have a cage 40 x 20 x 40.
————— 6. A hamster needs 10 to 15 grams of food per day.
————— 7. They produce litters in June and July.
————— 8. The female produces ten to fifteen litters in a lifetime.
————— 9. The gestation period is ten days.
————— 10. You might be able to sell some hamsters to laboratories.

Check your answers with the article itself to find how well your vertical field of vision worked for you.

Selection 5

Try skimming a longer selection with the use of the same techniques. Allow yourself no more than 10 seconds.

Sweet But Nonfattening[6]

ABSOLUTELY NONFATTENING. . . . Thrills your taste, trims your waist. . . . All the flavor is in, all the sugar is out. . . . Insist on frosty, taste-tingling refreshment with this revolutionary new sweetening discovery!

With just such high-pitched promotional fanfare, soft-drink manufacturers this year have been vigorously pushing the sales of dietetic beverages—products in which the sugar normally present has been replaced by a synthetic, nonfattening sweetener. These products go under various trade names, and many of them are booming. One company which only recently began selling low-calorie soft drinks expects its gross sales of these products during the year to total about $5 million in the metropolitan New York area alone.

Today, dozens of beverage manufacturers are hopping aboard the bandwagon, not merely to keep the diabetics of the nation happy but primarily to appeal to the millions of calorie-conscious folk trying resolutely to lose weight—or at least to hold their own. Incidentally, it's no trade secret that the leading users of dietetic soft drinks are women.

Most of the new dietetic beverages contain between 0.1 and 0.3 percent of a calcium salt usually designated as calcium cyclamate or Sucaryl. (There is also a Sucaryl based on sodium and more closely related to common salt, but it is not used so much.) Because a noncaloric sweetner is used in place of sugar, the average 12-ounce bottle of dietetic beverage supplies only about 3 calories, as compared to the 200 or more found in the conventional soft drink.

As manufacturers hasten to explain, synthetic sweeteners are definitely not sugar substitutes. The key distinction is that the synthetics, unlike sugar, provide flavor only, not food value. Thus far, only two synthetic sweeteners have been approved by the Food and Drug Administration for use in foods. These are saccharin and Sucaryl.

Saccharin, produced by Monsanto Chemical Co. and intermittently by Lapaco Chemicals, has been manufactured commercially in the United States ever since the turn of the century. In fact, John F. Queeny's first production of saccharin in St. Louis in 1901 not only broke Germany's monopoly on saccharin but also marked the birth of Monsanto Chemical itself. Sucaryl, on the other hand, is a relative newcomer. Abbott's commercial production of sodium Sucaryl began in the spring of 1950.

A year later, Abbott began producing calcium Sucaryl, which has a special appeal to people on sodium-free diets. Both salts have approximately 30 times the sweetness of sucrose.

The relative advantages and disadvantages of saccharin and Sucaryl have been the subject of continuing debate. The principal point of contention is the relative aftertaste of both products. There are people who rave about saccharin, will use nothing else. Others would go without any sweetening whatever rather than subject themselves to what they regard as saccharin's objectionably bitter or metallic aftertaste.

Of course, in anything as subjective as taste, there are bound to be clashes of opinion. Although it is frequently stated that Sucaryl in normal use is less apt to impart an aftertaste than saccharin, it is still true that, at concentrations greater than 0.5 to 0.8 percent, most people think Sucaryl also tastes bitter.

Moreover, because saccharin has 14 times the sweetening power of Sucaryl, it is vulnerable to overuse. The problem of aftertaste, therefore, is often accentuated. On the other hand, Monsanto claims that its saccharin does not contain the trace of impurity responsible for saccharin's bitter aftertaste.

Today, producers of synthetic sweeteners not only must face the competition of rival manufacturers but also a welter of national and state regulations. For example, the use of saccharin in foods is prohibited in 27 states in the United States. In 17 of these states, all synthetic sweeteners are banned. Despite these handicaps, the market for synthetic sweeteners is expanding.

With horizons broadening, what about possible new synthetic sweeteners? Oddly, there is very little research being done today that is directed specifically toward the synthesis of new sweeteners. One reason is that not much is really known of why certain select compounds actually taste sweet.

In all likelihood, new synthetic sweeteners will continue to be discovered by accident in totally unrelated fields of research. Thus, new sweeteners await the fortunes of laboratory workers who have the foresight—and courage—to taste their own compounds.

Checking Comprehension

Write "True" or "False" before each statement.

_____ 1. The sales of nonfattening beverages are booming.

_____ 2. The manufacture of dietetic beverages is being conducted by two manufacturers only.

_____ 3. Calcium salt and Sucaryl are one and the same thing.

_____ 4. The synthetic sweeteners provide real food value.

_____ 5. Saccharin has been produced for over two centuries.

_____ 6. Sodium Sucaryl has been produced only recently.

_____ 7. The principal point of contention over the relative advantages of saccharin and Sucaryl hinges on the aftertaste of the two products.

_____ 8. Saccharin has much more sweetening power than Sucaryl.

———— 9. There are no state regulations in regard to these sweeteners.

———— 10. Very little research is being conducted in regard to these sweeteners.

See the Answer Key on page 286.

Comprehension Score: ————

Skimming Page-Wide Material with Vertical Eye Movements

In the selection below the content appears in full-page width. See if you can use your vertical eye movements and vertical field of vision in skimming this article which contains wider lines than the ones with which you have been working.

This selection will also offer you a good opportunity to try the technique of converting subheads into questions and then skimming to find the answers to these questions.

Follow this procedure:

1. Preview to determine the pattern of writing.
2. Set up as your general purpose reading to find the answer to the question in the title.
3. Preview the subheads and convert each one into a question as you glance at it. Perhaps your converted sub-heads will take forms similar to those below.

Subheading	*Converted*
It Was Clearly Petunia	Who considered it to be "Clearly a Petunia?"
Entrée to Kitchen Gained	How was the entrée gained?
Unsettling Discovery Was Made	What was the "unsettling discovery"?
Gardener Forced to Confess	What did the gardener confess?
If Not a Petunia, Then What?	What Was It?

4. Skim the selection, trying to move your eyes straight down through the middle of the page, "catching" all you can as you swiftly pass over the central portion.

5. With watch in hand allow yourself exactly 10 seconds for skimming. Ready. Start!

Selection 6

WHAT WAS IT[7]

It Was Clearly a Petunia

It all began sometime ago when the days were still warm. The lady of the house started it by saying she would like to have a potted geranium in the kitchen window during the winter, since there would be no garden to look out upon until late next spring. Later, the gardener, inspecting a small bed where perennials for next season were taking root, found growing between two rows of carnations what clearly was a misplaced petunia—very small, very young, and very determined. With a true gardener's sense of thrift, instead of pulling up and throwing away what clearly was a petunia, the gardener obtained a large flower pot, carefully lifted the plant into it, and brought pot and plant into the house well before the first frost.

Entrée to Kitchen Gained

As tactfully as possible the gardener suggested to the lady of the house that a potted petunia might be a more welcome addition to the kitchen window during the winter than a potted geranium. The lady of the house demurred, commenting that she never had heard of anyone having a potted petunia in the kitchen. It was, however, such a small petunia that, resting in the center of the big flower pot, it had somewhat the appeal of a lost small child. The gardener thoughtfully observed that he had to put the petunia somewhere, and inquired if he might leave it in the kitchen until a better place could be found. As the days passed he observed with interest that what plainly was a petunia was being watered regularly and growing, and that he heard no

[7] "Topics of the Times," *New York Times*, November 20, 1954.

more requests for geraniums—which, privately, he did not care for, anyway.

Unsettling Discovery Is Made

Some days later the gardener noted, casually, that what plainly was a petunia was growing rapidly, the picture of health. He mentioned the encouraging growth to the lady of the house, who, as if waiting for just this opening, asked if he would mind very much moving the plant, in its pot, to some more desirable location, as its spreading leaves were beginning to get in the way at mealtimes. Obligingly the gardener picked up the flower pot and moved it into the dining-room window, as he did so getting a good view of the plant's leaves for the first time in weeks. What plainly had looked like a petunia when it was transplanted was beginning not to look like a petunia at all.

Gardener Forced to Confess

Having advertised his importation as a petunia the gardener was, understandably, reluctant to mention his discovery, and decided to let matters rest. Unfortunately, they did not rest long; the next day, looking out of the dining-room window over her second cup of breakfast coffee, the lady of the house asked the gardener if he was sure that what he had planted in the pot was in fact a petunia. The gardener had to confess that, whatever it was, indeed it did not now seem to be a petunia. It surely was not a geranium. It plainly was not a number of other things. But what it really was, he said, he did not know.

If Not a Petunia, Then What?

The gardener now wishes he had confessed nothing and had stuck to his story that this was a petunia. For the plant—now a foot tall with spoon-shaped leaves perhaps ten inches long—occupying a conspicuous place in the dining room, has become a conversation piece; all who come to dine ask about it, or if they fail to do so the lady of the house tells them the story of her "geranium," much to the gardener's discomfiture. The gardener, after consulting a number of books, has tentatively concluded that he is wintering a fine specimen of Nicotiana, but he is not positive. If it is indeed Nicotiana and grows no more rapidly than the Nicotiana in last summer's garden, it will be a long time before he can be sure. The gardener's only hope is that if he is nursing carefully an unidentified weed it will eventually bear large blossoms—resembling, preferably, geranium or petunia.

Checking Comprehension

1. Who considered it to be "clearly a petunia"? _____
   _____

2. How was the entrée to the kitchen gained? _____
   _____

3. What was the "unsettling discovery"? _____
   _____

4. What did the gardener confess? _____
   _____

5. What was it? _____
   _____

Check your answers with the Answer Key on page 286. Allow 20 for each correct answer.

Comprehension Score:_____

Skimming with the Technique of Your Choice

You have now tried skimming for main ideas, skimming with the use of key words, skimming with the use of vertical eye movements and vertical field of vision. Perhaps you have found that some one of these techniques has more promise for your own personal skimming use than the others; or it may be you have found that the combination of all three of these procedures serves you personally to the best advantage; or maybe you like to use one technique for one purpose and a different one for another purpose.

Choose the technique or combination of techniques which you think you personally can use to the best advantage in skimming the following article.

Selection 7

1. Skim this article to find out whom the author is writing about and why this person was a "Master at His Trade." In doing this you will of course gather general information on the topic.
2. Allow yourself 5 seconds for skimming.
3. Take the comprehension test which follows the article. This test will be based on general information—not details.

A MASTER AT HIS TRADE[8]

The ballplayers always said that Bill McGowan was the best umpire in the American League. No higher praise ever could be given an umpire, and perhaps that can serve as McGowan's epitaph. He'd have liked it that way because he was as devoted to his profession as Bill Klem had been. The American League had retired the ailing McGowan earlier in the week on a handsome pension. But he died yesterday before he had an opportunity to enjoy it.

The proudest moment of his life was in 1948 when the American League virtually admitted that he was its best arbiter. Once upon a time world series assignments were the supreme accolade, but they are on a rotating basis now and therefore meaningless. However, the junior circuit had the first and only play-off in its history in 1948 when the Indians and Red Sox tied for the championship. It was imperative that only the best of the Men in Blue handle that game. Significant indeed was the fact that Bill McGowan was named umpire-in-chief.

Bill was always an eager beaver, a hustler. And his enthusiasm never waned during his thirty seasons in the big leagues. But that's why he was so good, though his overenthusiasm twice drew him suspensions, a rarity in itself. Even then, the ballplayers never said grumpily, "Served him right." Instead they said softly, "Too bad about Willie, isn't it?"

In the Mirror

When McGowan entered the American League in 1924, he even brought his job into his hotel room with him, so unceasing were his efforts to improve himself. Soon he

[8] Arthur Daley, *New York Times*, December 10, 1954.

had his roomie, Roy Van Graflan, doing the same thing.

"Y're out!" Bill would bellow, jerking his thumb peremptorily in front of the mirror. Then he'd try it again with a different inflection and a different gesture, experimenting with his techniques. And pretty soon Van Graflan was doing the same thing.

"Y're out!" Van would scream, as the two of them practiced for hours on end. Finally a booming voice came echoing up from the hotel courtyard.

"Shut up!" howled a complaining nonsleeper. "Hey, don't you guys ever call anyone safe?"

It also was in a hotel that McGowan had one of the most soul-shattering experiences of his career. It happened when he was a young and green umpire. He'd noticed how well dressed his fellow arbiters were and asked for an explanation. After all, umpirical salaries were stringently modest in those days.

Wholesale Price

"It's easy," one of them said. "We lead lonely lives, apart from the ballplayers. But we're constantly coming in contact with traveling salesmen. So just butter up to a few of them, entertain them a bit, and you'll be able to get shirts, suits, shoes, and everything you need at wholesale prices. Sometimes they'll even give you samples for free."

McGowan cased the lobby and picked on a likely prospect. He struck up a conversation with him, learned that he was a salesman, and buttered him up. The stranger couldn't pick up a tab. McGowan wined and dined him, carefully avoiding even a hint of the nefarious purpose behind his hospitality.

"It's been a wonderful evening, Bill," said the stranger as they parted.

"By the way," said Bill, "you never did mention what firm you're traveling for. Which one is it?"

"The Baldwin Locomotive Company," said the stranger.

McGowan's two suspensions deserve mention. The first was the outcome of an incident at home plate in a game between the Senators and Indians in Washington. Joe Papparella ruled that Eddie Stewart was out at home with the winning run, and the Washington players came storming out of the dugout in violent protest.

New Man on Job

Technically speaking, the call was none of McGowan's business. But Papparella was a new man on the job, and Bill rushed to his rescue. But in taking the heat off his fellow worker, he set himself ablaze. Words were spoken that should never have been spoken. So McGowan was suspended to cool off. But that was why he got even more than the normal satisfaction out of being named umpire-in-chief a few months later in the play-off game. It was a vindication of sorts.

The other suspension resulted primarily from a run-in with players and then erupted in the wrong direction, toward the press box. It was a Tiger-Brown game in St. Louis, and McGowan thought the Tigers were unnecessarily rough in their riding of Satchell Paige. He furiously ordered them to stop and cleared off part of the Detroit bench. The baseball writers asked for details of the still-seething McGowan.

"Tell 'em I'll write a letter," snapped His Nibs.

"We didn't know you could write," was the unnecessarily rude message he received in return.

"If you guys could write, you'd be in New York," was McGowan's final insult. The press-box tenants took umbrage and filed formal protest with President Will Harridge of the American League. McGowan was suspended.

For all of that, though, he was a mighty fine umpire. The fellows who'll miss him most will be the ballplayers who always affectionately called him "Willie."

Checking Comprehension

1. Bill McGowan was famous in (a) tennis, (b) basketball, (c) baseball, (d) football.

2. At the time the article was written, McGowan was (a) retired, (b) working in connection with a World Series game, (c) just elected an official, (d) deceased.

3. The proudest moment in his life was when the American League named him (a) captain, (b) coach, (c) director, (d) umpire-in-chief.

4. Bill was (a) a pessimist, (b) optimist, (c) enthusiast, (d) chronic complainer.

5. Bill even practiced (a) in his kitchen, (b) while traveling on the train, (c) before the mirror in his hotel room, (d) in his locker room.

6. It was indicated that McGowan's salary was (a) high, (b) exorbitant, (c) modest, (d) increased three fold during his last ten years of work.

7. Bill picked a man from the lobby to entertain, thinking that this man was a good prospect for (a) helping Bill get a salary raise, (b) helping him get a promotion, (c) letting him have clothes at wholesale prices or for free, (d) teaching him a new trick in baseball.

8. The article mentioned that McGowan was suspended (a) once, (b) twice, (c) many times, (d) never.

9. One of Bill's suspensions resulted from (a) unfair play, (b) ill health, (c) a hot exchange of words with the press, (d) a quarrel with the President of the American League.

10. Ballplayers regarded Bill with (a) jealousy, (b) animosity, (c) pity, (d) affection.

Answers: 1)——, 2)——, 3)——, 4)——, 5)——, 6)——, 7)——, 8)——, 9)——, 10)——.

See the Answer Key on page 286.

Comprehension Score:——————

Selection 8

1. Skim the following article on tipping for the purpose of finding the answer to the author's question in the subtitle, "A National Racket?"

2. In realizing this purpose you will on the whole skim only for general ideas, but you will also have to grasp some of the details in the way of figures. So you will use a combination of techniques in skimming this article: general skimming, and grasping and remembering details.

3. Allow yourself ten seconds to skim this article, then take the comprehension test.

TIPPING[9]

A National Racket?

We Americans hand out approximately $750,000,000 annually in tips, or three quarters of a billion dollars,

[9] Oneta Aldrich Wakeford, *American Mercury*, June 1954, pp. 127-129.

according to the United States Department of Commerce. Of this amount about $450,000 goes to restaurant employees. The rest greases the open palms of hotel "gimme" boys, taxi drivers, beauticians, barbers, parking-lot attendants, bartenders, and a host of others who expect gratuities from the public for their services.

In spite of these magnanimous figures, however, tipping is generally an unpopular and disliked custom in the United States, and it always has been. As far back as 1896, the secretary of the Journeyman Barbers International Union of America condemned tipping as "humiliating and degrading." In 1905 the Anti-Tipping Society of America had 100,000 members, the majority of them salesmen. Within the next few years anti-tipping laws were passed in Arkansas, Iowa, Mississippi, South Carolina, Tennessee, and Washington. This legislation was short-lived, however, for in 1919 the Iowa law was repealed as unconstitutional and the other states soon followed suit.

Today, of course, we're all aware of how widespread the practice of tipping is, and how many categories of workers it covers. It has become mainly a "pressure" custom. And while we go along with it outwardly, the majority of us actually feel that it is wrong in principle. According to a recent survey on the subject, 65.1% of the persons queried definitely disapprove of tipping, only 22.2% approve, 12% are undecided.

A laborer should be worthy of his hire, no matter what his field. He shouldn't have to depend on the gratuities of the public. Yet, the United States Chamber of Commerce reports that there are 1,800,000 persons who depend on tips for the major part of their income.

Tipping itself has a servile aspect. One does not tip an equal. Even the way tipping is usually handled is undignified payment. Either the coin is slipped under the edge of the plate, out of sight, or into the servitor's hand quickly, almost stealthily, as if the transaction weren't quite above board. In the words of Edward Corsi, Industrial Commissioner of New York, who conducted hearings several months ago on proposed minimum wage laws that would affect his state's 250,000 restaurant workers: "Tipping is unworthy of labor in the twentieth century. It makes a servant out of the worker. It is a disgraceful thing that the worker has to depend on tips for a living."

This dependency on tips puts the worker in an unfair position. He has grown to expect them as his earnings, and not as a token of appreciation for extra service he has given. He is often filled with resentment when he isn't tipped, or not tipped highly enough because, to him, those gratuities are important as bread-and-butter money. Of course, there are a few servitors who, after the essentials are paid for, can well afford a shiny new Cadillac! Some headwaiters, for instance, who work in expensive nightclubs which dot the country from east to west, have reported yearly incomes of $35,000. At least six in New York earn $50,000. These naturally, are the exception.

The customer, on the other hand, is placed in an uncomfortable position, as well as what he thinks is an unfair one. The uncomfortable feeling comes usually from not knowing exactly how much he should tip. Practically everyone above the age of fifteen has read the "etiquette rules" of how much to tip and when. But if these rules were printed in books or magazines four or five years ago, he can be sure that they're substandard for today's tipping. Prices have gone up, and if the customer doesn't know it, or acts as if he doesn't, he'll receive bullet glances which denounce him as subhuman. For instance, ten or fifteen cents to a train porter for carrying one bag used to be acceptable. The present price is twenty-five. Ten per cent of the restaurant check was a standard rule a few years back. Today, it is fifteen, and in the so-called better places, more. As one waiter put it: "When I work in a swanky hotel I count on at least twenty per cent."

Because there are so many variations to the rules, a customer is often in a quandary as to whether the "rule" holds good in his particular situation. Take the case of a woman going into a beauty shop. She is armed with the "social knowledge" that she'll be expected to tip the operator fifteen per cent of her total bill. However, by the time she's had a haircut, shampoo, set, and manicure, not one operator but four have waited on her. If, for instance, her bill is $6.00 won't the required 90 cents tip, divided four ways, look stingy, and not be what each expected?

The term "tip" originated in a London coffee house in Fleet Street where Samuel Johnson and his cronies frequently visited during the eighteenth century. On the table was a bowl with the words, "To Insure Promptitude," printed around it. The phrase was later shortened to "Tip," taking the first letter of each of the three words.

Today, a person is expected to leave a tip even though the service has been slow and indifferent. The unfairness of the tipping racket, as far as the customer is concerned, hinges on the feeling that he is being pressured into carrying part of the employer's burden. If he pays a good price for his haircut, why should he tip the barber? Isn't it up to the employer to provide a decent wage for him? Or, when he stays in a hotel and pays that bill, why should he give the maid extra money for coming in to clean his room? Isn't her salary a definite duty of hotel management?

It seems to him that tipping is the employers' way out of responsibility. They pass the buck of their workers' salaries on to the customer.

Most of us continue to tip, even though we dislike the practice, for one or all three of the following reasons: (1) Conscience. We recognize the injustice of the worker's meager wage and feel that we must add to his take-home pay. (2) Social pressure. We don't wish to look like cheapskates to our associates or to the workers themselves. (3) Moral weakness. We lack the courage of our convictions that the principle of tipping, as it is being used today, is inherently wrong for our democratic way of life.

It is with a kind of mental relief that passengers ride the airlines, where no tipping is allowed. Many supermarkets which hire boys to carry bags or boxes of purchased groceries out to the car for the customer have signs requesting no tipping. A few (too few!) restaurants in various parts of the country have similar signs. To the customer, such signs are like a beautiful oasis in a "gimme" desert.

In some foreign countries such as Finland, a service charge is added to restaurant and hotel bills. I believe most of us would prefer this system to our present one.

The tipping racket can be stopped only when the three groups—employers, workers and customers—decide that it is an archaic and unfair practice and proceed to do something about it.

Checking Comprehension

1. The United States hands out in tips each year (a) millions of dollars, (b) hundreds of dollars, (c) thousands of dollars, (d) a very small amount.

2. In the United States tipping (a) is generally approved, (b) is generally disliked, (c) attracts indifference, (d) is regarded as unconstitutional.

3. Anti-tipping laws in the United States have (a) been short-lived, (b) been suggested but never passed, (c) been a success where they have been tried out, (d) been successful in only a few cases.

4. Tipping places the worker in the class of (a) a laborer, (b) a servant, (c) one's equal, (d) one who deserves recognition.

5. In following the rules for tipping, a customer may (a) acquaint the person who serves him with the rules, (b) always tip exactly the right amount, (c) disregard the rules entirely, (d) be in a quandary because of variations in rules.

6. As the years go by the amount given for tips (a) has become standardized, (b) is generally less than previously, (c) is generally higher than previously, (d) is higher for some services and less for others.

7. The word "tip" originated in (a) a French restaurant, (b) a Norwegian Smörgasbord, (c) a London coffee house, (d) an American hotel.

8. Nowadays you are supposed to leave a tip (a) only when the service is as good as usual, (b) only when you ask for something special, (c) only when the person serving you is unusually attentive, (d) even though the service has been slow and indifferent.

9. It seems that tipping is a good way for an employer to (a) recognize his help, (b) avoid his responsibility, (c) aid his help in avoiding income tax, (d) find out which one of his employees have special abilities.

10. In Finland tipping is (a) regulated, (b) not emphasized, (c) added to the bill, (d) paid by the employer.

Answers: 1)——, 2)——, 3)——, 4)——, 5)——, 6)——, 7)——, 8)——, 9)——, 10)——.

See the Answer Key on page 286.

See the Answer Key on page 286.

Comprehension Score:_____

Vocabulary Department

The italicized words appeared in the selections which you have just read. One of the phrases, *a*, or *b*, or *c*, completes each sentence. Check the phrase which correctly completes each of the sentences.

1. A *capricious* person would
   a. do surprising things
   b. usually be angry
   c. make a good soldier

2. He *reiterated* the
   a. machine
   b. building
   c. statement

3. An *assiduous* worker would
   a. work with chemicals
   b. be indefatigable
   c. try to please the boss

4. The president *demurred* because
   a. he disliked the plan
   b. he favored the plan
   c. he was using the plan

5. The *detritus* consisted of
   a. fleecy clouds
   b. tree-trunks
   c. tiny particles of rock

6. To take *umbrage* is to
   a. accept a bribe
   b. be resentful
   c. take the total weight of a cargo

7. A man in a *quandary* is
   a. successfully resisting temptation
   b. engaged in mining
   c. perplexed

8. Munificent *gratuities* were dispensed by
   a. a kindly old beggar
   b. the deacon of a small parish
   c. an industrial tycoon

9. *Nefarious* deeds were performed by
   a. iniquitous men
   b. chivalrous knights
   c. indigent but righteous men

10. The *peremptory* statement was made to
    a. encourage discussion
    b. ensure fairness
    c. silence all objections

11. The *exhumation* was done by
    a. a physician
    b. an undertaker
    c. a gravedigger

12. The *paleontologist* was examining
    a. blood cells
    b. fossils
    c. minerals

13. The boat slowly approached the *vortex*

a. to dock
b. to take it on board
c. because it was drawn to it

14. *Doldrums* occur when
a. stimulants are imbibed
b. life becomes meaningless

c. The wind is from the south

15. An *arbiter*
a. will work diligently
b. will settle the dispute
c. will record the proceedings

Check your answers with the Answer Key on page 286.

Vocabulary Score: ——————

Follow-Up Practice

Using materials of your own selection. Continue with your daily practice periods and, beginning with your next period, devote a part of your time to practice in skimming. Skim to find an article that you want to read. Skim to locate a certain fact or figure. In a factual article skim to get main ideas. In easy narrative material skim to follow the trend of thought. Set a time limit of one minute and see how much you can get out of an article in that time.

Also try skimming quantities of the material which you meet in your daily work or recreational activities. Use various combinations of the techniques suggested in this chapter, for these changing combinations aid in accomplishing your different purposes. As you become more and more expert, try the flashing-from-top-to-bottom-of-the-page technique more frequently. With practice you can really become very skillful in gathering meanings through the use of one vertical sweep of your eyes right down through the middle of the column or page. When you can do this effectively, you will know that you are an expert skimmer.

Answer Keys

Chapter One

Selection 1, pages 16-23:
1) d   2) c   3) c   4) b   5) c   6) d   7) b
8) a   9) d   10) c

Selection 2, pages 23-28:
1) d   2) c   3) c   4) b   5) d   6) c   7) c
8) c   9) c   10) d

Chapter Two

Selection 1, pages 38-40:
1) c   2) d   3) c   4) b   5) d

Selection 2, pages 40-41:
1) d   2) a   3) c   4) b   5) c

Selection 3, pages 41-42:
1) b   2) c   3) a   4) d   5) d

Selection 4, pages 43-44:
1) c   2) b   3) a   4) d   5) b

Selection 6, pages 46-49:
1) a   2) c   3) d   4) b   5) a   6) a   7) c
8) b   9) a   10) d

Chapter Three

Selection 1, pages 54-57:
1) c   2) b   3) a   4) c   5) d   6) d   7) b
8) d   9) d   10) b

Selection 2, pages 58-61:
1) d   2) b   3) d   4) b   5) a   6) d   7) c
8) c   9) b   10) d

Selection 3, pages 61-66:
1) d   2) c   3) d   4) b   5) a   6) d   7) d
8) b   9) c   10) c

Vocabulary Test, pages 66-68:
1) disintegrating, 2) collateral, 3) horticulture, 4) obsolete, 5) progeny, 6) agenda, 7) derelict, 8) distaff, 9) decrepit, 10) burgeon.

Chapter Four

Selection 1, pages 77-78:

Go-ahead Words		Turn-about Words
and	moreover	nor
and	consequently	rather
and	and	not
and	and	but
and	and so	but
and	and	even though
and	and	not
and	and	on the other hand
and	and	but
therefore		

Selection 2, pages 78-83:
1) c   2) d   3) b   4) a   5) c   6) b   7) d
8) b   9) c   10) f

Selection 3, pages 83-87:
1) c   2) c   3) b   4) c   5) b   6) d   7) a
8) b   9) d   10) c

Vocabulary Test, pages 87-88:
1) reinvigoration, 2) artisans, 3) several, 4) honesty, 5) convincing, 6) flippantly, 7) resource, 8) exclusion, 9) associates, 10) insecure.

Chapter Five

Selection 1, pages 93-102:
1) d   2) d   3) c   4) b   5) c   6) a   7) b
8) c   9) d   10) b

Selection 2, pages 103-111:
1) d   2) c   3) d   4) c   5) b   6) d   7) c
8) a   9) b   10) d

Vocabulary Test, pages 111-112:
1) shoals, 2) lichen, 3) myriad, 4) fecund, 5) bushwhack, 6) vindication, 7) encompass, 8) wraith, 9) chute, 10) bend, 11) estuary, 12) vulnerable, 13) escarpment, 14) spate, 15) veritable, 16) muskeg, 17) tributary, 18) domain, 19) pessimistic, 20) portage

Chapter Six

Exercise 1, pages 120-122:
Paragraph 1)a   Paragraph 2) b   Paragraph 3)c

Exercise 2, pages 122-127:
Paragraph 1) b   Paragraph 2) c   Paragraph 3) c
Paragraph 4) d   Paragraph 5) d

Selection 1, pages 129-137:
1) a   2) d   3) c   4) a   5) b   6) d   7) d
8) b   9) c   10) a

Vocabulary Test, pages 137-138:
1) enhances, 2) dynamic, 3) ethereal, 4) incendiary, 5) accentuated, 6) permeates, 7) animosities, 8) therapeutic, 9) regeneration, 10) consonance

Chapter Seven

Paragraph 1, Pages 143-144

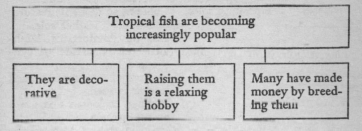

Tropical fish are becoming increasingly popular

| They are decorative | Raising them is a relaxing hobby | Many have made money by breeding them |

Paragraph 2, Page 144

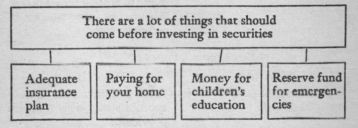

There are a lot of things that should come before investing in securities

| Adequate insurance plan | Paying for your home | Money for children's education | Reserve fund for emergencies |

Paragraph 3, Pages 144-145

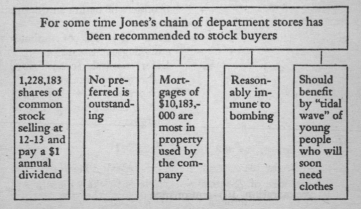

For some time Jones's chain of department stores has been recommended to stock buyers

| 1,228,183 shares of common stock selling at 12-13 and pay a $1 annual dividend | No preferred is outstanding | Mortgages of $10,183,-000 are most in property used by the company | Reasonably immune to bombing | Should benefit by "tidal wave" of young people who will soon need clothes |

Paragraph 4, Pages 145-146

Main Idea	Major Details
A leather sole has been developed which possesses qualities of composition soles.	Developed by shoe manufacturer rather than tanner.
	Contains all desirable features of orthodox leather sole.
	Has the comfortable "cushiony" characteristic of synthetic soles.
	Ordinary chrome-tanned leather is used.
	Pumped to loosen fibers and create air cells.
	Claimed that it is strengthened by this process.
	Tests indicate it wears better.
	About half the weight of ordinary sole.

Paragraph 5, Pages 146-147

Main Idea	Major Details
The history of production is easily sketched.	Early primitive man merely appropriated what nature provided.
	Through the centuries man learned to work over the products of nature more and more.
	Later the use of animals caused great expansion.
	Later natural forces were harnessed to production.
	At present U.S. has more than a billion horsepower of energy.

Paragraph 6, Page 147

Main Idea	Major Details
I. The essence of Cambridge is in its surroundings.	A. It is in the crocuses and daffodils

B. It is in the roses and lu-
   pines
C. It is in the sounds of the
   bells of the church
D. It is in the swifts
E. It is in the meadows

Paragraph 8, Pages 149-150

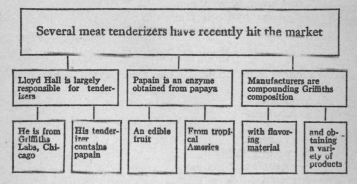

Paragraph 9, Pages 150-151

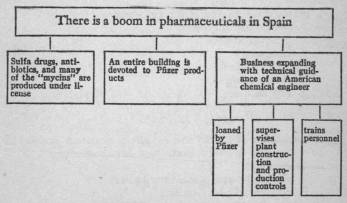

Paragraph 10, Pages 150-152

I. Public industries are less important in the United States
than in some other countries.

II. What are the two major sub-topics and details belonging under each?
A. European countries and public industries controlled by the government
    a. Australia, New Zealand, Canada—railroads
    b. France, several other countries—tobacco
    c. Various cities in the world—public utilities
B. Our government has no important industries except:
    a. Post office
    b. Certain types of banks
    c. A few hydroelectric plants
    d. None of these yield revenue

Paragraph 11, Pages 152-153

1. We know a lot about air but there is still more to be learned.
A. Properties
    a. substance
    b. weight
    c. pressure
    d. compressibility
    e. expands and contracts
    f. inertia
    g. resistance
B. Inventions made possible
    a. instruments to measure air pressure
    b. pumps to compress it
    c. pneumatic tires
    d. air engines
    e. blast furnaces
    f. vacuum tanks
    g. (1) balloons, (2) dirigibles, (3) airplanes.

Paragraph 12, Pages 153-154

1. A knowledge of forces and resources of nature enables us to appreciate and understand our environment.
A. Science has:
    a. changed waste places into gardens
    b. conquered germ diseases
    c. controlled sources of power in nature
    d. promoted travel under water and through air
    e. illuminated cities
    f. improved fruits, root crops, cattle, horses and sheep.

Paragraph 14, Pages 154

I. Characteristics which make automobiles the generally comfortable, smooth-running vehicles they are—(as distinct from simple conveyances providing places to sit and engines to move them around)—are built into every American passenger car today in varying degrees.
   A. They are the end-products of
      (1) A great amount of research
      (2) expert guidance
      (3) technological know-how
      (4) management prejudices
      (5) consumer studies
      (6) dumb luck, and
      (7) shrewd guesswork.
   B. As a result, the various brands of cars are notably unlike each other
      (1) in handling
      (2) economy
      (3) ease of repair
      (4) power and speed
      (5) riding qualities
      (6) noise level
      (7) driver vision and safety

Paragraph 16, Page 156

In the Hudson, opposite West Point, is a famous little island that recalls heroic days of the Revolutionary War. From one end of the island a great chain was stretched across the river to the cliffs below West Point, to keep back the British fleet. The links of the chain were forged in a blacksmith shop at New Windsor, New York, and were carried down the river on a log boom. A part of the chain is today on view at Washington's headquarters, Newburg, New York. Another section of the chain is to be seen at West Point.

Paragraph 19, Pages 158-159

1. Plastics
2. (a) molden (b) bent (c) carved

3. (a) rubber (b) resin
4. (a) 1. carbolic acid, (2) formaldehyde
   (b) 1. phenols, (2) aldehydes

Selection 1, pages 160-163:

1. (a), (b), (c) Any three of these: weaving, embroider-
   ing, making furniture, carving wood, building houses.
2. (a) London, (b) Paris, (c) Rome
3. (a) Architecture: made more progress than in others,
   (b) Painting: still dependent on Parisian influences, (c)
   Music: contributed new motifs, but not a composer of
   first rank, (d) Drama: achieved some individuality, (e)
   Motion pictures: set world standards but not high.
4. (a) art education, (b) advertising, (c) higher incomes,
   (d) shorter working days, (e) need for leisure time activities
5. (a) Yes, (b) No
6. (a) commercial, (b) industrial

Selection 2, pages 164-171:

1) c 2) c 3) b 4) c 5) b 6) d 7) a
8) b 9) c 10) b

Selection 3, pages 172-176:

1) c 2) d 3) d 4) a 5) d 6) b 7) d
8) b 9) b 10) b

Vocabulary Test, pages 176-177:

1) c 2) b 3) b 4) b 5) c 6) b 7) a
8) c 9) c 10) c 11) b 12) c 13) b
14) b 15) a 16) b 17) a 18) c 19) a
20) b

Chapter Eight

Practice Section 1, pages 187-190:

1) Sharing experience, 2) Question-answer, 3) Sharing experience, 4) Question-answer, 5) Question-answer, 6) The
Great Plains or remote sections of the West, 7) Baby food
formulas, 8) A man lying in the bottom of a pitpan, or
dugout canoe, 9) Emotional stress, 10) Heavy snowfall

Practice Section II, pages 190-195:
1) Substantiated fact, 2) Opinion-reason, 3) Information, 4) Substantiated fact, 5) Opinion-reason, 6) 5,000, 7) Rise of Soviet-Union, 8) 1913 Liberty Nickel, 9) The Cradle Society, Evanston, Illinois, 10) secure

Practice Section III, pages 195-222:

Selection 1, pages 196-201:
| 1) d | 2) c | 3) d | 4) b | 5) c | 6) d | 7) a |
| 8) b | 9) d | 10) d | | | | |

Selection 2, pages 201-208:
| 1) d | 2) a | 3) c | 4) d | 5) b | 6) b | 7) a |
| 8) b | 9) c | 10) c | | | | |

Selection 3, pages 208-212:
| 1) b | 2) h | 3) a | 4) c | 5) c | 6) d | 7) b |
| 8) a | 9) b | 10) c | | | | |

Selection 4, pages 212-217:
| 1) a | 2) d | 3) c | 4) c | 5) d | 6) d | 7) d |
| 8) a | 9) b | 10) c | | | | |

Selection 5, pages 218-221:
| 1) d | 2) c | 3) a | 4) b | 5) c | 6) d | 7) a |
| 8) d | 9) a | 10) d | | | | |

Vocabulary Test, page 221:
1) unpremeditated, 2) commotion, 3) marvel, 4) incongruity, 5) examiner, 6) terminology, 7) ingenious, 8) discerned, 9) dominantly, 10) insertion, 11) pine, 12) provisional, 13) puissance, 14) encroach, 15) surpassing

Chapter Nine

Selection 1, pages 230-233:
| 1) b | 2) b | 3) d | 4) c | 5) b | 6) c | 7) a |
| 8) a | 9) c | 10) c | | | | |

Selection 2, pages 234-238:
1) c   2) a   3) d   4) d   5) a   6) c   7) d
8) d   9) c   10) d

Selection 3, pages 239-243
1) b   2) a   3) a   4) d   5) a   6) c   7) d
8) a   9) c   10) a

Selection 4, pages 243-249:
1) a   2) c   3) c   4) c   5) c   6) b   7) b
8) c   9) b   10) d

Selection 5, pages 259-262:
1) True, 2) false, 3) true, 4) false, 5) false, 6) true, 7) true,
8) true, 9) false, 10) true

Selection 6, pages 263-265:
1) The gardener, 2) The gardener suggested it to the lady
of the house, 3) It was beginning to look not like a petunia
at all, 4) He didn't know what the plant was, 5) Gardener's tentative conclusion was that it was Nicotiana

Selection 7, pages 266-269:
1) c   2) d   3) d   4) c   5) c   6) c   7) c
8) b   9) c   10) d

Selection 8, pages 269-274:
1) a   2) b   3) a   4) b   5) d   6) c   7) c
8) d   9) b   10) c

Vocabulary Test, pages 274-275:
1) a   2) c   3) b   4) a   5) c   6) b   7) c
8) c   9) a   10) c   11) c   12) b   13) c
14) c   15) b

INDEX